Soft Skills

AN INTEGRATED APPROACH TO MAXIMISE PERSONALITY

Soft Skills

AN INTEGRATED APPROACH TO MAXIMISE PERSONALITY

GAJENDRA SINGH CHAUHAN
Head and Associate Professor
Department of Humanities and Social Sciences
BITS Pilani

SANGEETA SHARMA
Associate Professor
Department of Humanities and Social Sciences
BITS Pilani

WILEY

Soft Skills

AN INTEGRATED APPROACH TO MAXIMISE PERSONALITY

Published by Wiley India Pvt. Ltd.,
Plot No. 382, 383 Shahabad Daulatpur, New Delhi-110042

Printed at: Manipal Technologies

Edition: 2016
Reprint: 2026

ISBN: 978-81-265-5639-7

Other Wiley Editorial Offices:
John Wiley & Sons, Inc. 111 River Street, Hoboken, NJ 07030, USA
Wiley-VCH Verlag GmbH, Boschstr. 12, 69469 Weinheim, Germany
John Wiley & Sons Australia, Ltd (ACN:009 673 081) at Level 4,600 Bourke St, Melbourne Victoria 3000
John Wiley & Sons Singapore Pte. Ltd, 134 Jurong Gateway Road, #04-307H, Singapore 600134
John Wiley & Sons Canada Ltd, 22 Worcester Road, Etobicoke, Ontario, Canada, M9W ILI
John Wiley & Sons, Ltd, New Era House, 8 Oldlands Way, Bognor Regis, West Sussex, PO22 9NQ, UK

www.wileyindia.com

Preface

Presently we have two incredible virtues as a nation: one, the youngest population in the world; and second, the vibrant emerging knowledge economy. To build upon this strength, we need a workforce suitably trained in *soft skills*. Several researches unequivocally support that people and their skills are very critical in order to sustain or make a business successful. The book is designed with a clear objective to identify the need of the present generation and empower them with the right set of skills to make them employable. Authors feel that there is a distinct mismatch between the expectations of the economy and skills of the graduates, calling for immediate partnership of academia and industry to fill this vacuum of soft skills in young graduates leading to poor employability. As a result, students have good theoretical knowledge, but they lack problem-solving skills due to lack of exposure to practical projects. The good news is that soft skills can be learned and mastered. Therefore, the training of soft skills for prospective professionals is gaining momentum, as 9 in 10 employers believe that graduates with soft skills will become increasingly important as globalisation speeds up, according to a survey by Talent Q, part of Hay Group.

With the bunch of soft skills, the book chips in to fill this void between the university curriculum and current industrial needs. The proposed book intends to work on core skills with practical approach based on authors' own academic experience and research with management and engineering graduates, and also forms the backdrop of the book to bring valuable inputs for the overall development of the students. The book includes various stories, illustrations and cases from the real world to prove the argument: "how soft skills do wonders when rightly combined with hard skills in life."

Book Sections

The book strategically divides soft skills under three domains: **Social**, **Academic** and **Professional**. Although they are strongly inter-dependent and complementary to each domain, the division makes it easy to represent the different soft skills depending upon their direct source of learning and application to the practical world. **Part I** is designed to bunch the skills which people learn from the society; like, how to nurture a good personality, etiquette and emotional intelligence. **Part II** delves into the realm of academic skills; like, to be a good communicator, to make presentations, to write resume and to participate in group discussions and interviews effectively. **Part III** explores the skills which are of immediate relevance and utility to the market and enables the graduates to learn these skills along with social and academic skills to build a strong prospect in the competitive job market. These skills prepare the graduates to be good leaders and decision makers, to have critical thinking, to cope with stress, to work as team players and how to learn and unlearn at workplaces.

Snapshots of the Book

Learning Roadmap

These are the lampposts that highlight the key issues covered in the chapter and steer the expected learning outcomes for the students.

Learning Roadmap

After reading this chapter you will be able to:

- Differentiate between soft skills and hard skills.
- Appreciate why soft skills are essential for employability.
- Comprehend the importance of collaboration bridge between the academia and the industry for building knowledge economy.
- Know about the plans of various departments for skill enhancement of their professionals.
- Appreciate the importance of the employability skills in global perspective.
- Know about the roll-out of the new Skilled India programme for better employability and productivity.

Perspectives

These box items feature in-depth discussions of a particular soft skill covered in the chapter and its application and significance in real life.

PERSPECTIVE

We are one of the youngest populations in the world with a huge reservoir of English-speaking youths. Fortunately, to enable this young force to contribute to nation-building, the present government has taken up skill development as a thrust area. Along with 'Digital India' and 'Make in India', the government has launched a momentous programme called 'Skill India' to overcome the scarcity of skilled manpower. It intends to create more opportunities for skill enhancement of the young Indians and train them to optimise productivity in all sectors. 'Skill India' is a massive movement for young India where the academia and corporates join hands to fill skill gap for better employability. It aims to train the youths in a way that would make them a valuable human resource for the society and the nation. With such skill development initiatives, our young generation can create history by making our nation developed and knowledgeable. Our nation would become a land of opportunity and prosperity if we mould and train our youths to be skilful and tech-savvy. Simply knowing things may not help us. We need to master skills to practise what we have learnt. It is time we realised that college degrees and campus placements are not the ultimate

Instant Idea Boxes

These idea boxes are the most instant connector to the concepts discussed on the page.

Your resume should be designed to match the job advertisement and complement the skills asked for.

Worldly Wise Comic Strip

The comic strips set to gear you up to understand the relevance of the concerned concept by projecting some faux pas in a lighter vein.

Experts' Speak

These present a quote or statement imbued with wisdom and winning edge from the stalwarts across the various spheres of life.

> *"Lots of people want to ride with you in the limo, but what you want is someone who will take the bus with you when the limo breaks down."*
>
> — Oprah Winfrey

Communication today!

Exhibits

These provide an informative visual display that furthers students' knowledge through tables, diagrams, objects, photographs, etc.

Chapter Review Questions

These are presented to assess what all the students have learnt in the given chapter.

Chapter Review

1. What is communication?
2. What are the features of non-verbal communication?
3. Explain why listening is most important of all communication skills?
4. Why does the communication cycle need to be repeated?
5. How has technology affected workplace communication? Discuss the pros and cons of the same.
6. What measures will you suggest to improve the intercultural communication?

Direct Questions

1. Discuss GSC's3M model of communication?
2. What do you mean by the barriers to listening? Name some barriers to listening.
3. Why is feedback necessary for effective communication?
4. Why there is need for intercultural communication at the workplace? Justify your answer.
5. How technology has facilitated faster communication in the business world? Discuss some new communication technology tools that have been practised recently in the workplace.

Direct Questions

These are presented to assess students' basic understanding about some of the key concepts covered in the given chapter.

Critical Thinking Questions

These are planned to put students in a situation where they are required to apply critically what they have learnt in the chapter so far.

Analytical Questions

1. As the saying goes that there is a difference between listening and hearing just as there is a difference between seeing and knowing. What can you infer from this saying? Justify the saying in the context of professional communication.
2. As a project manager of a team comprising members from different cultures and nationalities, how would you plan your cross-cultural communication strategies to avoid any confusion and achieve your business objectives with everyone's participation?
3. How can listening skills be a decisive factor in a workplace environment such as a business setting or a negotiation meeting? How can listening skills make or mar prospects of a significant business venture?

Resources for further Reflections

These are presented to the students various allied learning sources to access online videos, newspapers, magazines and books for sharpening their understanding of the concepts.

Resources for Further Reflections

1. Example of effective communication skills: video of President Obama's first public address after being elected as the president of the Unites States. https://www.youtube.com/watch?v=rPG-6g2AAWo.
2. A relationship between body language (non-verbal communication), communication and confidence. http://www.ted.com/talks/amy_cuddy_your_body_language_shapes_who_you_are?language=en#.
3. A guide to effective cross cultural communication. http://www.colorado.edu/conflict/peace/treatment/xcolcomm.htm.
4. Technology and workplace communication http://www.forbes.com/sites/unify/2013/12/10/how-technology-has-changed-workplace-communication/.
5. Effective communication for managers http://www.business.vic.gov.au/hiring-and-managing-staff/staff-management/communication-skills-in-the-workplace-for-managers.

Caselet 1

The Stressed CGM of Maruti Udyog

Vikas, Chief General Manager (CGM) of Maruthi Udyog, is 41 years old. Born and brought in Delhi, he graduated in Mechanical Engineering from Delhi University. He got married at 28. As the CGM of Maruthi Udyog, he is responsible for INR 500 crores of annual sales. He is accountable to the President of Maruthi Udyog, Indian division. When the President asks Vikas to go to London for this year's annual meeting, he agrees to go to London.

One day before his departure to London, Vikas wakes up in the morning and looks at the wall clock in his bedroom. It is 6 am. Then it occurs to him that today he has a meeting with his president in preparation to his London trip. He also has to pack his travel bag and review a few bills. "Oh God!" he exclaims angrily. "I need to fresh up fast." With pouncing heart, Vikas jumps out of the bed and starts brushing his teeth. After taking bath, he prepares coffee for himself. He knows that soon other members of the family will up and hence he must be ready to leave for the meeting before they start their day. While sipping coffee, he starts looking at his company's quarterly report, which he had received last evening. As he is short of time, he skims the report instead of reading it thoroughly and comes to know that his division has fallen short of its annual profit target by more than INR 2 crores.

When Vikas is about leave the home, his wife Priya comes running and informs him that their son Gautham has missed the school bus. Then Vikas asks angrily, "What am I supposed to do?. I have warned Gautham many times about this lazy conduct in the morning". When Priya asks him if he could drop Gautham to school on the way to his office, Vikas refuses, saying, "I have other important things to do than driving him to school. Do not waste my time now." His wife retorts, "You will never do anything for us. Come on Gautham, Mom will drop you to your school".

After arguing with Priya, Vikas leaves for the meeting, driving 40 km to reach his office. The long drive to the office has added to his stress. In the office, he is greeted by a bad news that few labours have boycotted the employee attitude survey, which was his initiative. He mutters to himself, "How dare they? I should take strong action". Then looking at his watch he realises that he was 5 minutes late for his meeting with the President. He gets furious and rushes to the meeting room where the President is waiting for him. When the meeting begins, the president asks him about his tour plan for London and his understanding of the company's quarterly preparation. Though Vikas responds to the President's queries, the latter is not satisfied by his answers. Then the President tells him frankly, "Look, Vikas! I'm sending you to London with this report because I feel you are capable to explain the audit professionals in London why we fell short our annual target by INR 2 crores. But if you get stressed like this and do not manage your time, you'll be replaced by some other person next time". And saying this, the President leaves the meeting room.

Questions

1. Vikas should have taken his son to school. Oppose or support this statement with justification.
2. How Vikas's meeting with the President would have happened had he not been so stressed before the meeting?
3. What kind of a manager Vikas is?

Caselets

These represent particular instances used or analysed in order to illustrate the topic under discussion and presenting an opportunity to take the decision and justify the same from the learnings.

CD

It includes videos that facilitate understanding about Interviews, Group Discussions and Professional Presentations.

Instructor manual assists the instructor with indicative notes. These manuals can be obtained from the publisher on request by writing to acadmktg@wiley.com.

Acknowledgement

Book writing is a culmination of ideas and experiences from the working place, and for us that is BITS, Pilani campus. We owe a lot to all the people who have supported and motivated us to pursue this project. We are astutely conscious of the importance of *soft skills* in the predominant world of technology, and it is the dire need for the students who had led to the germination of this book. So we admit that contribution made by the present and past students has been immense on this mammoth project.

This book became reality because of the positive attitude and readiness to print from the Wiley team. There are multitalented people from Wiley who were closely associated with the book. They had tirelessly worked on the chapters to see the book in an immaculate shape. We are extremely thankful to Siddhartha Deb, Publishing Editor; Meenakshi Sehrawat, Executive Editor; Sayani Bhattacharyya, Assistant Editor and Rakesh Poddar, Senior Production Editor who had put an extra effort to ensure the book is launched in time. Their ability to get the best out of us had made us work with rigour and kept us on schedule.

We also take this opportunity to express our gratitude to our department colleagues for their aspiring guidance, invaluably constructive criticism and friendly advice during the entire project. Students are the people who inspired us to design this idea for book writing. Our special thanks to the coterie of students who readily contributed the case studies, graphics and question banks for this book – Raja Tirumalesetty, Alekhya Kaki, Siddhant Bhardwaj, K Surya Narayana Manoj, Divya Vaswani and Mayur Saxena.

On family front, Gajendra acknowledges his wife Yogita's wry smile and miss calls for his regular late comings from the department and his children, Rajeshwari and Chandrahari, for allowing him to work on their computer on weekends instead playing computer games. Hope one day they could read and understand this book.

Sangeeta wants to mention her husband Suresh's motivation and her sons Amrit and Anuj who gave valuable inputs and ideas from students' perspectives. It is the love and affection of children that let the ball rolling!

Gajendra Singh Chauhan
Sangeeta Sharma
(September 2015)

Authors' Profiles

Prof. Gajendra Singh Chauhan

Gajendra Singh Chauhan is presently the Head, Department of Humanities and Social Sciences, BITS Pilani, where he teaches various courses on professional communication, advertising and media studies. He is an Associate Professor of Communication and Media Studies who specializes in applied linguistics, advertising communication and media writing with a focus on linguistics of advertising in India. He earned his Master's degree in English language and literature, MPhil in ELT and a doctorate in advertising communication. His academic interest also helped him get a Bachelor's degree in Journalism. His contributions to the literature include four books, numerous articles and radio talks on All India Radio. As a communication professional, he has conducted Management Development Programmes for corporate executives on "Workplace communication" in IIM Rohtak and regularly delivers for private and public sector organizations. He has participated in several professional conferences and seminars over the years and is always learning from his colleagues and students. Besides academics, he loves sports, yoga, travelling and interacting with students.

Prof. Sangeeta Sharma

Prof. Sangeeta Sharma has been working as faculty of communication, creativity and advertising for last 25 years in the department of Humanities and social sciences at BITS, Pilani and has been in the leadership roles as head of department and coordinator of centre for women studies. She is an active and lively person who participates in sports and related activities. Dr. Sharma is an academician of par excellence for last two and half decades. She has excelled in all aspects of academics such as classroom delivery, corporate connect and training, writing of books and research papers, paper presentation in national and international conferences, editorial work and organising academic events etc. She has to her credit more than 15 books published by reputed national publishers such as Oxford University Press, Prentice Hall of India and Jain Brothers and others. She has published research papers in National and International Journals and has delivered more than 100 invited lectures to MBA and Engineering students at prominent institutes and Universities across India. Dr. Sharma's forte is training in the art of communication which she has been practicing for last 15 years by conducting MDPs for the corporate managers and FDPs for academicians in higher education.

Contents

Chapter 3 Emotional Intelligence 31

Chapter 4 Etiquette and Mannerism 43

Chapter 9 Group Discussion 129

Chapter 11 Ethical Values 163

Chapter 12 Capacity Building: Learn, Unlearn and Relearn 175

Chapter 1

SOFT SKILLS VS HARD SKILLS: AN INTRODUCTION

Learning Roadmap

After reading this chapter you will be able to:

- Differentiate between soft skills and hard skills
- Appreciate why soft skills are essential for employability
- Comprehend the importance of collaboration bridge between the academia and the industry for building knowledge economy
- Know about the plans of various departments for skill enhancement of their professionals
- Appreciate the importance of the employability skills in global perspective
- Know about the roll-out of the new Skilled India programme for better employability and productivity

PERSPECTIVE

We are one of the youngest populations in the world with a huge reservoir of English-speaking youths. Fortunately, to enable this young force to contribute to nation-building, the present government has taken up skill development as a thrust area. Along with 'Digital India' and 'Make in India', the government has launched a momentous programme called 'Skill India' to overcome the scarcity of skilled manpower. It intends to create more opportunities for skill enhancement of the young Indians and train them to optimise productivity in all sectors. 'Skill India' is a massive movement for young India where the academia and corporates join hands to fill skill gap for better employability. It aims to train the youths in a way that would make them a valuable human resource for the society and the nation. With such skill development initiatives, our young generation can create history by making our nation developed and knowledgeable. Our nation would become a land of opportunity and prosperity if we mould and train our youths to be skilful and tech-savvy. Simply knowing things may not help us. We need to master skills to practise what we have learnt. It is time we realised that college degrees and campus placements are not the ultimate things. But to be a successful professional and human being, we need to master those skills that could have everlasting values and applications. Let's prepare the youth of India, one of the youngest nations, with skills and the achievement-oriented mindset for a better future and commendable life.

"Lots of people want to ride with you in the limo, but what you want is someone who will take the bus with you when the limo breaks down."

— Oprah Winfrey

1.1 INTRODUCTION

Today's workplace demands a manager to be a team leader who can interact and collaborate with others easily. To communicate effectively with co-workers from different divisions and sections, technical professionals acting as team leaders need to hone their soft skills.

Soft skills are the valuable set of skills needed to accomplish the various job requirements that may not be taken care of just by mastering hard skills. These skills strengthen your job profile and personality quotient. Being an accountant, you may have the hard skill to crunch numbers and manage balance sheets. But your ability to gel with others, work in teams, communicate effectively with your business partners and manage things timely is termed as soft skills. The term soft skills with respect to a professional signifies that he/ she is a team player and has an inquiring mind, innovative spirit and interpersonal communication skills. A successful professional is expected to be a fine blend of soft and hard skills, so that he/ she could adapt easily to any job assignment and work environment. These are 'mobile skills', that is transferable in nature, and thus are highly important in every sector unlike hard skills which are just confined to their respective domains. Every job that you get with your technical domain knowledge needs a set

of soft skills for handling it efficiently and boosting your career. One needs to walk the extra mile to identify and acquire soft skills as they are the toughest to learn and master. Unfortunately, there is a disconnect between hard skills and soft skills at the level of formal education, as no technical degree teaches specifically how to handle people and crisis at workplace, analyse a problem and arrive at apt solutions, show leadership and entrepreneurial capabilities and communicate with empathy.

1.2 SKILLS TO MASTER

Recruiting managers and placement officers strongly feel that it is our will to keep learning that equips us with the aptitude and skills that are essential for professional growth and personal excellence. There is no doubt that soft skills can be learned over a period of time. Today many organisations are looking beyond the technical knowledge of a candidate to explore his/her real worth by focusing on smart personality and behavioural traits. Explaining this shift in the hiring process, Jayashri Ramamurti – Head of People Operations for Engineering and Product, Google India, says, "Nowadays, close attention is paid to a person's ability to work in a team, lead projects independently, work collaboratively and communicate well."

In view of the growing importance of soft skills in the employment market, a young graduate may ask: "What soft skills I should learn in order to get a good job?". The answer lies in his/her willingness to learn new skills beyond the hard skills (like budgeting, analysing, programming or coding expertise) of his/her domain. Young graduates enhance their value immensely in the job market when they open up to learn the people skills

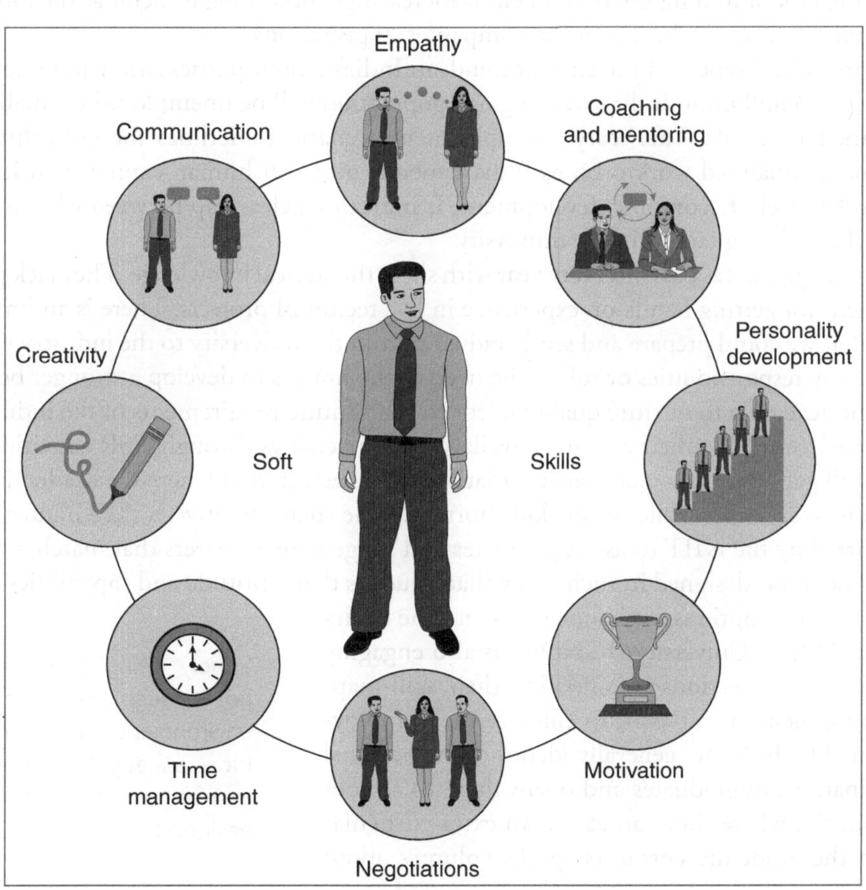

and other self-management skills. These skills empower them by teaching them how to communicate with co-workers, superiors and juniors confidently; cope with stress; inspire their team using their leadership ability and take right decisions. Their familiarity with the people skills helps them win more friends, secure jobs and get promotions in their careers. With these skills, they enjoy the trust and support of their colleagues and consequently lead them to better productivity by developing an inspiring work culture. Successful professionals never stop learning and training themselves. They keep adding to their skill basket by learning work ethics, positivity and business etiquettes. As they learn, they grow higher and become a magnet for others with their positive attitude and the way they behave, dress and communicate at workplace. A workplace cannot always be fair to all associated with it and we cannot complain about others' unprofessionalism and control external situations that have a bearing on the workplace environment. However, our mastery of soft skills provides us the cushion to overcome these jerks and make our sailing to new directions smooth and rewarding.

1.3 ACADEMIA – INDUSTRY CONNECT

A major challenge that we face in the present scenario is how to make the academia align with the corporate world to build in the youths skills needed for their employability and better productivity. Experts agree that soft skills are just as essential for professional success as domain-specific abilities. Nowadays, in their recruitment drives companies are careful and specific in identifying the talents they require as they are placing more emphasis on a graduate's multidisciplinary skills, academic abilities, cultural sensitivity and creativity. But the task of finding the right talent is increasingly becoming difficult as the job skills of college graduates in India are just nowhere near the companies' expectations.

According to a Crisil report, if the current trends in India's labour participation and unemployment rate continue, about 423 million in India's working-age population will be unemployed or unable to participate in the job market by 2030. This scary unemployment scenario underlines the criticality of closing the skill gaps of India's qualified workforce, as India depends more on human capital than its peer countries that have a similar level of economic development. It indicates a clear gap between what is expected in the industry and what is being taught in the university.

More and more graduates pass out every year with sheer theoretical knowledge. They lack problem-solving skills due to their not getting hands-on experience in live technical projects. There is an immediate need to fix this gap so that we could prepare and send graduates from the university to the industry where they could easily take over any responsibilities or roles. The need of the hour is to develop a stronger bond between the industry and the academia to nurture quality talent to fulfil future requirements of the industry. Corporates can come forward and make their resources available to universities through CSR activities and do a great job to fill the skill gap. Recently many such initiatives have been started where the academia and the industry joined hands to face the challenge of skill shortage. One such initiative is the Graduate Employability Test (GET) started by the NIIT to assess graduates and suggest them careers that match with their abilities and interests. The test is designed in such a way that it judges their aptitude and capabilities and accordingly suggests new-age career options to channelise them. The Indira Gandhi National Open University (IGNOU) is also engaging its students in newer directions by initiating their skill-mapping and training them in soft-skills to enhance their employability quotient. The IGNOU generally identifies the personal traits and inclinations of graduates and opens them to a series of job opportunities where they can excel. An extra-curricular exposure from the academic corridors speaks volumes about

> Simply being good at your job is not enough. In global competitive environment, you prove your mettle, have an appetite for new learning and be curious to work beyond your assigned job.

a candidate's personality and helps him/her get a job, not merely a good CGPA. Few years back, even the Union Ministry of Human Resource Development in collaboration with Nasscom had floated the concept of 'Finishing Schools' for engineering students' to help young technical graduates become industry-ready.

1.4 SOFTENING OF THE HARD SKILLS

Technical professionals are often hired for their core skills and may or may not be tested for their people skills which are considered necessary for corporate managers. As a group leader, they need to hone their soft skills to handle the team and projects to be relevant in their new role. Today we have these technical professionals self-proclaimed as 'techies' or 'geeks' in every industry including aerospace, electronics, information technology, manufacturing, software and telecommunications. Their contribution in terms of scientific and technical knowledge cannot be ignored. Technical professionals due to their technical acumen can climb the corporate ladder easily but their inadequate leadership and management skills make it tough for them to get the job done by others at the workplace. But the fast changing global economy expects them to perform a manager's duties as well as use their technical expertise. Today's workplace demands a manager to be a team leader who can interact and collaborate with others easily. To communicate effectively with co-workers from different divisions and sections, technical professionals acting as team leaders need to hone their soft skills. But the lack of their grounding in social sciences or psychology creates problems for their effective coordination with the non-technical workforce. The type of training technical professionals receive makes them more task-oriented and less people-oriented. They believe more in scientific excellence and technical precision and are not comfortable with public dealing and social events. They lack soft skills such as communication, negotiation, interpersonal, team management because mastering these skills was not their priority when as they were busy securing their technical/ engineering grades and degrees. This situation puts technical professionals at a disadvantage in the global business scenario where success depends a lot on one's mastery of soft skills.

> *The greatest challenge seems not to be about mechanics of management – budgeting, strategy development, etc. – but about the people skills that enable effective communication to get things done.*
>
> — Hurd & Juri

1.5 INTERDISCIPLINARY RELEVANCE

Whether it is a call centre job or a flight attendant role or jobs in the service and manufacturing sectors, graduates are expected to have the ability to acquire and use interpersonal skills, empathy, assertiveness, problem solving skills and positivism. Imparting the required soft skills to their staff is gradually becoming a priority of the human resource division in every organisation. They regularly conduct competency building workshops to improve the vocational and technical skills of their employees. *Atithi Devo Bhavah* (guest is like a God) is a social awareness campaign by the Ministry of Tourisms to educate the local population about the civic sense and good behaviour towards tourists and build a better image of India as a favourite tourism destination. The ministry of tourism has designed a skill development programme to train guides, ticket vendors, porters and cab drivers to serve tourists with a smile. Such programmes touch almost every sphere of the professional world. A cop slouching at a traffic-light signal or police check-post, talking in chaste regional dialect could be a thing of the past. Recently, a batch of new recruits of traffic police had undergone soft skills and English speaking training in Chandigarh. It is meant for beat cops, traffic cops and all other officials who are engaged in public dealing. While diagnosing and treating a disease, sometimes a doctor and his/her a patient face the problem of poor communication. To overcome this problem, Nashik-based Maharashtra University of Health Sciences introduced several modules of soft skills in medical education. Along with training medical students in communication skills, the institution also planned to introduce formal lectures on topics like professionalism and work ethics.

Whether it is a call centre job or a flight attendant role or jobs in the service and manufacturing sectors, graduates are expected to have the ability to acquire and use interpersonal skills, empathy, assertiveness, problem solving skills and positivism.

1.6 GLOBAL PERSPECTIVES ON SOFT SKILLS

It is common concern worldwide that businesses cannot sustain unless they have the skilled workforce that is employable. In today's digital age, the business boundaries have shrunk geographical and cultural distances. This scenario has thrown many opportunities and challenges for the global society at large and youth in particular. To strengthen the recruitment scenario and professionalism, many global business giants and work organisations advocate strongly the need of imparting soft skills to the young talent along with the functional knowledge of their respective domains. UNESCO in its annual report "Youth at Work" clearly advocates that "If young people are to maximise the benefits of technical and vocational training, foundation and transferable skills are essential – even more so in today's dynamic global economy, where labour market demands and the skills for specific occupations are constantly evolving."

An independent study conducted on CEOs, by Stanford Research Institute and Carnegie Mellon in the USA, found that long-term job success depends 75% on people skill and only 25% on technical knowledge. The Australian Chamber of Commerce and Industry and the Business Council of Australia undertook a comprehensive study of the skill, called 'key competencies', commonly required by both new and existing employees to work successfully in organisations. They derived a set of key skills which they called 'employability skill'. It is industry's preferred term for soft generic skills. It has been the buzzing field of study the world over for last one decade. While discussing the importance of investment in soft skills, Shari Caudron, the author and career freelancer reports, the studies of close to 500 organisations worldwide indicate that people who score the highest on EQ measures rise to the top of corporations. She brought together years of research to show that emotional intelligence — which can loosely be described as a person's ability to manage him or herself and relate to other people — matters twice as much as IQ or technical skills in job success. However, Zielinski D, points out that "If you had asked project-management gurus five years ago to name the most important competencies project managers should have, most would have said technical skills. Today they'd be more inclined to place communications or negotiations acumen at the top of their lists."

Sampson B, in his research, observes that the skills required for project management are now often divided 50/50 into traditional 'hard' skills, such as risk management and scheduling, and 'soft', people-oriented skills, such as interpersonal communication. Greg Netland, president of the IT division at New Boston Systems, reflects that "about 70% of managers we do business with feel soft skills are more important than they were five years ago." Technical skills get you in the door, but soft skills keep you in the job. Companies sink or swim based on soft skills regardless whether their technologies keep them afloat temporarily. The AICPA Vision 2011 Project has added soft skills to the list of core competencies that successful accountants should possess. While taking cue from available research, the present work would be a step ahead in this direction to suggest a workable model for the young graduates.

> *"We can each define ambition and progress for ourselves. The goal is to work toward a world where expectations are not set by the stereotypes that hold us back, but by our personal passion, talents and interests."*
> — Sheryl Sandberg

1.7 NATIONAL INITIATIVES AND PRIORITY

Skill development has become the top agenda of the Indian Government. It has also been reflected with the formation of the new Ministry of Skill Development and Entrepreneurship under the new government. Prime Minister Narendra Modi, in his first Independence Day speech, invited companies across the world to make their products in India and create jobs in the labour-intensive manufacturing sector. To supplement this mission, he called upon the nation to take a pledge to make India the 'skill capital' of the world. In this direction, the new government is taking a leap forward by launching the 'Skill India' programme to train the youths in a way so that they could become proficient and economically independent. The Ministry of Skill Development and Entrepreneurship has a clear plan of coordinating with various government departments who are part of the skill mission to converge some of their programmes and sync their policies with the Prime Minister's most promising project 'Make in India'. With the similar objective, the National Skill Development Corporation (NSDC), as the first model of public–private partnership in skill development, is also working in this direction to address the challenge of inculcating the right set of skills necessary for a growing economy of India. It channelises effectively the skilling and up-skilling process in India and produces a skilled manpower across the sectors and shrinks the present gap between the demand and supply of skills through various skill training programmes. Its main motive is to encourage private sector and industry participation in skill training and development.

> Skills are vital to a knowledge economy desperately in need of job creation. Skill India mission will be a game changer for the country where government, industry, and academia must focus on scaling up skill training efforts to meet the demands of employers and drive economic growth.

Summary

Continuous learning is closely associated with the career growth of a professional. Gone are the days when the classrooms were the ultimate bastion of learning and personality development. The concept of soft skills is being increasingly discussed in corporate lounges and academic corridors of higher learning. There has been a growing awareness of the importance of soft skills because the workplace has transformed drastically. In this increasingly skill-driven scenario, soft skills serve as a means to bridge the gap between educational curriculum and actual job credentials. While considering the power of knowledge economy, graduates are to be groomed in a way so that they could absorb and deliver their best in any industry they aspire to join. Today MNCs that are visiting academic campuses want graduates who are team players, can communicate effectively and work under pressure, are good at problem-solving and can perform with integrity and ethics to motivate a team and enhance productivity. So the soft skill development initiatives facilitate moulding of graduates into professionals who are adjustable dynamically to the changing demands of employment and technologies. This promotes excellence by meeting the requirements of the knowledge economy. As soft skills find their application in every sector, job managers and skill trainers affirm that these skills can be learned and practised seamlessly to support and strengthen the individual and the industry.

Chapter Review

1. Why it becomes necessary to have a fine blend of soft and hard skills to be a successful professional?
2. How do soft skills help in dealing with unprofessional behaviour? Explain with examples.
3. What disadvantages do you think are associated with being task-oriented and not people-oriented?

4. Why do you know by 'Skilled India' programme initiated by the Indian government and how it helps to strengthen the knowledge economy?
5. Why is communication an essential part of soft skills? How does clear communication improve the performance of an organisation on the whole?
6. Why it becomes crucial for technical professionals to acquire soft skills?

Direct Questions

1. What you mean by hard skills?
2. Why soft skills are considered mobile skills?
3. What types of soft skills could help make a person employable and how? Explain each in detail.
4. State the significance of soft skills in a workplace.
5. How can soft skills help employees work well even under pressure?
6. Explain how grades and degrees have become a secondary factor when it comes to hiring for jobs?

Analytical Questions

1. State an example of any organisation that has moved on to focusing more on development of soft skills than hard skills. How do you believe has this affected the organisation's receptivity, demand, productivity and profits?
2. State and explain the plans that can be envisaged by universities and corporates together to enable graduates to improve their soft skills for employability.

Resources for Further Reflections

1. 28 soft skills to working smart https://in.newshub.org/28-soft-skills-working-smart-14743819.html.
2. Soft skills matter: Can they be taught? http://www.businessnewsdaily.com/7907-improve-employee-soft-skills.html.
3. Soft skills videos for individual trait development: Communication: https://www.youtube.com/watch?v=X0voPlW2pSs.
4. Enthusiasm and attitude: https://www.youtube.com/watch?v=-vk-99seC_I.
5. Critical thinking and problem solving: https://www.youtube.com/watch?v=hPiI44XEKgs.
6. Professionalism: https://www.youtube.com/watch?v=7dPWVjQSad4.
7. Teamwork: https://www.youtube.com/watch?v=sMFh9QYFh2I.
8. Workshop on soft skills IIT Kanpur: https://www.youtube.com/watch?v=EyMZDMLYk8w.
9. 6 soft skills that guarantee your success http://www.forbes.com/sites/alexmcclafferty/2014/10/21/soft-skills/.
10. Why soft skills matter http://www.mindtools.com/pages/article/newCDV_34.htm.
11. Soft skills can't be taught, but they can be learnt http://schoolsweek.co.uk/soft-skills-cant-be-taught-but-they-can-be-learned/.

Caselet 1

Management of Teachers

Priya Patel was an intelligent student with a flair for entrepreneurship. This trait she inherited from her family who had been in business for four generations. When working independently, she had been a great performer. Following the footsteps of her entrepreneur father, Priya founded a start-up, a coaching institute. She became Managing Director of the institute, managing its teachers and other employees. The objective of the institute was to teach children of higher secondary schools and prepare them for various entrance tests. Priya's plan was to teach students in the institute and also virtually through a live classroom on the Internet. She thought the Internet classroom option would bring a lot of business from those students who wanted to enjoy the luxury of being taught by home tutors. She hired teachers for each discipline and some web developers who would help the teachers go online. Looking at the good public response, Priya was initially very positive about her business turning out a success but slowly things began to change. She could not get the teachers work according to a set schedule or convince them to give live video lectures according to the demands of the students. She felt the teachers and other employees did not take her seriously. She was also unable to talk to them calmly with a positive attitude.

It was becoming increasingly difficult for Priya to handle the teachers she hired. She did not know what they wanted. Nor would they communicate with her about their problems. She definitely had several amazing strategies to increase her profits but her staffs were not supportive enough to help her apply those strategies. To set things right, first she tried firing those teachers who she thought were not giving their best, but this adversely affected her reputation as an employer and even the good teachers started resigning. She could not afford to let go these teachers because after all her business ran on their shoulders. If things continued this way, Priya feared her hard work for transforming her idea into a flourishing business fading away slowly. She realised if she did not learn to handle her employees and difficult people effectively, she would have to shut down her institute.

Finally, to save her nascent business, Priya hired an image consultant and apprised him about her experience of running the business and the problems she faced in her engagement with her staff. When the consultant submitted his report suggesting ways to overcome her business problems, Priya was shocked to know that the major problem in not getting her people's support was her own behaviour and personality. She was badly lacking in soft skills. The consultant suggested her to develop a set of soft skills, especially communication skills, emotional intelligence, team spirit and leadership skills. The consultant made her realise that though she had been a great performer while independently, she required different skills and some extra work to succeed while leading a team. Priya learnt that all she was lacking was her ability to adjust with people who had views and personalities which were quite different from her own. She needed to read their minds, learn to convince or encourage them to follow her ideas and strategies, connect with them emotionally and ensure their welfare.

Following the consultant's suggestions, Priya did unlearn what was hurting her business and mastered the art of socialisation for better bonding with her staff. In a few months, this positive change in her personality started reflecting in her business, which again started flourishing with her staff giving their best for the success of business plans and strategies.

Questions

1. Describe the qualities that Priya lacked in her personality which made her business fall apart.
2. What all the consultant suggested her to follow in order to revamp her dying start-up?

SECTION

1

SOCIAL SKILLS

Chapter 2

PERSONALITY DEVELOPMENT

Learning Roadmap

After reading this chapter you will be able to:

- Know why personality of an individual is important
- Learn about positive thinking and its impact on personality
- Understand Johari's window
- Know the role of communication skills in personality development
- Understand the connect between physical fitness and personality development

PERSPECTIVE

A couple went to a towering institute of great repute to meet the president. The secretary did not like the sight of the couple and accordingly she informed the President about these visitors. The President pretended to be busy and said he had no time for the people who appeared uncouth, uneducated, dishevelled and uncultured. When the secretary informed the couple they said they could wait till the President would get free. However, the presence of them in the outer office was irritating for the secretary and the President, so finally the President thought he could meet them briefly to get rid of them fast. He strutted pompously towards them and asked what they wanted. The lady informed the president that her son died while studying in the institute so they wanted to create a memorial in their campus. The president retorted that in that case their campus would become cemetery, if they accept their proposal. She patiently answered that probably he did not understand what she meant; she wanted to donate land to them. The president was flummoxed and asked if she knew what the land would cost – it would cost over nine and a half million dollar! The lady quipped, 'only that much?' It is better construct one of their own then to donate land to the people who least respected them. The couple walked away with pride to establish their own institute. The President was discombobulated! All can be said is that personality cannot be judged by only external outlook.

Personality has power to uplift, power to depress, power to curse, and power to bless.

— Paul Harris

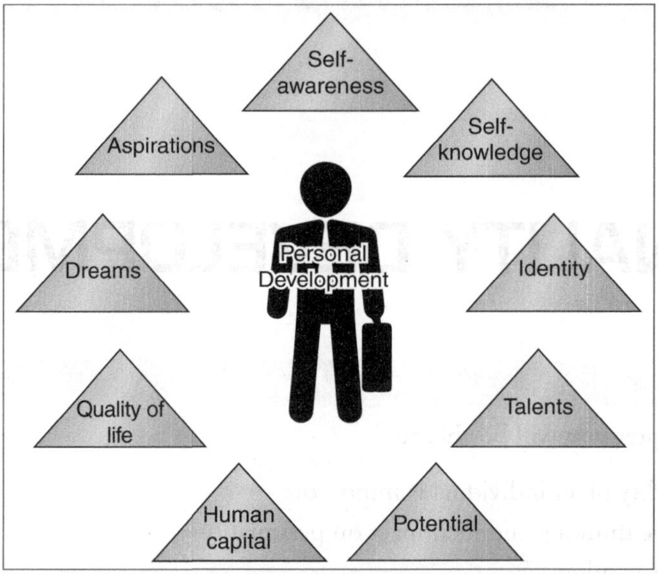

There are different kinds of people in the world, and all of them have different personalities. No two faces are exactly alike, nor are their body structures. In fact, there are as many personalities as the number of people in this world. Some personalities fascinate you while others put you off. It is important for us to know which personalities are universally liked by everyone.

People form images about your personality mostly by your dressing style, behaviour, walking posture, ways of talking and how you present yourself in a group. Your expressions play an important role in your personality. If you have pleasant expressions, people feel like approaching and talking to you. If you have stultified looks, nobody would want to get closer to you. When you become part of an organisation, you have to behave as per the norms of the organisation. More you conform to the expectations of the organisation, better chances you have of acceptability.

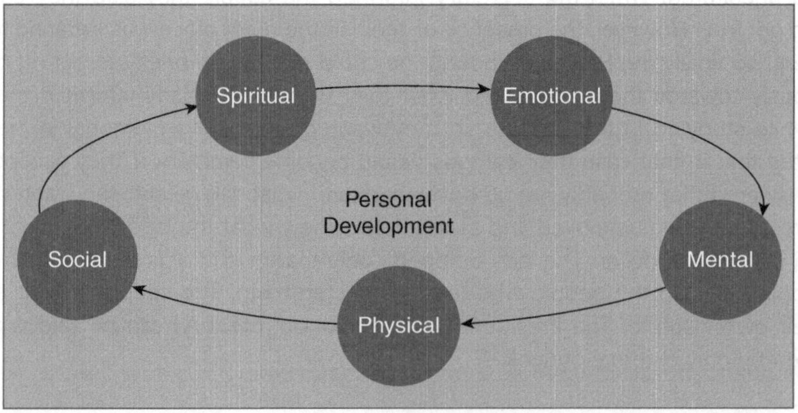

2.1 KNOWING YOURSELF

No human being is completely satisfied with what he/she has. Most people want to bring certain changes in their personalities. Some even aspire to emulate the behaviour, dressing style and other characteristics of celebrities. And, it is possible to polish one's behaviour and personal characteristics in desirable ways through personality development.

Personality development means modifying one's individual behaviour and attitude which would distinguish one from other people. It is an ongoing process which is largely dependent on the environment and communication. Personality development can also be defined as the growing personal characteristics of individuals.

It is important to know about yourself if you have to develop your personality in a desired way. Once you know your limitations and strengths, it is easy to find ways to overcome your shortcomings.

> Personality development is an important part of the individual which never stops growing.

For example if you know that you are introvert, then you can speak in a group more often to become a confident speaker. Similarly if you become nervous on seeing your seniors around you, then you can talk to your friends more often and overcome that fear.

Knowing or understanding yourself, therefore, is very important. It is different from knowing your favourite friend, favourite pastime, favourite number, favourite dress, etc. Knowing yourself is not going against your parents, but it is more profound than that. To know yourself, you have to see how confidently you deal with different situations. To know yourself is not an easy job, it is a long and slow process. It is like a meandering road where you do not see the end, and you have to travel yourself to reach the end. This travelling helps you clear your doubts and increase your confidence while moving towards your destination or goal. You can then cherish the journey because it gives you a new experience at every stage.

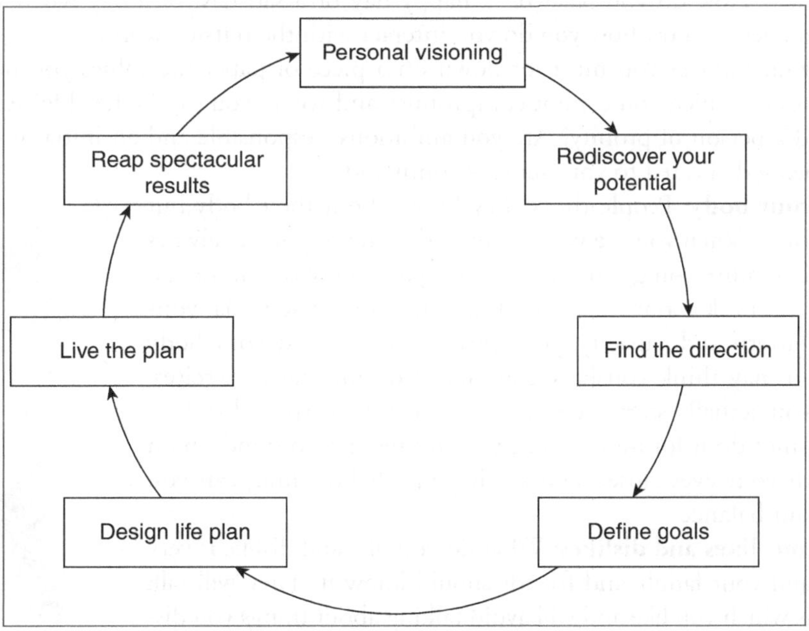

Knowing yourself is understanding your beliefs, moods, body language, personality and relationships. For some people it could be the priority to indulge in exercises or yoga, as that is the time when they feel their true self and they know more about themselves.

Know yourself in the following ways:

- Be aware whose company you like
- Know your strengths and weaknesses
- Be aware of your moods, emotions and feelings
- Examine your interaction with others
- Understand how the external environment affects your mood

You must know your strengths and weaknesses, passion and fears and pain and ecstasy. You can deal with your life in a better way if you know about your weirdness and idiosyncrasies, tolerance and limits and hatred and likings. You must also know the purpose of your life. You do not know about yourself right from the birth. As you grow, you get to know about yourself at every stage. It is a conscious effort and you should do it with proper intention and purpose. You may get frustrated if you have not spent time to know yourself. For example, if in an interview you are asked about your positive traits, you will be tight lipped and will not have an answer if you have never introspected.

The main purpose of knowing yourself is to make you a better leader, which would enable you to take right decisions and reach your goals faster. So how do you get to know yourself? Knowing some essential things about yourself, which are explained below, will help you understand yourself.

Style is a reflection of your attitude and your personality.

— Shawn Ashmore

1. **Knowing your personality:** There are several personality and assessment tests which you can find online. By taking these assessments, you will get to know about your hidden qualities. Just ponder over them. What does your name signify? What are your characteristic traits? What people think about yourself? How do you react on a happy day or a sad day, or a day when you get a reward? Basically, you get to know how you do you interact with the outside world.
2. **Knowing your values:** You must jot down on a piece of paper the values you possess. Like, what are the things on which you cannot compromise and where you can be flexible? Are you honest and truthful and a person of probity? Are you ambitious, responsible and an initiator or a follower? Do you value being dedicated to your senior's commands?
3. **Knowing your body:** People think they know about their body but they are wrong. When you see your body in the mirror you are always surprised. The more you get to know about your body the more you get surprised. Think about it! Do you know about your stamina, your breathing pattern and capacity, your physical limits and your body balance? You may think you have stamina to do lot many exercises. But when you actually start exercising, you may be surprised to find that you cannot do it for more than two minutes. Try to stand up on one leg with your eyes closed and see it yourself how long can you maintain your balance.

4. **Knowing your likes and dislikes:** What do you like and dislike is very important and your family and friends should know it. They will talk about things which you like and will avoid talking about things you dislike. For example, if you do not like talking to strangers or travelling to

other places, do not do it. But if you like dancing or shopping online or chatting on Facebook, do spend some time on these things.

5. **Knowing your mood:** There are many adjectives which can be used to describe your mood. It can be good or bad, sorrow or delightful. Identify what irks you or what gives you peace of mind. Learn about the ups and downs of your mood so that you can find ways to enhance the ups. Try to get rid of your bad mood by doing meditation or by pursuing the hobbies you like.

2.2 POSITIVE THINKING

If you remain positive you will reflect a lot of energy to motivate yourself as well as others. So have a positive self-image of yourself because it is an important factor for learning new skills, for maintaining your emotional health and for overall development of your personality.

Negative thinking about yourself will lead to acquiring the following negative characteristics:

1. Insecurity, scepticism and fearfulness
2. Low or no self-confidence
3. Dearth of pride in achievements
4. Often feeling embarrassed in public

Positive thinking enables you to accept yourself as you are and also accommodate others as they are. You will have the feeling of security and confidence for whatever you do and you will accept people's compliments with pleasure.

> Positive thinking enables to have a feeling of security and confidence.

Late Dr. Eric Berne studied attitudes of people towards themselves and others. Through his research he had identified the following four attitudes which people generally have towards their life:

1. **I am not okay, you are not okay:** People with this attitude are introvert and cannot accept themselves, as they always feel inferior. They suffer from inferiority complex. Things in their life are not worth and they get negative vibes.
2. **I am not okay, you are okay:** Such people cannot get along with others easily. They reject themselves thinking their life is not worth living. They blame others for their problems and give and get negative vibes.

3. **I am okay, you are not okay:** Such people forcibly impose themselves on others. They behave like bullies and are demanding. They think their life is more important than others and give negative vibes.
4. **I am okay, you are okay:** Such people are positive about life. They get along with others with mutual respect, accept themselves and others as they are and give and get positive vibes.

To create a positive image about yourself keep the following five points in your mind:

1. **You are the best:** God has made you a unique person and gifted you with special talents. Do not make a mistake of comparing yourself with others. Like an entrepreneur, compete only with yourself; must learn from Usain Bolt, the fastest runner, who is the champion for 50 metres and 100 metres run and is constantly reducing time duration because he wants to be his best.
2. **Polish yourself:** Know your weaknesses and work on them or know your strengths and develop them. Keep polishing yourself because you have control over you and you can change. If you think you have something which you dislike, it is time you got rid of it.
3. **Observe others:** You have made friends for what they are and not because what they should be. Accept the people around you as they are and influence them to change by posing yourself as a role model.
4. **Think of success, not failures:** Most of the time you may be recalling your bad times and failures and keep sulking. Instead, you keep telling yourself that you are born to succeed. Think of the success stories and the good times you have had in the past with your near and dear ones.
5. **Choose the righteous path:** Many people influence you by telling what you should do and what you should not, but nobody has a clear idea of ethics. It is your responsibility to keep your moral standards high and live up to them. Certainly you will be respected by all.

2.3 JOHARI'S WINDOW

To have a positive outlook and good personality one has to assess oneself at every stage. For this assessment Johari's window model is a handy tool which is being used by a number of individuals for improving self-awareness and developing fruitful relationships with their colleagues. The name Johari's window has been coined from the names of American psychologists Joseph Lift and Harry Ingham who had developed this model. Today this model is very popular in the field of personality development as it emphasises and influences soft skills, interpersonal relationships, empathy, cooperation and intergroup development.

Johari's window model is specifically helpful for understanding the employer–employee relationship, which is very important for the progress of an organisation. People across the world have adapted the four regions of this model described by psychologists Joseph Lift and Harry Ingham. It is indeed a very simple model.

Some people refer to Johari's window model as a disclosure/feedback model of self-awareness while others call it an information processing tool. Johari's window refers to oneself and others. Self indicates the subject and others are people of other groups. Actually, this model provides information about the experience, attitude, feelings, motivation and depression of a person or group in relation with other people in four main perspectives.

The four perspectives of Johari's window are called areas, regions or quadrants. Each perspective represents information, feelings, etc. related to a person. It also tells whether the information is known by the person and whether the information is known or not known by other members in the group.

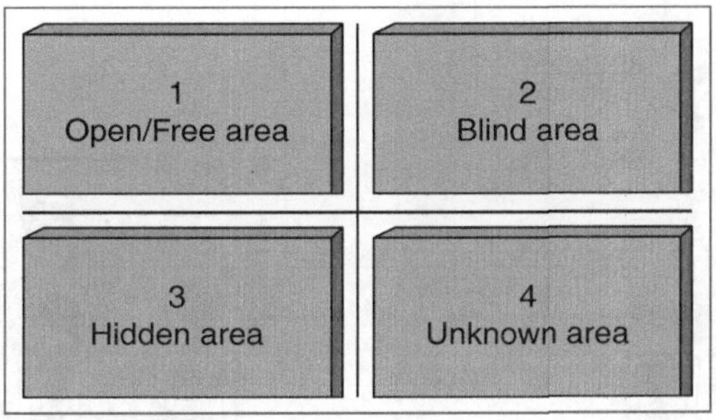

Four quadrants of Johari's window for self-assessment.

The first area of Johari's window is called open or free area which is also known as the area of free activity. This contains complete information about a person – his/her attitude, knowledge, skillset, views, opinions etc. – which is known by the self and others. The aim should be to develop the open area for every person in a group. When working in the free area, as you have no inhibitions you are more efficient and productive and the group is also very productive. It is in the open area that frank communication and cooperation occur that is free from mistrust, confusion, hindrances and misunderstandings. The existing members of a group have larger open areas than those of new entrants in the group. This is because the new members begin with relatively small areas due to the insufficient knowledge they have about the other members. Gradually, the size of this area of a new member is expanded horizontally into the blind space by his/her proper listening of the feedback of other group members. This is known as feedback solicitation. One can help other members expand their open area by listening to them and providing feedback sensitively.

> Johari's window model emphasises and influences soft skills, interpersonal relationships, empathy, cooperation and intergroup development. It is, therefore, helpful in the field of personality development and is specifically helpful for understanding the employer–employee relationship.

When people start hiding their information and feelings, then the size of their open area is expanded vertically downwards into the hidden space. Good leaders play an important role by facilitating feedback among group members. The responsibility of the leaders is manifold. They have to promote the culture of open environment, positive thinking, helpful conduct, sensitive communication and knowledge dissemination throughout the organisation. Progressive organisations always have the culture of openness and healthy environment. Therefore, they encourage positive development of the open area of everyone.

Johari's second quadrant is called the blind area or blind spot. It represents what is known about the subject by others and the subject is oblivious about this information. By seeking feedback about oneself from others and responding positively to it, one reduces this area, thereby increasing one's open area. The blind area is not productive for individuals or groups. It represents the ignorance about individuals or issues in which one is involved. It also includes those issues that others are purposely withholding from a person.

People who are difficult to work with do have big blind areas. Managers should take responsibility to reduce this area of the people working under them and expand their open area by giving feedback and encouraging them to come out of their shells. Leaders can serve as conduits to promote non-judgmental feedbacks and group responses rather than individual disclosures. They can reduce fears breeding among people and encourage them to be less resilient.

Johari's third quadrant is called hidden self or hidden area or facade. This area represents feelings or information known to an individual, but is kept hidden and, therefore, not known to others. The hidden feelings or information can be about anything which an individual does not want to reveal to others. It may include one's fears, hidden agenda, secrets or anything that one does not want to reveal. Some information pertaining to the third quadrant may not have any repercussion on the work of a team or group and so can and should remain hidden. However, a lot of hidden information may have a bearing on one's work performance or the work of the entire team, so it is better to place that information in the open area. The aim should be to share information with others as far as possible. Sharing information in the terminology of Johari's window is called as self-disclosure or exposure process, which helps in increasing the open area. We must share information about ourselves with others. By doing this we can reduce our hidden area and increase our open area which will bring better trust, understanding, cooperation and productivity in our team or group. This will remove confusion, misunderstanding and mistrust which are instrumental in undermining teamwork.

Johari's fourth quadrant is called unknown self or area of unknown activity. It represents information about an individual's latent abilities, aptitude and feelings, which is unknown to the individual as well as people around him/her. This information could be about one's behaviour, attitude, capabilities which can be positive and good, but it is hidden deep in an individual and impact one's personality in different ways. Bigger unknown areas are more prevalent in the younger people who have less work experience.

The fourth quadrant can be reduced by self-discovery or by learning from keen observation of oneself by others in different kinds of situations. Counselling can also unravel many unknown issues which could either be done by one person or by a group.

The 'self-image' is the key to human personality and human behaviour. Change the self image and you change the personality and the behaviour.

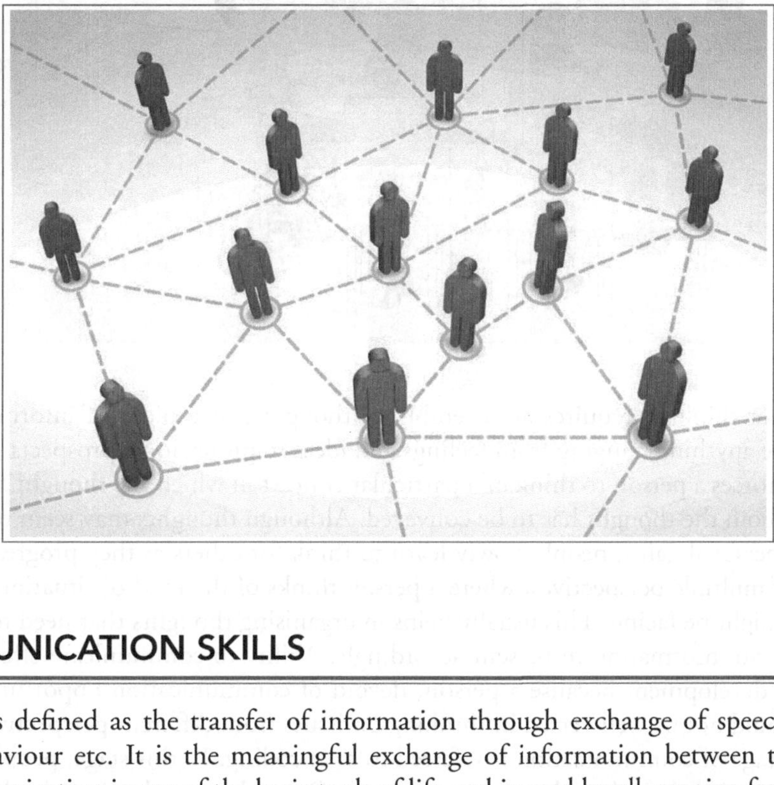

2.4 COMMUNICATION SKILLS

Communication is defined as the transfer of information through exchange of speech, messages, signs, visual effects, behaviour etc. It is the meaningful exchange of information between two or more living organisms. Communication is one of the basic tools of life and is used by all, ranging from microorganisms to full-grown animals like mammals as well as trees that have been living for centuries. In relatively intelligent species, such as mammals, communication is effective not only as a survival trait but in the case of humans it is also essential for the development of personality.

Communication is viewed in three stages, which represent thinking, encoding and decoding. In the case of humans, psychology research has showed that people living in closed environments with little stimulus from the outside world tend to have

Communication is viewed in three stages, which represent thinking, encoding and decoding.

comparatively less mature mental profiles in comparison to those who have been in a wider range of contact with living beings surrounding them. The latter people have a more mature mental profile than the former because of the frequent communication they do have with the wider range of people around them.

Communication in itself might seem to be a simple process but actually it is complex process comprising three stages, which can only be noticed when observed closely.

The first stage of thinking requires an assembly of thoughts, or a piece of information in a person's mind. This could be anything, ranging from feelings and ideas to professional prospects. The need to send a particular thought forces a person to think of a particular context in which the thought settles, and of a particular person to whom the thought has to be conveyed. Although thoughts may seem to arise mostly from the motivation of personal gains, people slowly learn to think for others as they progress in their life. This leads to the idea of multiple perspectives, where a person thinks of the kind of situation another person or a group of people might be facing. This usually helps in organising thoughts that need to take into account these people and form information to be sent accordingly. Ability to communicate effectively is a primary step to personality development because a person, devoid of communication opportunities or hesitant in communication would not be well versed in thinking on issues from different perspectives.

In the second stage of communication is referred to as encoding. In this stage, people choose a method that best fits for conveying their thought to the receiver(s). Depending on the thought that needs to be conveyed, there are different modes of communication. Each mode has its own specialty and requires specific effort and creative inputs.

For example, information to be communicated to a young audience can be better presented using illustrative visuals such as animations and comic strips to grab their attention. For people of older age groups, information can be presented in the form of news, books, blogs, etc. A great quality of people possessing a developed personality is their insight about how to react in the particular situations and environments to get optimal transmission of information. Keeping in mind the sort of effect that different types of media can cause on the receiver, the sender has to choose an appropriate criterion. For example, an obituary message needs to be as short, respectable and subtle as possible. On the other hand, the advertising slogans should be aggressive and persuasive to draw the attention of prospective customers. These sorts of variations contribute greatly to personality development as they teach how to act in a given situation appropriately.

The last stage of communication consists of decoding a received transmission. It means understanding the transmitted information by its receiver. In daily life, people have to do much more decoding as compared to encoding as the world is witnessing an ever-increasing connectivity thanks to proliferation of new-found media sources such as blogs, social websites, news channels and newspapers. School education, which was earlier feasible only through reading a book physically or through teaching by someone, is now available over a vast range of media such as audio tapes, television and the Internet. All this requires lots of decoding by the receiver of information.

In decoding the information existing in a person's mind is combined with the information being received by the person to gain new understanding in wider contexts. Two people simply talking to each other can share experiences and insights that none of them has shared with anyone. On a much bigger scale, learning new languages or taking new courses can broaden a person's range of thinking and help him/her tackle the problems faced in daily life. One can hone one's communication skills by reading books and taking part in activities such as group discussions. A person travelling to a new country may experience wide cultural and behavioural differences with people living there. It is in such a situation that people who have been exposed a wide range of cultures, either by reading books, talking to other people or simply browsing the Internet have better chances of settling with the people of that country without much difficulty.

Personality development takes place in a person through all the three stages of communication. It is critically important to have a smooth experience with little or no friction while interacting with people through communication. A task as simple as giving a speech in front of ten colleagues may make some people nervous. They may forget what they were about to say. But with proper communication experience or training, such as having long one-on-one talks as well as understanding other people's perspectives can really help reduce nervousness and enable them give speech without much difficulty. Other tasks, such as writing letters, essays and blogs and exchanging them with others leads to a much healthy conversation or exchange of information as the persons involved can express their views in more easily decodable forms. Conversation usually contributes to improvement of speaking skills and also helps develop listening skills in a person. Other forms of expression such as drawing, paintings and photography are also used to communicate certain views that are hard to put forward in words.

Communication is not used for only exchange of information. It also helps one pursue one's interests. For example, people interested in music, literature or photography will feel happy if they could find other people or communities with similar interests. Interaction with co-artists or co-professionals opens before them broader horizons in of their fields, enabling them to upgrade their skills. YouTube, for example, has helped people across the world post their films, music, art, etc. on the Internet and interact with people of similar interests. Recently, YouTube has also introduced an income generation programme where people can earn money by simply attracting lots of viewers and by the likes recorded on their videos. As for the viewers, it has become a really efficient source of learning that teaches skills such as playing guitars to assembling a robot in a simple and straight forward experience. Finding music of a particular genre to searching live footage of the civil war going on in a neighbouring country, have all become easy, hence contributing to personality development.

2.5 NON-VERBAL COMMUNICATION

The process of communicating information through wordless (non-verbal) cues, is called non-verbal communication. It involves the use of cues related to voice, touch, distance, physical surroundings, appearance etc.

2.5.1 Importance of Non-verbal Cues

Many times our words and non-verbal cues do not match. In such instances, it is the listener's choice whether to believe the verbal message or the non-verbal message. Mostly the listener will choose to believe the non-verbal message because it is an instinctive and natural expression that showcases our true feelings and intentions.

The way one hears, sees, moves and reacts tells people whether one is interested in a particular task, whether one is being truthful, and also how much attention is one paying. Trust, clarity and understanding increase if non-verbal signals complement the words; otherwise they lead to tension, mistrust and confusion. Thus, in order to communicate effectively, it's important to give due attention to non-verbal cues.

In *The Importance of Effective Communication*, Edward G. Wertheim says that non-verbal cues can play the following five roles:

1. **Repetition:** They can repeat what a person is speaking.
2. **Contradiction:** They can also contradict a message that a person is trying to get across.
3. **Substitution:** They can substitute for a verbal message. For example, a person's facial expressions may sometimes convey much more than his words do.
4. **Complementing:** They may complement a verbal message. For example, an approving nod from a listener can imply understanding.
5. **Accenting:** They may accent or enhance a verbal message. Banging the table, for instance, can accentuate a message.

2.5.2 Components of Non-verbal Communication and Body Language

There are various components that contribute to non-verbal communication. Together, they combine to communicate one's interest in a particular thing. These components are described in the following sections:

> The process of communicating information through wordless cues is called non-verbal communication. It involves the use of cues related to voice, touch, distance, physical surroundings, appearance etc.

2.5.2.1 Facial Expressions

Our faces are capable of emoting countless feelings. Interestingly, unlike some forms of non-verbal communication, facial expressions are universal. Facial expressions for emotions like surprise, happiness, sadness, fear, anger, disgust, etc. are the same across countries and cultures.

> The various components of non-verbal communication are facial expressions, body movement and postures, gestures, eye contact, touch, space, voice etc.

2.5.2.2 Body Movements and Postures

People's perceptions of others are affected by the way they walk, sit, stand up, etc. The way one moves and carries speaks volumes about one's personality. This type of non-verbal communication includes one's postures, bearing, stance, etc.

2.5.2.3 Gestures

Gestures form an inseparable trait of our personality. We express ourselves with gestures on auto-pilot when we wave, point, beckon and use our hands while arguing or speaking animatedly. However, the meaning of gestures may vary across cultures and regions, so it is important to be careful to avoid misinterpretation. Thumbs up, facial expressions, palm movements, etc. are examples of the gestures that we regularly use in communication.

2.5.2.4 Eye Contact

Visuals are much more powerful than words as most people give importance to visual perception in communication. Eye contact is one of the most important types of nonverbal communication. The way one looks at someone can convey many things, including interest, affection, enmity, jealousy or attraction. Eye contact is especially important to continue conversation and for determining the other person's response.

2.5.2.5 Touch

Touch is a very effective means of communicating one's feelings. For example, a pat on the back may reinforce praise while a controlling grip on the arm may convey aggression. Think about the messages conveyed by the following types of touch: a timid handshake, a weak tap on the shoulder, a warm embrace and a patronising pat on the head.

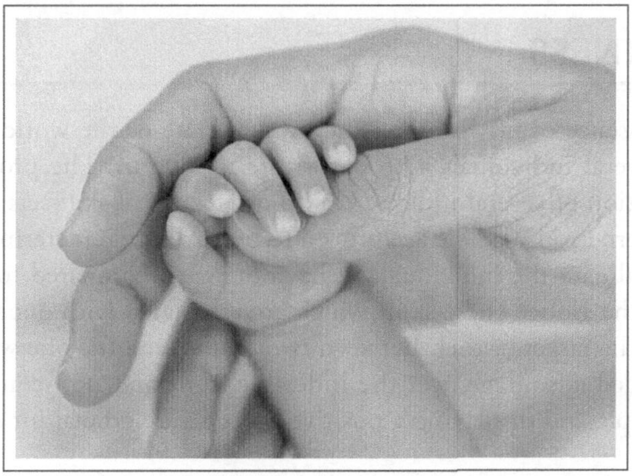

2.5.2.6 *Space*

Everyone needs a physical space although one's need for space depends on factors like culture, situation and the proximity that exists in a relationship. Physical space can be used to communicate many different nonverbal messages, including those like intimacy and affection or aggression and dominance. Sometimes people may feel uncomfortable if someone stands very close to them while talking. They feel that their personal space is being violated.

2.5.2.7 *Voice*

In a communication, other than what one says, it is also important how one says it. Listeners judge a speaker by the quality of his/her voice. They pay attention to the quality, timbre, tone etc. of the speaker's voice. Sounds that convey understanding like 'Hmm' and 'Uh-huh' are important. Think about how someone's tone of voice, for example, can indicate sarcasm, anger, affection or confidence.

2.5.3 Tips to Improve Non-verbal Communication

Developing stress management skills to handle stress in the heat of the moment is one of the most important things one can do to improve non-verbal communication. Stress compromises one's communication abilities. When under stress, people are more likely to misread others. They send confusing or off-putting non-verbal signals and lapse into unpredictable patterns of behaviour. Furthermore, emotions are like a contagious disease. If someone is upset, it is very likely that the people around him/her become upset too, making a bad situation worse. More is explained on this topic in chapter 13 on stress and time management later in the book.

To cope with stress, it is best to take time out. Efforts should be made to calm down before jumping back into the conversation. Only after one regains emotional equilibrium does one become better equipped to deal with the situation in a positive way. You will learn more on this in Chapter 13 — Stress and Time Management.

> *The most basic of all human needs is the need to understand and to be understood.'*
>
> — Ralph Nicolas

2.6 PHYSICAL FITNESS

Growth, being the quintessence of life, signifies the present state of the world today, which is indeed an aggregate of growth of several individuals who constitute the world. The progress and prosperity of an individual is an amalgamation of several indices. Of which, technical skill-sets and interpersonal skills are of highest importance. Interpersonal skills have proven to be auxiliary in determining the growth trajectory of an individual as they validate the individual's behaviour when compared to the technical skills which are taught vividly all over the globe. These skills which are associated with one's emotional intelligence are more bankable to achieve the target farther. Between two employees, the one with a positive, pleasant and upbeat attitude has an added advantage over the inflexible, sour and non-communicative one. Knowing how to get along with people and displaying a positive attitude are crucial for success. Tasks like problem solving, delegating, motivating and team building are all much easier if you have good soft skills coupled with physical fitness.

Interpersonal skills when coupled with physical fitness can help one excel in one's vocation. Fitness has copious benefits – the physical ones being the most evident. The mental and emotional benefits, on the contrary, are the ones which help in developing an amicable personality. Physical fitness increases the endorphins (the happy chemicals of human body) in the body, boosts brain functioning, improves concentration, alleviates stress and helps tap into the creativity of an individual. It also bestows on the individual added benefits like improved self-confidence, greater enthusiasm and the ability to inspire others.

Physically fit people are less likely to get sick. They are generally more resistant to disease. They have more energy. One of the many benefits of regular exercise is increased and sustained energy throughout the day. This energy allows a person to stay focused on the task, handling it efficiently and giving the best of themselves to each task.

Fit and healthy individuals tend to have a high level of self-confidence because they have proven to themselves that they can do what is required to obtain a high level of physical fitness. This self-confidence empowers them to challenge themselves and strive for higher levels of achievement in the workplace. They inspire confidence. A person who maintains a high fitness level, tends to be a person in whom others have confidence.

Because of the many positive benefits of a healthy lifestyle, fit individuals tend to make good leaders. They do not hesitate in taking more leadership roles. They tend to have a physical and mental balance that results in a more positive attitude at the workplace. They are less stressed. Regular exercise releases physical and emotional tensions that life brings your way.

Perceptions of physical attractiveness contribute to generalised assumptions based on those attractions. Across cultures, what is beautiful is assumed to be good; attractive people are assumed to be more extroverted, popular and happy. The bias in favour of physically fit people is robust, with attractive people being perceived as more sociable, happier and more successful than physically unfit people.

Technical skills are like the soul while the interpersonal skills form the countenance of a person's abilities. Good interpersonal skills when coupled with physical fitness enhance the overview of one's life. It makes one more confident to address the needs of an explicitly demanding world. It helps a person strike a balance in life. This balance and fullness provide one with an edge over one's competitors. One can be a decisive game changer by keeping calm and focused through adversities of life and by providing solutions in taxing times. Such attributes can be developed by exemplary physical fitness – a precursor of sharpened technical skills and remarkable interpersonal skills.

On a conclusive note, physical fitness enhances both mental and emotional intelligence. It brings about a phenomenal change in the attitude of a person. This positivity could be leveraged to attain improved creativity, health and relationships on personal and professional levels.

Summary

People of this world have different kinds of personalities. Some have appealing personalities, whom you want to meet more often than others. You must know what kind of a personality you are. You should know of your likes and dislikes and other characteristic traits. If you understand your personality and know your strengths and weaknesses, you can always improve. Positive thinking helps you have a good personality as it reflects positive energy and outlook. People with positive thoughts are respected more than others and are sought after for company. To create a positive image think you are the best, observe others, focus on success and choose ethical paths. Johari's window helpsone assess oneself so that one's relationship with others could improve. Good communication skills, both verbal and non-verbal, boost your confidence and hence your personality. Communication is defined as the transfer of information, knowledge, ideas, behaviour etc. An individual needs to communicate effectively while participating in group discussions, facing an interview, giving instructions etc. The communication ability is also needed while writing reports, policies, notices, agenda and minutes. It can be improved by reading books and newspapers, participating in group discussions and by talking to others. Non-verbal communication through gestures, postures, eye contact and space distancing is equally important as they communicate a volume. Physical fitness is another attribute which must not be ignored. Regular exercises help one attain a high level of physical fitness. By keeping healthy you can spread positive energy and work efficiently to go up in your career.

Chapter Review

1. Explain some ways in which you could know more about yourself.
2. Describe the ways with which you can create and keep a positive image about yourself.
3. Explain the roles played by non-verbal cues in communication.
4. What determines a person's personality?
5. List ways to enhance self-awareness for proper personality development?
6. What role does communication skills play in development of a positive personality?
7. What is the importance of body language in overall personality development?
8. How can Johari's window be used to create better and stronger relationships?
9. What do you think can be the ways for self-motivation for a positive personality development?
10. What can be the features of a good personality for making a positive first impression?

Direct Questions

1. Define personality development?
2. What do you mean by an introvert?
3. What is non-verbal communication?
4. What are the critical features of development of positive personality and attitude?
5. What are the traits of a positive personality?
6. How are the following important in personality development:
   a. Personal grooming
   b. Self-esteem and confidence

c. Emotional stability
d. Diverse experiences

7. What are the four quadrants/perspectives of Johari's window?

Analytical Questions

1. Imagine that at an interview you are asked to tell about your weaknesses. What would be your answer? Justify.
2. Imagine you are facing an interview for your dream job. You are being asked where you see yourself in fiveyears. Give your answer with proper justification.
3. You are being invited to a college to give a motivational speech on personality development to the students. Write down your speech.

Resources for Further Reflections

1. Some questions to ask yourself: http://www.oocities.org/halzmarty/3rdedition/QFPD.html.
2. Personality interview question and answer: http://www.job-interview-site.com/personality-interview-questions-and-answers.html.
3. A blog on personality development: http://sadhuji.blogspot.in/.
4. Personality development: http://vrsiddhartha.ac.in/cse/files/Personality%20Development%20study%20material.pdf.
5. Johari's window: https://www.usc.edu/hsc/ebnet/Cc/awareness/Johari%20windowexplain.pdf.
6. Building relationships with Johari's window: http://www.theinnovationcenter.org/files/doc/A4/CLW%20pp%20120%20Building%20Deeper%20Relationships%20with%20the%20Johari%20Window.pdf.

Caselet 1

Harsha Real Estates

Harsha Real Estates is a company known for its development teams, whose members wear T-shirts with this quote: 'We work long and still love it!' Starting as a very small firm in 2006 in Chennai, Harsha Real Estates had grown to become one of the most sought-after companies to work with by the end of 2007, that is, in just two years of its inception. It captured 14% of market share just two years. Its employees enjoy the flexibility, given to them, to work from home. The company's career portal says, 'Apply only if you have a personality to work round the clock.' Actually, the company has found out that its employees work more from home as compared to their output in the office.

Harsha, CEO of Harsha Real Estates, started off his business along with his friend as partner.

He was highly confident of his ability to make his venture out perform all the existing players in the market. Hence did not take a long time to start his company.

Harsha has a high level of optimism and he also wants his employees to remain optimist. A noticeable feature of Harsha's approach to business is to keep all his employees motivated. That's why he always tells his people, 'If you see a person seeking some concession, do not ask the supervisor, just take care of it. Erase the extra amount (i.e. the cut that the company gets which can be reduced), inform the customers about it and make the deal at the earliest'. In fact, there were rewards to employees who made the highest number of customers to join Harsha Real Estates. Recently, a woman employee was given the employee of the year award. Harsha brought her parents from London and arranged a party. For all this he spends a lot of money but he says it is an investment.

Although the employees have to work for longer hours, there are very less number of employees who feel they are stressed. The employee turnover ratio is very low. New customers are delighted to join Harsha Real Estates because they are served at a very fast pace. The CEO has been very popular in the company and his employees are extremely hard working. They compete among themselves to get reward parties directly from Harsha.

Questions

1. Why do employees work for long hours at Harsha Real Estates?
2. How do they still manage to be happy?
3. What did Harsha do to make his employees happy and do stress-free work?

Chapter 3

EMOTIONAL INTELLIGENCE

Learning Roadmap

After reading this chapter you will be able to:

- Understand what is emotional intelligence
- Differentiate between emotional intelligence quotient and intelligence quotient
- Explain why emotional intelligence is the driver of life
- Learn about self-management and self-awareness for personal excellence
- Know about social awareness and relationship management for social and professional success
- Understand the art of being emotionally intelligent

PERSPECTIVE

We humans are a bundle of emotions. Our emotions are a reflection of what we are and what we want to be. They also create our image for others. It is important to understand how we control emotions or how emotions dominate our lives. By controlling emotions we can bring a desired transformation in our personality because emotions influence our behaviour and also have a bearing on our lifestyle. It is emotional intelligence (EI) that enables us to control our emotions and feelings. Being emotionally intelligent can empower us in various ways – by knowing ourselves, bonding with others, overcoming stress, etc. Emotional intelligence saves us from living an emotional rollercoaster life. When we look at the lives of people around us, we find that they have their own shares of frustrations, anger and failures. Some of them cope well with these adverse situations while others just get carried away by the negative emotions generated in these situations. From Mahatma Gandhi to Nelson Mandela and from Mother Teresa to Dalai Lama, EI was the constant companion of these great souls in their struggle for the causes that were dear to them. EI was a dominant trait of their personalities which enabled them continuously adapt with changing times, use their strengths, overcome their weaknesses and build strong relationships with people around them. There are many stories of the people who made a huge difference in the world and left indelible marks on the annals of history because they could use their emotions righteously. Indeed, our ability to develop EI and use it effectively goes a long way in bringing contentment and professional excellence.

> *Emotional intelligence is the sine qua non of leadership. Without it, a person can have the best training in the world, an incisive, analytical mind, and an endless supply of smart ideas, but he still won't make a great leader.*
>
> — Daniel Goleman

3.1 MEANING AND DEFINITION

Emotional intelligence (EI) is a unique ability bestowed upon or acquired by individuals to understand, control and regulate their emotions. It impacts different aspects of our daily life such as our behaviour and interaction with others. It also prepares us to perceive and react to the emotions and feelings of others. EI is measured by emotional intelligence quotient (E-IQ/EQ). It primarily gives a measure of one's ability to use, understand and manage emotions in ways that positively affect oneself and others, and help in relieving stress, communicating effectively, showing empathy, resolving conflicts and overcoming challenges.

EI is an important personality trait that enables us to recognise our own emotions and understand how they may affect others around us. It involves understanding perceptions of others which helps in effective management of our relationships. Whether we are in office or home, the ability to engage with friends and colleagues and interpret their emotions is essential for professional excellence, social acceptability and personal contentment. The emotionally intelligent working environment is the backbone for amiable social life and professional excellence. It enhances people's competence and makes them more supportive, healthy and productive. Psychologists worldwide hold different views about the inherent nature or otherwise of emotional intelligence. Some believe it is something which can be groomed or nurtured, whereas others feel it is an instinctive behaviour.

> Emotional intelligence is the "something" in each of us that is a bit intangible. It affects how we manage behaviour, navigate social complexities, and make personal decisions that achieve positive results. — Travis Bradberry

3.2 NEED FOR EMOTIONAL INTELLIGENCE

Certain important aspects of a person's life are greatly affected by the level of the person's EI. Some of these aspects are explained below:

1. **Professional excellence:** Higher EI is a great motivating factor in life. It helps us achieve many things professionally and socially. We plan and lead our career in a better way by setting new goals and working hard for achieving them, engaging people and leading them and thus contributing to the growth of our employer or own business.
2. **Physical wellness:** EI has a direct correlation with our physical and mental wellness. In other words, EI plays a significant role in maintaining our body and nervous system in good shape. It helps improve our stress management and strengthens our immune system.
3. **Mental health:** Poor management of emotions leads to psychological disorders and other serious ailments. EI keeps us mentally alert and calm. It is a great help in tackling stress and mood swings and generating creative ideas.
4. **Relationship management:** By understanding our emotions, we can better reciprocate to others' feelings and moods. In this respect, EI makes it easy for us to engage with new people and share our ideas with them. It brings compatibility among the members of groups and teams and empowers them to work and deliver effectively.

5. **Leadership:** Research has proved that those who show outstanding leadership at the workplace or in any other field are endowed with a high level of EI. Leadership comes naturally to such people as they understand, motivate and build strong rapport with the people across an organisation. This aspect of EI makes them acceptable as leaders of choice to everyone.
6. **Crisis management:** EI brings people closer. So it helps people working in groups resolve their conflicts and misunderstandings amicably preventing any blow-ups. With this ability, they are open and receptive to each other and try to control explosive situations swiftly.

> *The only way on earth to influence the other fellow is to talk about what he wants and show him how to get it.*
>
> — Dale Carnegie

3.3 INTELLIGENCE QUOTIENT VERSUS EMOTIONAL INTELLIGENCE QUOTIENT

Generally people strive to have a high intelligence quotient (IQ) thinking that it is all they need to be successful. Not long ago, the business world used to emphasise that smart and dynamic leaders with high IQ were the only people capable of writing the success story of growth and fame for companies. But soon they realised that professionals with high IQ may not always be the right choice for building successful businesses. Research carried out by the Carnegie Institute of Technology shows that 85% of your financial success is due to skills in 'human engineering, your personality and ability to communicate, negotiate and lead. Shockingly, only 15% of financial success is due to technical knowledge. Therefore, high IQ would improve marginally the prospects of a successful life. It is EQ that is the essential ingredient of social and personal bliss. There are many examples of leaders worldwide who are acclaimed for their high IQ, but they are frustrated and unsatisfied with themselves regardless of their high IQ level.

Usually, a degree from a reputed university and a high IQ are the most cherished values in any job scenario, but these do not guarantee a professional's successful career or high social status. Though people

with high IQ and low EQ manage to reach top positions sometimes, they are usually bland, condescending, critical, uncomfortable and stressful. Such people are not liked by others and are not the first preference to be included in any team. On the contrary, people with a high EQ are poised, outgoing, committed, sympathetic, caring and comfortable with themselves and those around them. Having a good IQ with a high EQ is like having the icing on the cake. Such people are the most successful and are the most preferred for roles of team players, leaders, higher managers and entrepreneurs. They know how to interact with people and are loved and supported by all.

Several studies that support the benefits of EQ over IQ have generated a notion that sometimes a high EQ can compensate for a very low IQ. However, it is important to understand that only EQ with no IQ also cannot lead a person towards success. We must not ignore the fact that IQ is important to pass pre-requisite examinations for certain jobs. EQ certainly helps in handling interviews and team work and giving good job performances, but the role of IQ in professional excellence can never be completely ruled out. There has to be a balance between the two. IQ is something a person is presumed to be born with or enhanced by a person's intellectual ability. There is a lesser scope for IQ development in a person. However, unlike IQ, EQ can always be improved by social interactions, observation and practice.

Classification	EQ	IQ
Stands for	Is a measure of a person's level of emotional intelligence	Is a number derived from a standard mental test
Definition	The ability to perceive, evaluate, and express ones own emotions and others	Is used to determine academic abilities and apply information to appropriate conclusion
Brain	Right Brain	Left Brain
Prospect	Gets you promoted	Gets you hired
Domain	Social and emotional competence	Academic and technical competence
Workplace	Team leader, good at networking, and collaborator	Highly talented professional with analytical and research aptitude
Tests	Mayer-Salovey-Caruso test Daniel Goleman model score	Stanford-Binet test; Wechsler; Woodcock-Johnson tests of cognitive abilities

3.4 COMPONENTS OF EMOTIONAL INTELLIGENCE

Daniel Goleman, in his landmark book *Emotional Intelligence: Why It can Matter More than IQ,* argues that we need a special kind of competence that he called emotional intelligence to conduct ourselves and interact with others effectively – whether to work in teams, to overcome differences or to motivate people for achieving goals. He proposes the following five components of EI which have become essential guiding principles for any professional to practise meaningfully in the workplace:

1. Recognising emotions
2. Understanding emotions
3. Regulating emotions
4. Motivating yourself
5. Using emotions/managing relationships

The first three components of EI (recognising emotions, understanding emotions and regulating emotions) fall into personal competencies.

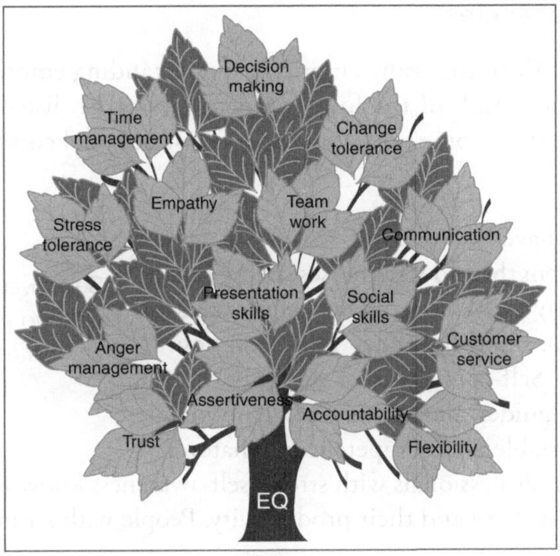

Emotional intelligence is the foundation for critical skills.

3.5 COMPETENCIES OF EMOTIONAL INTELLIGENCE

The five components of EI proposed by Goleman are generally grouped in the following four clusters:

1. Self-awareness
2. Self-management
3. Social awareness
4. Relationship management

These four clusters are categorised in the following two broad categories of competencies of EI:

1. Personal competencies
2. Social competencies

	What I see	**What I do**
Personal competence	Self-awareness	Self-management
Social competence	Social awareness	Relationship management

Emotional intelligence is made up of four core skills.

3.5.1 Personal Competencies

The first three components of EI (recognising emotions, understanding emotions and regulating emotions) fall into personal competencies. And, of the four competencies of EI, listed above, the first two — self-awareness and self-management — come under the category of personal competencies.

3.5.1.1 Self-awareness

The best virtue that you can have is to become self-aware. It is the power to evaluate your strengths and weaknesses. Being self-aware means you can perfectly feel and accurately understand the level of your own emotions and how they reflect on your behaviour and performance. Self-confidence is an important aspect of self-awareness that guides and trains your emotions in a way that you feel comfortable and competent in whatever situation that comes up in life. Professionals with strong self-awareness know what their behaviour is, how it affects others and how it drives them and their productivity. People with strong self-awareness are:

> Self-awareness is the power to evaluate your strengths and weaknesses as well as their effects on others.

1. Aware of their strengths and weaknesses
2. Self-believers and are capable of learning from experiences
3. Open to candid feedback and new perspectives
4. Always honest to themselves and others
5. Able to speak directly and correctly
6. Capable of reacting sensibly, neither over-critical nor over-joyous
7. Interested in continuous learning and self-development
8. Able to show a sense of humour and perspective about themselves

3.5.1.2 Self-management

Self-management is built on the understanding that has been gained by self-awareness. It involves controlling emotions and not allowing them to control you. In other words, it can be termed as self-control which includes maintaining equilibrium while facing any problem or provocation. It is important because it establishes your trustworthiness and conscientiousness. It also reflects on how motivated and how optimist you are.

People with great self-management show several noteworthy virtues some of which are described below:

> Self-management is a training to control our feelings and impulses and channelise them in positive ways. It helps in creating an environment of trust and fairness.

1. **Self-control:** It is your ability to remain composed and balanced whatever the situation you are in. It is your capacity to keep unruly thoughts and impulses under control. People endowed with self-control effectively manage their impulsive feelings, urges and distressing emotions in order to stay composed, positive and unflappable even in difficult moments.
2. **Trustworthiness:** Your trustworthiness implies that you always stick to your words and people always look for and trust your wisdom. People with this ability are known to act with high standards of honesty and integrity. They develop their credibility through their actions and are not hesitant to admit their own mistakes. Such people are not reluctant to take tough, principled stands, even if they become unpopular and regardless of how much they have to fight for the right. When managers behave reasonably while controlling their impulses, they are able to create a healthy ambience of trust and harmony. They minimise infighting at workplaces and improve relationships among employees and their productivity.
3. **Conscientiousness:** It is the quality of being a highly caring and competent employee. People with this virtue attempt to set new standards in professionalism and excel in every task they undertake. Highly conscientious employees do their jobs perfectly. They set their goals and work hard to achieve them, reach office on time and are supportive and thoughtful towards their co-workers. They hold themselves accountable for meeting their objectives and are organised and careful in their work. They do have the knack of keeping themselves motivated and organising their lives well.
4. **Adaptability:** It is one's capability to adapt oneself to the prevailing circumstances. It is a much needed job skill, as workplaces today offer multiple roles and responsibilities for the employees to perform. When professionals adapt themselves to the changing business needs, technical skills and multitasking roles, they make themselves the most sought after employees in any organisation.
5. **Orientation towards achievement:** It refers to the driving force in individuals to raise their excellence bar to new heights. People endowed with this virtue challenge themselves by setting goals and measure their own performance against those goals. They actively seek the information needed to get their work done and use their time productively.
6. **Initiative:** It refers to one's ability to identify new opportunities and execute them proficiently. People with this ability are enterprising and proactive in everything assigned to them. These professionals are highly motivated and contribute something new and innovative at the workplace. Through their initiatives, they take control of adverse and risky situations and help in amicable resolution of problems.

3.5.2 Social Competencies

> Social competencies enhance our abilities to interact positively and get along well with people using a range of skills aimed at resolving conflict.

The last two components of EI (motivating yourself and using emotions/managing relationships) are effectively expressed in social competencies. These competencies expect you to expand your awareness to include the emotions of the people around you. These skills look at how well you manage your relationships with others, including their emotions. Social competencies are sub-divided into two clusters called social awareness and relationship management.

3.5.2.1 Social Awareness

Social awareness refers to one's ability to understand the interconnectedness between people's emotions. It is significant to appreciate differences and similarities among the views and emotions of different people to create a cohesive working environment. Our understanding and acceptance of our co-workers and citizens enable us to grow as a society and nation. People with social awareness demonstrate the following characteristics:

> Social awareness is the key to understand others' perspectives, to realise the needs of an organisation and to serve the needs of the clients.

1. **Empathy:** It refers to one's ability to see the world from other people's perspectives and discerning what they are thinking by putting oneself in their shoes. In other words, empathy is the skill to engage with and relate to others. It is like glue that keeps people working together for the growth of their organisation. People endowed with empathy are gifted listeners. They listen with focused attention what others say and sense their feelings perfectly. They pursue their goals or tasks without conflict and are willing to accommodate other's plans and suggestions for effective work culture.
2. **Organisational awareness:** It is the ability to know what is happening across the organisation. It enables one to understand organisational structure, culture and dynamics, power relationships and organisational issues. In short, organisation awareness enables employees to understand the very philosophy of their organisation. This understanding helps them get things done within the organisation both formally and informally.
3. **Service orientation:** It is how your liberal social standing or reach helps you serve better business interests of your organisation. People endowed with this competency are able to identify issues that hamper their organisation's business. They engage their clients through an empathetic discourse and counselling to improve their satisfaction while doing business with the organisation.

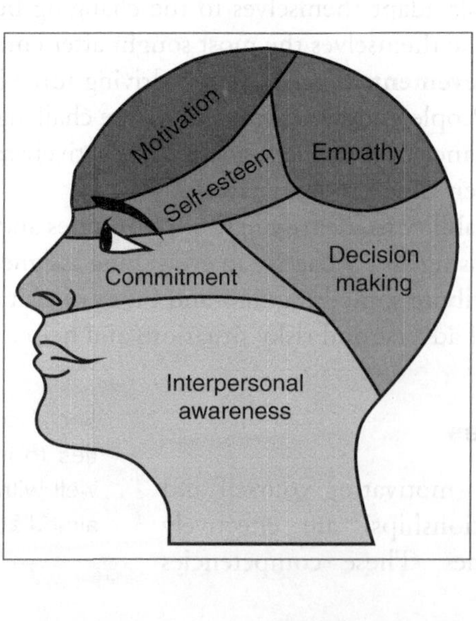

3.5.2.2 Relationship Management

Whether you have your own business or work for a company, your prowess to manage and work with people effectively makes you a magnetic professional and a great team leader. It is your effective relationship management across the organisational hierarchy that sets you ahead of your peers and helps you win accolades. The ability to build effective interpersonal relationship is an essential ability for those aspiring to work and win in the global workplace. This competency equips a professional to identify, negotiate and manage with different sets of people in the practical world. The following skills are the key to successful management of relationships:

1. **Influence:** One of the most vibrant relationship management skills is your ability to influence others. It is reflected in the way you get along with others through your arguments and behaviour.
2. **Leadership:** Your quality of being a people-friendly leader makes you acceptable to one and all in your organisation. Genuine leaders always get the support of their teams and deliver the best in rain or shine.
3. **Developing others:** It refers to your ability to make your team members or colleagues perform to the best of their abilities. Professionals endowed with this competence not only recognise their co-workers' qualities and performance but also inspire them to change and grow with the organisation.
4. **Communication:** It refers to your ability to communicate and build bonds with people and bring new clients and more profits for your organisation. An open communication climate would improve the loyalty of the staff, create healthy relationships and enhance productivity in the organisation. Professionals need to master the communication ability to build rapport with their colleagues and clients. Many ways are available to acquire or improve this competency which will help you devise better ways for soliciting information, giving feedbacks, putting an argument forcefully and listening attentively.

Fortunately emotional intelligence can be developed. It helps you manage better relationships, achieve your professional goals and find peace and happiness in life.

The noblest pleasure is the joy of understanding.

— Leonardo da Vinci

3.6 SKILLS TO DEVELOP EMOTIONAL INTELLIGENCE

Whether or not is it possible to learn EI — This is a subject of continuous debate among those working in the fields of psychology and personality development. The basic human nature or personality traits are hard to change in any individual. But EI can be acquired through effective training programmes. Such training is necessary because every organisation needs people who manage themselves and others well, understand work dynamics and influence the workforce to achieve organisational goals. It is rare to find a successful manager, social leader and personally motivated person who is not emotionally intelligent. It is one of the essential human skills that organisations look for in aspiring team leaders/managers. For, EI drives people to professional excellence and helps create social bonhomie in the workplace. EI is also vital to lead a successful and satisfying happy life. To develop EI, your focus must be on acquiring or improving the following personal characteristics:

1. **Be an optimist:** When you are an optimist, your life is full of positivity and happiness. People come to you for seeking support and suggestions. You handle crisis well and bring harmony in an environment or system. You can adjust well in any given situation and overcome problems.

2. **Be stress-free:** Your strong and balanced mental attitude will never get you stressed by any tough situations. This attitude you can develop by doing physical exercises, performing meditation and following your passions and hobbies. Actually, it is your lifestyle that enables you to be emotionally intelligent and free from fatigue and stress. You spot stress triggers and get through them quickly.
3. **Be an eternal learner:** Your quest for learning new skills and acquiring knowledge can help you lead an enriching professional and social life. You are swift to adapt to new changes and understand people's aspirations easily in the workplace. This helps you stay updated in life and opens up you to learn more skills to be emotionally intelligent.
4. **Be expressive:** The primal urge of human beings is to express themselves. Your ability to communicate empathetically with others dispels from the minds of co-workers doubts and fears about your behaviour at the workplace and establishes your identity as a reliable, approachable and helpful professional. You become an excellent communicator because you control your thoughts and others trust you.
5. **Be responsible:** The way you manage your social and professional relationships makes you a truly responsible citizen. It is how you take care of your and others' interests without any conflicts. You are the one who is needed by everyone on their projects as a team player.

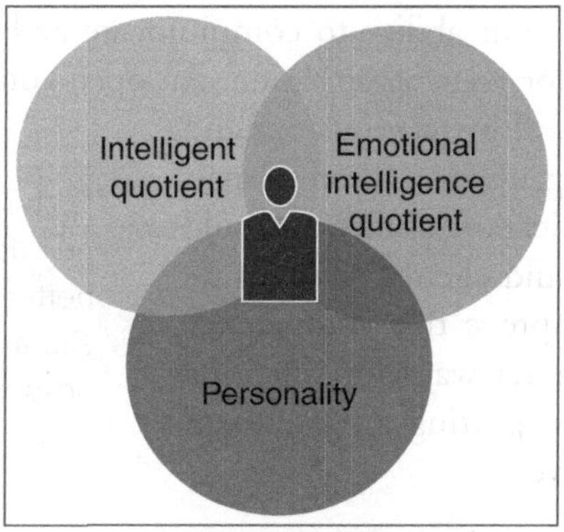

Emotional intelligence is an essential part of the whole person.

Summary

In simple words, emotional intelligence (EI) can be termed as emotional sensibility, that means being sensible in knowing and managing your own emotions as well as those of others. EI is the ability to recognise your emotions, understand your mind-set and, most importantly, realise how your emotions affect the people around you. It also involves your perception of others' emotions, that is, your understanding of how they feel in a particular situation. EI enables you to manage your relationships effectively. It is highly important not just in social life but also for a successful professional life. It empowers you to lead and adapt, change and recreate, and act and react sensibly in all situations in your organisation. With EI, you emerge as the most social, compassionate and creative individual who makes a fine balance between personal and professional worlds and serves them well. Unlike intelligence quotient (IQ), emotional intelligence quotient (EQ) is more flexible and easy to develop at any age with practice and persistence. Certain attributes and domains govern EI. It can be developed by taking care of these attributes and domains to add value to our life.

Chapter Review

1. What are the attributes affected by emotional intelligence? How are they affected?
2. Why is emotional intelligence quotient (EQ) an essential ingredient of social and personal bliss in spite of intelligence quotient (IQ) being a well-accepted measure?
3. What are the five components of emotional intelligence described by Daniel Goleman?
4. What are the attributes which people endowed with great self-management show?
5. What are the characteristics which people endowed with great social awareness show?

Direct Questions

1. What role does effective communication play in emotional intelligence?
2. Define emotional intelligence.
3. Why is EQ more important than IQ?
4. What do you understand by the term empathy? Why is being empathetic important in professional life?
5. What are the key skills for successful relationship management?
6. Describe the skills to develop emotional intelligence.

Analytical Questions

1. How do you use your emotional intelligence when you are negotiating certain issues in an important deal for your company?
2. If you were an employee, which causes/factors do you think would make you angry at the workplace and how would you resolve them with emotional intelligence?
3. As a leader of a project team you have a day left from the deadline to submit the project but you do not expect it to be complete in time. How would your emotions be? What possibly would you do to tackle this disturbing situation?
4. What initiatives and methods would you employ to train employees in your organisation for developing or enhancing their emotional intelligence?

Resources for Further Reflections

1. Emotional intelligence by Daniel Goleman: http://www.danielgoleman.info/topics/emotional-intelligence/.
2. Emotional intelligence and why it matters: http://www.mindtools.com/pages/article/newCDV_59.htm.
3. How to build emotional intelligence: https://www.youtube.com/watch?feature=player_embedded&v=hlfPjCviTxA.

4. Emotional intelligence predicts job performance: http://www.forbes.com/sites/sebastianbailey/2015/03/05/emotional-intelligence-predicts-job-performance-the-7-traits-that-help-managers-relate/.
5. 10 reasons why emotional intelligence is critical: http://www.huffingtonpost.com/tracy-crossley/10-reasons-why-emotional-_b_6770864.html?ir=India.
6. How to know if you're emotionally intelligent: http://www.theglobeandmail.com/report-on-business/small-business/sb-tools/sb-how-to/are-you-emotionally-intelligent-heres-how-to-know-for-sure/article23148898/.
7. Jensen K. Intelligence is overrated: What you really need to succeed. Forbes, April 2014. http://www.forbes.com/sites/keldjensen/2012/04/12/intelligence-is-overrated-what-you-really-need-to-succeed/.
8. Goleman D. Emotional intelligence: What makes a leader? Harvard Business Review, January 2014. https://hbr.org/2004/01/what-makes-a-leader.
9. Bradbeey Davis. Emotional Intelligence – EQ. Forbes, January 2014. http://www.forbes.com/sites/travisbradberry/2014/01/09/emotional-intelligence/.

Caselet 1

Shipra Technologies

Vamsi Krishna was appointed as project manager at Shipra Technologies in Mumbai. He was aggressive and did not speak much, except when he was asked to share his thoughts or advise on something. He handled a team of 25 people.

Vamsi was given a project to provide support services to a client of the company, Kenstar India Pvt. Ltd, a leading manufacturer of airconditioners, coolers, washing machines, refrigerators and other electrical appliances. The support services contract was for three years.

While working on the Kenstar project, Vamsi always carried out his work with diligence and expected everyone to follow the same. As he started working with the employees under him on a critical aspect of the project, his team began to notice that their project manager was little indifferent and least bothered about their emotions and feelings. They felt Vamsi was not treating them well. Adding to their woes, he started conducting meetings at unusual hours of the day. His excuse was: it was waste of time to conduct meetings during working hours.

In the meetings Vamsi used to scold non-performers irrespective of their personal issues and technical glitches. He did not give much attention to their issues and asked them to perform. As the work progressed, workplace conflicts frequently arose between Vamsi and his team members. This led increase in absenteeism among the employees. This affected the work a lot. Soon due to high workload, it became difficult for Vamsi's team to continue providing support services to Kenstar.

Kenstar India sought explanation for inefficient handling of the service contract. Vamsi hardly had any valid reason to justify their inefficiency. This resulted in the project getting doomed, and the higher authorities at Shipra Technologies initiated a disciplinary action against their project manager.

Questions

1. Identify the various emotional issues because of which the Shipra Technologies team, headed by Vamsi, made a mess of the Kenstar contract.
2. What might Vamsi have done before things got out of his hand?

Chapter 4

ETIQUETTE AND MANNERISM

Learning Roadmap

After reading this chapter you will be able to:

- Know about etiquette and mannerism and their roles in professional life
- Learn how to inculcate various etiquette
- Know different mannerisms for desired behaviour in varied situations
- Understand telephone and email etiquette
- Learn tips to improve business etiquette

PERSPECTIVE

It was the inaugural function of a conference on 'The emerging trends in marketing'. The conference hall had a conglomeration of esteemed guests, delegates and academicians. All had high expectations from the conference in terms of learning and taking back a lot of experiences and inputs. Everyone was eagerly waiting with bated breath for the chief guest to arrive. He was already late by 15 minutes with no intimation to the organisers. When the conference secretary tried to call him up, his phone was out of reach. The gathering had almost lost hope of the chief guest coming to the conference. Suddenly, he barged in the conference room, one hour behind his scheduled arrival. He was perspiring profusely, his hair dishevelled. The organisers somehow made him feel at ease and seated him in a chair on the dais. Finally, the conference proceedings began and he was invited to give his conference speech from the lectern. Hardly the chief guest had finished his opening remarks that his mobile started ringing aloud in his pocket. Instead of excusing himself and switching off the phone, he took the call and started talking loudly. His voice was magnified because the microphone put in front of him was on. The audience felt embarrassed with his uncivilised behaviour. Nobody expected this sheer lack of etiquette and mannerism from the person of his calibre and position. Had he been sincere about time management, dressed nattily and ensured no interruption in his speech, the audience would have held him in high esteem.

Good manners will open doors that the best education cannot.

— Clarence Thomas

4.1 INTRODUCTION

The other day during my flight to New Delhi from Mumbai, I was put off by the highly uncivilised behaviour of a co-passenger who was seated beside me. The fellow was picking his nose frequently, scratching his ears and yawning loudly. I was on a window seat. He also irked me by leaning on me to have the outside view from the window. This guy showed an utter lack of etiquette and manners.

It is essential to follow etiquette and manners by everyone living in a society to make it civilised. Following etiquette and manners is also essential for creating one's positive image during one's interactions with others. As per the Oxford dictionary Etiquette is a customary code of polite behaviour in society or among members of a particular profession or group; and manners as per oxford dictionary is a way in which a thing is done or happens.

Although etiquette and manners both vary according to the culture of a society, few rules of behaviour are common to humankind.

They are different only in terms of etiquette being more specific and manners being more generalised. Manners teach you that you must respect your elders while etiquette consists of things like the desired way to address your teachers or, maybe, the prime minister. You must not think too much about the difference between etiquette and manners as most of the time you will find them overlapping. You will also find that many people who follow etiquette do have good manners.

> Etiquette and manners are integral part of a civilised society.

If you learn good manners at a young age, it will be easy for you to adapt and respond to the behaviour of others in socially acceptable ways. In other words, you will get tuned to the behaviour and norms of the society unconsciously. This tuning happens by practice and observation, not through instructions. One important reason why parents want their children to be part of social gatherings is that they would learn social etiquette and mannerism.

To appear decent and civilised in your interactions with people, it is desirable that you behave like a gentleman or a gentle lady. Remember, your etiquette and manners are tested in adverse situations when you tend to get rough. If you make a bad impression in such trying times, then it spoils your reputation. Later, you may regret your undesirable behaviour, but those bad impressions are indelible. And, you may not get a chance to explain the cause of your undesirable behaviour to the people who were affected by this behaviour.

The following sections throw light on some behavioural traits that are essential to inculcate etiquette and manners for behaving in a socially desirable way.

Etiquette is behaving yourself a little better than is absolutely essential

— Will Cuppy

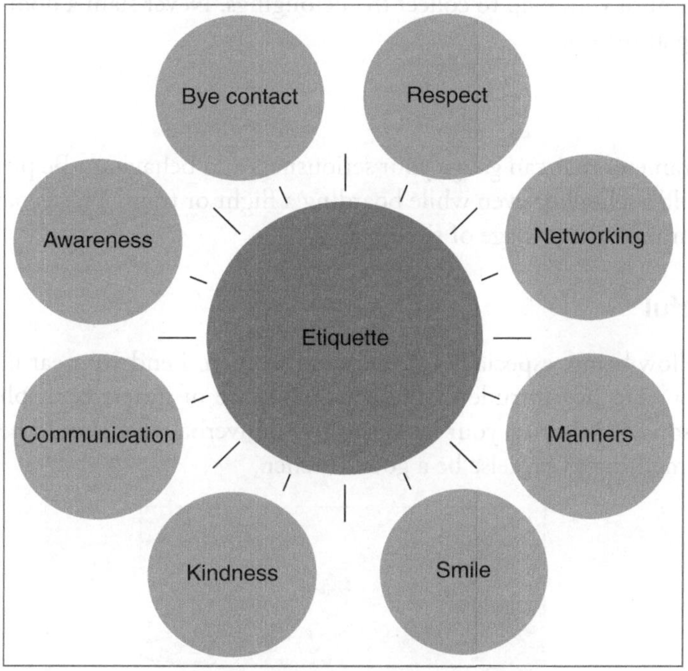

4.2.1 Be Polite and Amicable

At home or outside, your friendly behaviour can pull many people close to you. To appear friendly, you must wear a smile along with your neat clothes and perfume when you step out of your home. A smiling face does not cost much but it can make your interaction with others easy and friendly. Never wait for others to wish you first. Take the initiative and offer appropriate greetings to them. Have you ever realised that the smile you wear is contagious? Try it next time in your interactions with others by adding friendly words like 'please', 'thank you', 'so nice of you', 'good day', 'excuse me', etc. This way you can show kindness to others. This will certainly be reciprocated. Never think that people do not value your friendly behaviour. They certainly do.

4.2.2 Be a Sport

Not that you have to crave to be a helper, but if there is a chance, try to open the door for someone. If someone fell down infront of you, help to collect the belongings. Never slam a door on the face of someone if the person is standing at the door.

4.2.3 Value Time

To be in time is one parameter that can gauge your seriousness and behaviour. Be punctual whether in office or to doctor or your child's school or even while boarding a flight or train. This is part of your etiquette,and these habits cultivate through the passage of time.

4.2.4 Be Respectful

Show respect for the fellow being, especially to elders and women. Lend your ear if the other person wants to voice his/her opinion. Do not intrude in the personal space of others both physically and otherwise. If you are with the person of authority, your language and nonverbal cues should be full of humility. Speak out only if you have something to say, else be a good listener.

4.2.5 Allow Others to Go First

This is a sign of respect for others. How uncivilised and childish does it look when you push others to move ahead before them? Have patience and let others move first whether standing in a queue, driving or walking. If you come across an ambulance or a lady with child – give them priority. Also never try to overtake your senior colleague as it is disrespectful. Gesture the person if they are in hurry to go ahead and you do not mind.

4.2.6 Keep Mobile Ringtone Volume Low

The world is full of noise. Therefore, civilised behaviour demands that you keep the ringtone volume of your mobile low. You will realise the need for this necessity on observing your own adverse reaction to the loud ringtones coming from others' mobiles in the office premises. Also, do not talk loudly on the mobile. One must be sensible to know where and how to talk on one's mobile.

4.2.7 Follow Etiquette while Eating with Others

Observe good table manners while eating with friends and family members. Do not speak too much while eating. Keep your elbows off the table. Do not bend on others to reach out to something on the table. Use friendly expressions like 'please' and 'thank you' without hesitation.

4.2.8 Introduce Others

In a meeting if you know the participants, do not hesitate to introduce them to others. But do not mix up their names. If you do not feel confident enough for this task,ask the participants to introduce themselves.

4.3 PROFESSIONAL ETIQUETTE

The etiquette followed in the professional setting/work place is called professional etiquette. You may have profound academic knowledge, but if you lack in social skills at the workplace, you may not ascend the ladder of success. You reflect maturity and smartness if you have good social skills and the employer has confidence in you that you can represent the organisation in a better way. If you lack proper etiquette, it can tarnish your image and sour your professional and personal relationships with others. Sometimes you would be unaware of what went wrong in your professional and personal interactions with others. Remember, professional etiquette keeps changing, but a few remain the same. For example, earlier addressing your boss by his/her first name was totally unaccepted. Today, it is in vogue. Good manners do evolve with common sense, that is, if you observe what is going around you, you will learn manners automatically. However, when facing certain situations for the first time, a few tips will be useful. Of course there are some common courtesies which you must follow when you are interaction with people professionally.

4.3.1 Etiquette at Meetings

As you meet a person, you are expected to greet him/her. Your first impression on the person must be good. For this you should smile and do a handshake or Namaste, as appropriate in the given situation. During a handshake you should also make an eye contact to exude confidence and your interest in the meeting. If you make a firm handshake, it reflects your confidence. A limp handshake shows a lack of confidence and gives the impression that you are not interested in the person. To make a good impression at a meeting, adhere to the following etiquette:

- Do stand while introducing others or being introduced.
- While introducing the participants, provide essential information about them along with their names. For example, "Kalpana, please meet Dr. Sharma, Dean Research and Consultancy Unit, BITS, Pilani"; Or, "Seema, this is Kalpana Kannan, Professor at the IIT Bombay".
- Try to address people by their titles and last names. The way to address people varies country to country.
- Do a confident handshake along with a simultaneous eye contact.

4.3.2 Etiquette at Dining

Indian habits of eating and dining have a lot of variety; therefore, one has to learn the dining and eating etiquette consciously. Sometimes during a job interview you may be made to eat a meal so that the interviewer could observe your dining habits. If you do follow the dining etiquette, chances of your rejection increase.

Regarding the dining etiquette, you may be interested to know the proper use of your hands while eating, how to use table napkins, in which hand should you hold the fork and spoon, etc. The following tips help you to learn the dining etiquette:

1. Look for the host to indicate your seat on the table
2. Put the napkin in your lap before beginning to eat
3. If you have to order, always opt for easy to eat dishes
4. Do not impose your choice of food on others. Let others also give their choices
5. Wait for all to start

6. Put your hands on your lap if not eating
7. Sit in the right posture with arms close to your body
8. Do not bring your head to the plate, but take food to your mouth
9. Match your eating pace with that of others
10. Keep the conversations rolling on
11. If you have to excuse yourself, keep napkin on the chair
12. At the end, place the napkin close to the plate
13. Move the chair to its original position after you get up

Always eat with your mouth close.

4.3.3 Involuntary Awkward Actions

Sometimes certain awkward actions happen involuntarily, like sneezing, yawning and hiccups. How to cope with them? You must be prepared to deal with these reflexes. I remember in one of the senate meetings a senator started sneezing continuously and he did not carry a kerchief. He was wiping his mouth with his shirt. Such acts give wrong impressions about the individual.

> *You can get through life with bad manners, but it is easier with good manners.*
>
> — Lillian Gish

4.4 TECHNOLOGY ETIQUETTE

These days technology has become an inseparable part of our life. So it is imperative for us to learn technology etiquette for using technology professionally. The main gadgets we use are mobile phones and computers. Let us know about the etiquette for using these gadgets.

4.4.1 Phone Etiquette

You must know that the phone must be used in the right setting. You must not show the impropriety of using the phone as the chief guest had used in the example mentioned in the Perspective of this chapter. He picked a call while addressing an audience and his phone talk was audible to everyone as the mic was on. If you are at a funeral, you must not talk on the mobile. Some other settings where it is impolite to use the mobile are classroom meetings, worshipping places, public transports etc. Remember when others give you curious looks while you are talking on the phone, you must stop the conversation. The following are some tips for conducting phone conversations in a proper way.

1. When you talk in public space, remember everyone around is listening to you. To prevent your personal life becoming public, you must not talk something too personal at a public place.
2. While you are on the phone, do not converse with a person around you, as this will lead to a lot of confusion for the person at the other end of the phone. He/she will not understand what you are saying to him/her and what to the other person.
3. Avoid working on the computer while talking over the phone. Your attention will get diverted, and the person on the other side may also get irritated by the clacking of the keyword.
4. Avoid using cell phones completely in a social setting. If you remain occupied over phone for a long time in a social setting then it reflects that people in that social setting are not important to you.
5. Making phone calls during early hours of the day or late nights should be avoided unless it is urgent. Also avoid making use of the mobile during meals, work and meetings.

> While talking over phone in a crowd, be very conscious of the sentiments of the surrounding people.

4.4.1.1 *Incorrect Number*

Ensure the number dialled is correct; if not, say sorry to the person for disturbing him/her. Do not disconnect without apologising. If you receive a wrong call, do not shout at the person who has called. The person may be ill, old or desperate.

4.4.1.2 *Voice Quality*

Check how you sound on the phone. Your talk on the phone gives your impression to a person whom you are talking for the first time. He/she forms an image of your personality by the tone and quality of your voice. Your voice reflects your mood and thoughts for the person at the other end. Speak clearly and with a pleasant tone. Transfer smile through your voice and make a good impression through your talk.

4.4.1.3 *Be Courteous*

Whenever you have made a call, it is your responsibility to introduce yourself rather than putting questions to the person who has picked your call. Do not be in a haste to tell the purpose of your call, as it is abrupt and harsh to do so. So say, "I am Sunil Jain and I'd like to speak to Mr. Suresh Sharma. Is he available?" Either the desired person is on the line or if he is not available, you will be informed about that.

> Telephone etiquette speaks about your personality and behaviour. You might offend the other person by not following them properly.

4.4.1.4 Give Time to Pick the Call

When you call, give enough time to the other person to pick your call, as the person may be working in the kitchen, garden or talking to neighbours. If they come to take your call and you hang up, it is irritating for them. So give them enough time to pick your call.

4.4.1.5 Avoid Prolonged Talks

Phones are for convenience and should not be used for entertainment. You might waste others time by stretching your phone talk too long. Remember if they get bored by your talk, they will avoid picking your call next time.

4.4.1.6 Be Careful on Information Sharing

When you get a call, do not immediately reveal your identity unless you are sure who is on the other side. Just say a polite "hello" and always pretend there are others around you. It is unsafe to say you are alone. Be practical and smart. If the call is for someone else say, "One moment please, I'll just call them for you." Before calling the concerned individual, place the phone mouthpiece down. You must not shout in the mouth while calling him/her. If you don't find that individual, tell the caller that you will inform him/her and he/she will get back.

4.4.2 Email Etiquette

To run their business successfully, companies need to have a competitive edge over their competition. To win new clients a company needs to communicate with them in a professionally effective manner. Many companies do not give due importance to email communications with their clients. To deal professionally with their clients, it is essential for the company's employees to save themselves from awkward situations while writing emails to them. Following are some rules that should be implemented for writing better communication for their clients:

1. **Be concise and to the point:** Reading an email is harder than reading printed papers. Keep in mind that the other party may not be able to focus on and understand all the facts if your email is too long. The shorter it is, it is more likely that you will get a faster response. A thumb rule is to limit emails to one or two lines.
2. **Number your questions:** You must follow this rule. If you are not numbering your questions, it may be possible that your clients may answer those questions which are in the first line. By numbering questions you structure your email in such a way that every question gets the desired attention from your client and you do not have to ask again.
3. **Make usage of proper spellings, grammar and punctuation:** Improper spellings, grammar and punctuation not only leave a bad impression about your lack of writing skills but also make the sentences difficult to read and understand. Remember a good sentence should be not more than of 12 words.
4. **Mention deadlines:** One might think that mentioning deadlines may seem imposing conditions on a client, but it is not so. Professionals are very busy nowadays, so if a deadline is mentioned then they become conscious to fit that in their schedule and manage their accordingly.
5. **Avoid abbreviations:** Many of us have become habitual of using abbreviations like U for you, plz for please, etc. They may deem fit when we are talking to a friend but not with business professionals. Business emails should be more formal in nature in order to leave a good impact on the recipient.
6. **Try to reply fast:** Someone emails to you because they expect quick response, or else they could fax or send a letter. If an email is long and requires some thought, it is worth a reply that you will get back soon. This will assure the sender of your detailed response and he/she will wait patiently.

Keep your email short and sweet!

7. **Avoid attaching unnecessary files:** If you attach with your email the files that do not serve the purpose of your client, then you are annoying them. Also avoid sending large files as they take several minutes to download and also can bring down the email server.
8. **Do not write in capital letters:** If you write in capital letters people assume that you are implying things and that does not leave a good impression on your client. This may trigger an unwanted response from the client.
9. **Use expressive subject lines:** The subject line of your email is a key factor in setting the priority by your client – whether to read the email immediately or later. For example, if you do not want some actions on a matter but you want to just share, it would be good to have 'FYI' as the subject line.
10. **Go through the email once again before you click 'send':** A lot of people do not bother to revise their emails for correcting inadvertent mistakes. Such mistakes send a wrong signal to the email recipient. Have someone to read your email before sending it, as he/she would be giving you the perspective of the recipient.

4.4.3 Social Media Etiquette

The importance of social media is increasing at a very fast pace. Businesses have become so much dependent on social media that one gaffe by their social media handlers can lead to big losses. Therefore, it is necessary that you remain updated with the etiquette to be followed on social media. Do remember that etiquette on media keep changing according to time. You must learn the nuances of social media which may help you run your company social media network with ease. It is similar to driving; once you become used to it, you are more prone to accidents. You forget the etiquette on social media after you start using it excessively. Keep the following points for fruitful interactions on social media:

Courtesy and kindness cultivate confidence with good Netiquette. Doing things right makes you feel good. NetworkEtiquette.net

— David Chiles

1. **Your social media profile must be complete:** When someone visits your profile and finds that you have not uploaded complete information about yourself, the person gets disheartened. Photos are a good beginning as you can be identified with them. Complete the information about yourself in your profile as this will create a good impression.
2. **Avoid multiple profiles:** Remember the world is very small and everything is connected. If you have multiple social media profiles and they do not match, this will create mistrust. So you must be aware of what you have in private settings and what is to be revealed to the public.
3. **You become what you post:** Through your social media interactions you are leaving an imprint of your personality on the Internet, so do not be frivolous while making comments. If you keep quiet, then it shows lack of sensitivity. Be confident in voicing your opinion and stand strong on your views without hurting the sentiments of any community, society or class.
4. **Be minimal on automation:** Automation lacks personal touch and overuse of it is not very encouraging. If you do it very often you may get distanced from your social media circle.
5. **Do not be ubiquitous in all media:** Choose one or two sites – maybe Facebook and LinkdIn, as you will not have enough time to be everywhere; so be realistic.

> Keep abreast of social media etiquette as they are labile.

6. **Be amicable:** If someone asks you questions, try to send the reply. Do recommend your friend whenever required. Try to strengthen the connection by asking feedback or writing a helpful post on your blog.
7. **Do not be desperate:** Do not ask for 'Likes' and 'retweets'; go for creative solutions. Be smart enough to get what you want rather being direct.
8. **Be careful of spam:** Do not get carried away by the followers. If you have followers who do not have any followers, there are chances they are fake. Do not open the links sent by them. Avoid joining too many groups to post self-promotional messages and then not visiting them again. That is not polite at all.
9. **Be transparent to be trustworthy:** Remain transparent by not being indulging in activities that cause controversy. Neither keep secrets, nor delete comments. Do respond in the best possible way without getting defensive. Whenever possible, resolve the issues and let the other person know about it.
10. **Be careful about grammar and spelling:** You look uneducated with bad grammar and spellings. Ensure the language correctness before making your message public.
11. **Do not write in all capitals:** Writing in all capitals does not communicate anything significant because whatever you want to emphasise cannot be emphasised entirely by using capital letters. Nor does it reflect creativity. However, it just shows you are upset about something.
12. **Do not share the same message again and again:** If you share the same message repeatedly, it reflects your lazy attitude–whether on Tweeter, LinkedIn or any other site. Remember, social networks are smart to show your repeat posts to less number of people. Also, why do you want to have the epithet of lazy and careless?
13. **Engage in constructive comments:** While posting your comments do introspect if people really care to read about what you are posting. If something is of your interest, it is possible that others may not be interested. So go slow and find out the interest of others and once you have made connections, match your interest with that of others.
14. **Do not be miser in giving credit:** This rule is applicable in social media in the same way as in print media. If you are tempted to take up somebody's update, be polite in acknowledging it. Send tweets to the people whose work you like and enjoy. This will reflect humility and you will develop more connections.

15. **Think before tagging:** Before tagging someone, please find out from that person if they like tagging. Sometimes people get offended or surprised when they are tagged. Tagging is a good way to communicate about you and your businesses but you should be careful.

4.4.4 Video Conferencing Etiquette

Introduce politely to others: The first thing you should do is to tell your name to others and also know the others by names. Do inform others how they can address you- by name or whatever way you want.

1. **Clarity in voice:** Check the microphone before the conference begins. Ensure that everyone is able to hear you. Do not get conscious, be natural. Affected voice puts off the listeners. Do not yell to be audible. If you adjust the microphone properly, you will not face problems. Take care of obstructions between the microphone and your mouth – piece of cloth or your hand should not come in between.
2. **Control the body movement:** Keep the body movement to the minimum as the hand movements distract the attention. If your body moves back and forth or sideways your voice will get affected.
3. **Look at the camera:** Be focused and look at the camera. All your movements are noticeable, so avoid the temptation of looking at your mobile phone.
4. **Do not interrupt:** Let the speaker complete the statement before posing a question. Be a patient listener as it is a bad manner to cut in between the sentence.
5. **No side conversation:** The rules of video conferencing are exactly same as face-to-face meeting. Do not pass on the notes or start side conversation as it distracts the speaker.

6. **Dress appropriately:** Avoid visually distracting dresses. Bold colours like red, black, white must be replaced by pastel shades. Accessories should be kept simple.
7. **Be natural:** Enjoy and give opportunity to others to laugh and smile. People will be more focused if you give them chance to laugh and that can be done by indulging in jokes.

4.4.5 Web Interview Etiquette

Facing an interview is a challenge be it face-to-face or on web. The most common interview on web is Skype interview. In fact, some people feel it is tougher than interview in person. Keep the following points in mind while facing a web interview:

1. Download the software and get familiar with it before the actual interview
2. Have the similar name as your email id name so that it is recognised fast and look professional
3. Have immaculate sitting space, without clutters around
4. Keep track of time and log in at the right time; if you are in other country be more careful
5. Have your resume with you and ensure to send it as an attachment to the interviewer
6. Your web camera must be always focused
7. Do not allow others to prompt you during the interview
8. Have professional screen setting rather than pictures from informal settings
9. Microphone must be placed at the right place.

Summary

In a professional setting, it is essential to follow the right etiquette and mannerism. They are usually learned from the surrounding environment and by observing other sophisticated people. People around you will not accept you if you remain uncouth. Etiquette and manners are two terms with overlapping meanings and are interchangeably used. To follow the right etiquette, you must be polite and amicable and should take things in the right direction. You must value time and meet deadlines. While conducting a meeting, you must follow the meeting etiquette. Introduction of people should be rightly done followed by handshake and smile. In a professional setting, dining etiquette must be carefully followed as the seniors are keeping an eye on you. You cannot control a few awkward involuntary actions like sneezing, yawning and hiccups, but you should know how to apologise. The technology etiquette includes both phone and email etiquette. People behave very casually while talking on the phone or writing emails, making blunders and repenting later on. When you are using social media, remember its impact is great because of its greater reach; therefore, be alert and careful while using it.

Chapter Review

1. Explain the differences between etiquette and mannerism with examples.
2. Give some tips for dining etiquette.
3. There are a few settings where it is impolite to use mobile phones. Describe such situations in detail.
4. Describe email etiquette which may help a firm get as many clients as possible.
5. How does technology play an important part in business etiquette and mannerisms?
6. What etiquette can be followed during a business meeting?
7. How can you improve your business and workplace etiquette?
8. Discuss the role of social media in business etiquette?

Direct Questions

1. What does it mean to be polite?
2. Give your own example of being a sport.
3. How do you define being amicable?
4. What are the general mobile etiquette that can be followed at workplace?
5. List the ways by which you can make a successful positive impression of yourself at your workplace.
6. What is the importance of communication in business etiquette?
7. How can self-assessment help in improving your business etiquette?
8. How can dining etiquette be important for maintenance of a positive image at workplace? List some dining etiquette.

Analytical Questions

1. Imagine you do not like a picture of you posted by your friend on a social media website. How would you request him/her to remove and not share such pictures?
2. Imagine you were invited for dinner by your friend/workmate but could not make it due to an emergency. How would you inform him/her the situation on phone? Describe the conversation.

3. If you were to invite your work mates for dinner at you house, how would you invite them? Also, describe your responsibilities as a host.
4. Imagine a friend of yours who wants to work in the same company as you are. How would you introduce your friend to your boss?

Resources for Further Reflections

1. Life Lessons: http://www.realsimple.com/magazine-more/inside-magazine/life-lessons.
2. Indian etiquette:http://www.cyborlink.com/besite/india.htm.
3. A study on manners and etiquette:http://www.jstor.org/discover/10.2307/1879686?sid=21106373226383&uid=2&uid=4&uid=3738256.
4. Ask the etiquette expert:http://www.huffingtonpost.com/diane-gottsman/ask-the-etiquette-expert-_4_b_6547722.html?ir=India.
5. Workplace etiquette:http://www.careereducation.columbia.edu/resources/tipsheets/skills-business-etiquette.
6. International business etiquette: http://businessculture.org/business-culture/business-etiquette/.
7. Tips for business etiquette: shttp://www.businessmanagementdaily.com/glp/28411/Business-Etiquette.html.
8. Mobile phone etiquette: http://www.gov.ai/dg/documents/phoneEtiquette.html.

Caselet 1

TSMPL Steel

Dr. Rajashekaran is the Managing Director of Taboo Steel Manufacturers Pvt. Ltd. (TSMPL). He is an orthodox Brahmin from a State in South India. He started TSMPL 14 years ago and became one of the top business people in India. Mr. Xi Yung is a real estate contractor who is presently needs a huge amount of steel for constructing a series of apartments of 30 floors in China. A managerial cadre person, Mr. Vasudev, working with Mr. Yung, told him to talk to TSMPL MD, Dr. Rajashekaran, so that he can get some concession over the steel price. Mr. Vasudev arranged a meeting between them on a Sunday. Although initially Dr. Rajashekaran was reluctant to meet Mr. Yung on a Sunday, finally he agreed for this meeting.

Both met in the meeting room at the TSMPL head office. Mr. Yung came in a black blazer while Dr. Rajashekaran came in a white shirt. Mr. Yung extended his hand to greet Dr. Rajashekaran with a handshake, but the MD brought his palms together, bowed his head slightly and greeted Mr. Yung with Namaste. A surprised Yung repeated the same gesture,addressing the MD as Mr. Rajashekaran. He was not aware that the MD was a doctor.

Dr. Rajashekaran felt bad and thought Mr. Yung might not have known about him. To introduce himself properly to Mr Yung, Dr. Rajashekaran he gave him his business card. Mr. Yung took the card with the left hand and gave his card with the right hand. However, Mr Yung immediately put the MD's card in his pocket without looking at it and straightaway started talking about his requirement.

Dr. Rajashekaran felt that Mr. Yung was not paying any respect to him and decided against giving any concession to him even if he purchased steel in a huge quantity. So, even after Mr. Yung clearly explaining his steel requirement and informing about the project schedule, Dr. Rajashekaran did not pay any attention to Mr. Yung and gave him no concession.

Questions

1. What is the business etiquette to be followed while conversing with Indians?
2. What, according to Dr. Rajashekaran, were the mistakes made by Mr. Xi Yung during their meeting?

Caselet 2

IBM India Pvt. Limited

Vanitha Narayan is the Chief Executive Officer at IBM India Pvt. Limited. She got an email stating that a few officials from the USA are coming to India for an audit. On receiving the mail, Vanitha informed four managers under her to make arrangements for the officials' visit. The managers booked rooms for the officials in a four-star hotel near their head office in Bangalore.

When the auditing officials from the USA landed at the Bangalore airport, the managers assisted them in reaching the hotel where rooms were booked for them. The four auditors were: San Jose, Paul Adams, Peter Stirling and Stevenson. Following Vanitha's instructions, the managers waited at the hotel for the auditors to get ready for their visit to IBM India's office. After some time, the managers guided the auditors to the IBM office.

Vanitha greeted the auditors at the office. After completion of formalities, the auditors got on to their work. While they were doing the audit, coffee and snacks were offered to them. But as the auditors had come to India for the first time, they felt that the company people were trying to mislead them by offering coffee and snacks. So they did not them. After completing the audit, they started preparing the report.

Vanitha felt bad at the auditors' refusal to accept coffee and snacks. So, she decided to invite the auditors for lunch and told the managers to invite them for lunch and take them to particular restaurant. The auditors having finished the report accepted the invitation and went for lunch.

When the auditors arrived at the restaurant, Vanitha greeted them but they did not acknowledge her greeting and sat for lunch even before Vanitha took her chair. The auditors called a bearer and asked him to explain the items on the menu card. Even before Vanitha could guide them about the menu items, Stevenson ordered a dish about whose taste and other characteristics he was not aware of. San Jose ordered two glasses of wine. Paul Adams ordered some light food and one glass of wine while Peter asked a manager who came along with him for a suggestion to order. Later, an embarrassed Vanitha ordered very light food. As the orders came in, Stevenson, who did not know how to eat the ordered dish, took a knife in his left hand and started to cut it into pieces. Vanitha and her managers were perplexed seeing the auditors' awkward behaviour. Paul Adams started drinking wine and asked

Vanitha about the political happenings in the country to which she responded with a silence. San Jose while drinking told that her that the wine did not seem to be fresh. Finally, when the lunch was over, the auditors told the CEO that they would pay the bill. However, Vanitha politely refused the offer and paid the bill herself.

Although the auditors were her guests, Vanitha did not feel like a host as they did not behave with her in the way they were expected to. Hence Vanitha was utterly disappointed with the lunch.

Later when the company officials in the USA asked Vanitha about the auditors' visit, she responded bitterly, "It was the worst meet I ever had. They did not respect or pay attention to my words at all during their interaction with me".

Questions

1. Explain why Vanitha was disappointed.
2. Explain the lunch etiquette that has to be followed in India when eating with women.
3. Explain what the auditors should have done during lunch to behave decently.

SECTION

2

ACADEMIC SKILLS

Chapter 5

COMMUNICATION TODAY

Learning Roadmap

After reading this chapter you will be able to:

- Understand the importance of communication
- Define communication
- Explain the communication process
- Discuss the relevance of listening skill
- Understand the significance of intercultural communication
- Learn about the non-verbal communication
- Explore new ways of digital communication

PERSPECTIVE

We *homo sapiens* are gifted with the ability to communicate or express our thoughts and views to people around us. This remarkable ability makes us distinct and special in comparison to other species on this planet. In modern times, effective use of this ability has become all the more important for the progress of people and organisations. With economies scaling new heights and workplaces becoming competitive, we need to master communication skills to grab dream jobs and promotions.

Simply having communication skills is not enough for making an impact on others. Actually, we have to communicate our ideas/views clearly using apt language for their effective understanding by others, leading to the desired outcome. American business magnate, investor and philanthropist Warren Buffett once said that our art of communication can improve our success rate by 50%. The way we communicate makes all the difference between success and failure in every aspect of our life. We can observe that people around us, who are influential and powerful, have a great ability to communicate. Yet, imparting effective communication skills to students does not get the priority and focus it deserves from teachers. We train our youngsters to learn many values like honesty, sincerity and truthfulness. But students in schools and colleges are not properly guided to express or communicate their ideas clearly. Sadly, these students on entering the professional world realise that what they know about communication skills is just a complex set of grammar rules. Ironically, despite living in an era dominated by communication technology, we are yet to utilise its power to become good communicators. Such environment just adds more 'sounds' and no 'sensibilities' to make ourselves heard or communicated. Are we prepared to add more 'volumes' so that our 'voice' could be 'communicated' and 'heard' effectively?

Take advantage of every opportunity to practice your communication skills so that when important occasions arise, you will have the gift, the style, the sharpness, the clarity, and the emotions to affect other people.

— Jim Rohn

5.1 INTRODUCTION

Communication is a natural and essential bond for engagement among humans and a necessity for their progress. Every individual is blessed by the ability to communicate or express themselves by birth. This ability is bestowed on us in such an effortless way that we take it for granted. The need or urge to express themselves is a core activity of all human beings. And, most of us have this notion that we can communicate effectively in any given situation. But despite assuming the art of communication as something smooth and simple, we tend to make mistakes while communicating with others, failing to say what is appropriate at that particular moment. A sound understanding about how effective communication takes place and how to learn and practise it at the workplace will benefit every processional in their organisations.

How means of communication are changing with time.

5.2 SIGNIFICANCE OF COMMUNICATION

Communication is an intrinsic aspect of all our activities. The term 'communication' comes from the Latin word 'communicare', meaning 'to share, to transfer or to impart'; it literally signifies 'giving or exchanging information'. It is the effectiveness of this giving and receiving of ideas and opinions through speech, writing or visuals that determines the success of delivery of messages communicated by the participants in an interaction. Communication is a two-way process of connecting people through mutual understanding and sharing of ideas, emotions and news.

Ability to communicate effectively is a powerful skill to bring the desired change by engaging people productively at the workplace. Successful communication is critical for every business. Almost every organisation demands professionals with the ability to understand, speak and write convincingly. Some time ago, Forbes magazine had published a report on a survey conducted by the non-profit National Association of Colleges and Employers, USA. The survey asked the hiring managers what skills they prioritise while recruiting college grads. The survey findings reveal that the most important qualities employers seek are basic teamwork, problem-solving ability, the ability to plan and prioritise and the ability to communicate verbally with people inside and outside the organisation. So, despite all the emphasis on software and programming skills, the ability to express oneself is still ranked as one of the most desirable skills in prospective professionals.

Today's workplace is very diverse and complex, populated by individuals from different sections of society, cultures and nationalities. Diversity of people adds value to an organisation. But it also poses the challenge of streamlining the communication environment in the organisation to make it a common workplace for people coming from different backgrounds. Communication touches many different aspects of the workplace. The entire day people communicate meaningfully to each other at the workplace. It empowers professionals to execute multiple tasks every day, such as conducting team discussions, recruiting new people, writing negative or persuasive message, talking on the phone or giving presentations through video conferences.

Impressive communication skills are the gateway to success in life, workplace and relationships. It brings people together, creates harmony in environment and allows space for engagement and reconciliation.

Communication today!

5.3 GSC'S 3M MODEL OF COMMUNICATION: A SIMPLE APPROACH

All other things being equal in a situation, message, media and meaning determine the outcome of any communication process. These three elements combine to make GSC's 3M Model of Communication, as shown in the figure below. The message strongly reflects the idea to be communicated; the media facilitates transmission of the message; and the meaning as understood by the target audience provides the confirmation whether the audience response matches the objective of sending the message.

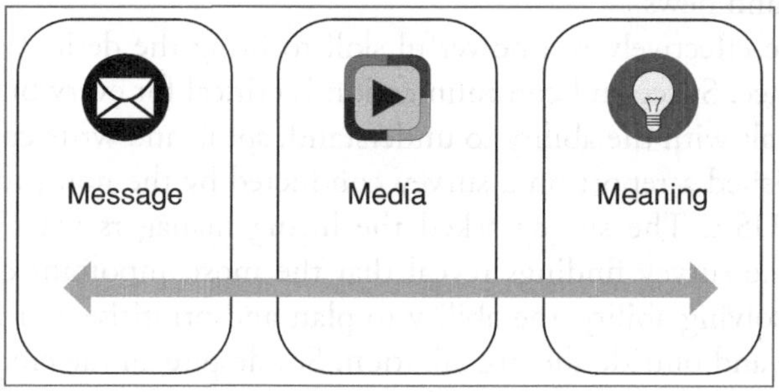

The 3M model of communication.

The 3Ms make the communication process quite easy and practical to achieve the desired result. The first M, that is, the message is strongly associated with the person who wants to initiate communication to convey an idea or thought. The type of message gives a clear understanding about the channel or media (the second M) through which the message travels. The message could be oral, written or non-verbal, but the urgency to deliver it also helps in deciding an appropriate media. The third M, that is, meaning is all about the understanding of an idea to communicate for which the message was initiated by the person. The communication process or cycle keeps repeating until the desired meaning of the message is delivered. There could be many internal or external factors that may lead to the distortion of meaning and consequently rendering the communication process incomplete. The workplace environment and physical distractions are also the critical areas to be taken care of while trying to execute the communication process effectively.

> Three elements combine to make GSC's 3M Model of Communication: Message, Media and Meaning.

What it needs to communicate.

5.4 VITALITY OF THE COMMUNICATION PROCESS

Today's workplace is demanding and volatile. Therefore, our understanding of the communication process becomes crucial to convey the right information from one person or team to another person or team at the workplace. The communication process consists of five steps: *ideation, encoding, transmission, decoding* and *response,* as illustrated in the figure below. Understanding the functions of these steps is essential to make our communication interactive and meaningful.

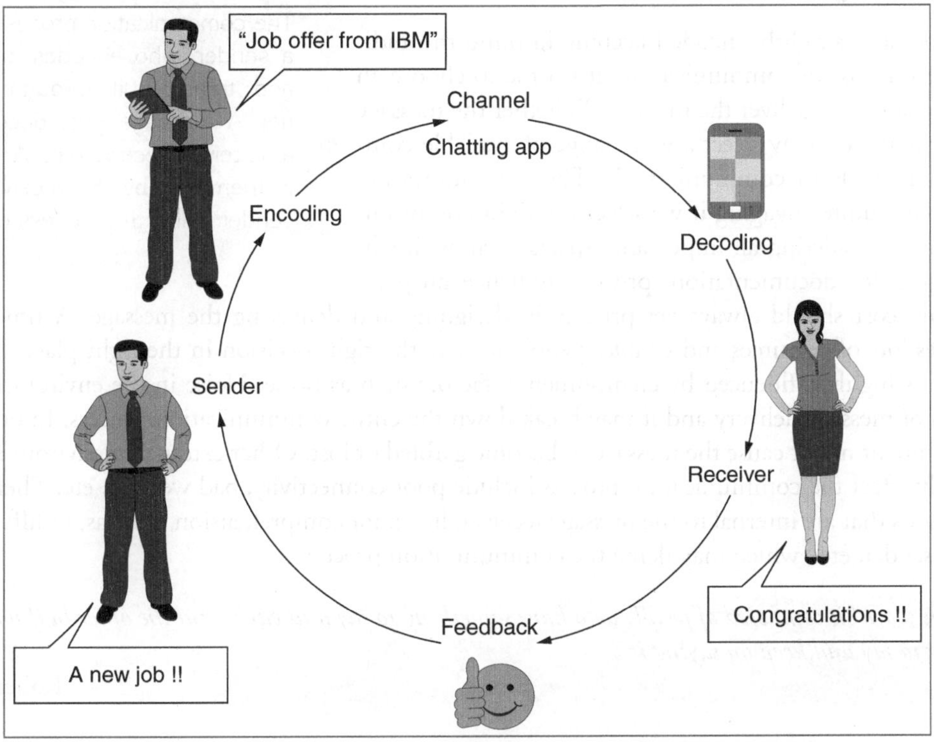

The communication process.

5.4.1 Sender Holds an Idea

Nothing takes place without an idea. A sender first has to conceive an idea, the very reason to communicate something with someone. It exactly defines the purpose of engaging or interacting with people. Conception is formed by internal and external forces. An idea that you conceive in the mind is an internal stimulus while external concepts are formed by your sensory organs: eyes, ears, nose, mouth and skin. An idea for communication at the workplace might be driven by anything: to discuss and brainstorm in a group about the better service to customers, to send an email, to update people in the team/organisation on everyday affairs, to hold a meeting, to revise a business proposal or to communicate with all business stakeholders through video-conferencing. A right idea leads to effective communication and bonding among professionals.

5.4.2 Encoding by Sender

In this step of the communication process, you translate your ideas into a proper message. As a sender, your understanding of the receiver and clarity of the purpose to communicate drive you to encode the message. Sometimes the communication process fails in its purpose when there is a gap between what you plan in your mind and how you put it into words. Encoding is a key factor in evaluating the success of the communication process which is achieved when both the sender and the receiver share a common understanding of the meaning of the message.

5.4.3 Selecting a Channel

> The communication process involves a sender, who encodes a message and transfers it through a channel. A message gets decoded and a receiver receives it. A feedback is then sent by the receiver to the sender. Thus, the process continues.

When the message is rightly encoded keeping in mind the audience and the purpose of communication, it is time to choose an appropriate channel to deliver the message. Whether the message is oral or written, you may select a wide range of available communication channels to communicate it. The communication process becomes quite engaging if we select the right communication channel considering all important aspects such as timeliness, cost, need for documentation, privacy, audience purpose, etc. Time and cost should always get priority in designing and delivering the message. A timely delivered message saves lots of resources and enables people to take the right decision in the right place. The message transmission is highly influenced by environmental factors such as noise. Noise in the environment disrupts the medium of message delivery and it may break down the entire communication process. In other words, a noisy environment might cause the message to become garbled or lost. Other external or environmental factors that adversely affect the communication process include poor connectivity, bad weather, etc. There could also be some reasons that are internal to the message receiver, like poor comprehension of ideas, indifferent attitude towards the sender, etc., which may derail the communication process.

> *Half the world is composed of people who have something to say and can't, and the other half who have nothing to say and keep on saying it.*
>
> — Robert Frost

5.4.4 Decoding by the Receiver

Once the message has been transmitted by the sender to the receiver, it is the responsibility of the receiver to decode the message and understand its meaning as intended by the sender. This process is called decoding. No communication is successful unless the sender and the receiver are able to deduce the same meaning from the message. In fact, in an ideal communication situation, both concur on the objective or meaning of the delivered message.

5.4.5 Response or Feedback

Response of feedback refers to the verbal or non-verbal response given by the receiver about the message. It is the most desirable aspect of the communication process for the sender. It reflects the effectiveness of the communication process by endorsing whether or not the message has been received and understood by the receiver in the desired manner. Feedback is significant in two ways: first, it indicates to both the sender and the receiver that communication has occurred; and second, if there is any problem with the message, it can be taken up by additional communication.

5.5 VIRTUES OF LISTENING

Listening is fundamental to successful communication. It is an important skill to understand and interpret the message correctly in the communication process. It is a paradox which means that the more sophisticated communication we have, the less sensitive we are as a listener. We are swamped with several digital means of communication, but still struggle to communicate and to understand what is communicated to us.

Though listening is considered a very easy and effortless activity, in reality it demands greater observation and adaptability from the listener. Adaptability is the capability that prepares a person to catch with other person's speed (delivery), message and sense of immediacy. Good listening skill is an asset for any individual. In fact, many corporate czars, political leaders and social activists attribute their success to listening skills. Effective listening skills are instrumental in fostering good relationships, optimising productivity, improving oneself and creating a harmonious environment at the workplace.

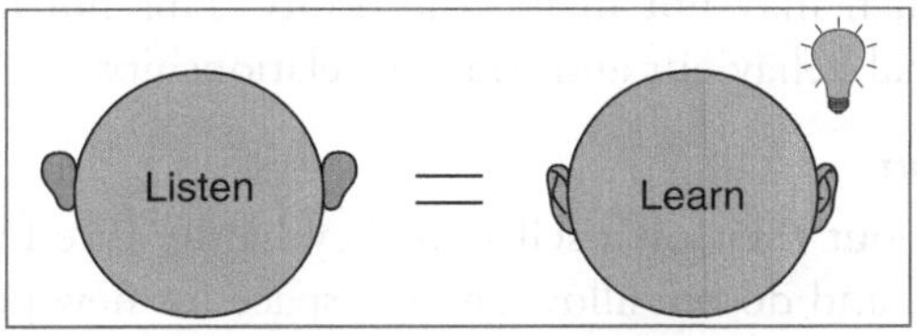

Importance of listening.

5.5.1 Listening is not Hearing

There is clear distinction between listening and hearing. Hearing is about perceiving sounds, whereas listening requires complete attention. Listening is an active process involving focus not only on the meaning, but how the meaning is formed through the type of the language used, the tone and voice and other physical cues. Listening takes note of both verbal and non-verbal content of a message. Any auditory message not received well would just create sounds. This is what happens with 'hearing' and we fail to understand.

Poor listening definitely creates a gap between the sender and the receiver of the message, generates a poor feedback and affects the productivity and moral of an individual.

5.5.2 Barriers to Listening

> Listening is fundamental to successful communication. It is an important skill to understand and interpret the message correctly in the communication process.

Listening is probably the most ignored of all communication skills. Fortunately, if you are interested, you can improve your listening. To be a good listener you need to take care of the following hindrances to listening.

5.5.2.1 Prejudice

Mostly people are driven by their preconceived set of beliefs and assumptions. When we are prejudiced about something, we usually are unreasonable and draw our own impressions and judgments which may not match the reality. This not only derails the communication process but also leads to irrational behaviour and strained relationships.

5.5.2.2 Self-concentration

People are so much obsessed about their own self that they hardly care for others' views and sentiments. They behave like Mr. Know-All and do not allow enough space for new perspectives of an information or better engagement with members in a team.

5.5.2.3 Distractions

If the distraction is physical it may be the problem of workplace. One such distraction is noise in the workplace environment, which disrupts flow of information and leads to unclear and insufficient listening by the target listener. These days noise is created at the workplace by people talking over phones and playing loud music. Traffic around the office also affects the listening process.

5.5.2.4 Selective Listening

Some professionals would see and hear only what they want to see or hear. These selective listeners pay attention to only specific information that serves their interest. Either they intentionally ignore other details or they are not present mentally at the workplace. Continuous selective listening is detrimental to the success of the communication process.

5.5.2.5 Language Background

Different language backgrounds of the sender and the receiver pose a hindrance to effective listening, as both fail to understand each other's ideas. Sometimes even when the sender and the receiver have a common linguistic framework, the communication process breaks down due to use of jargons, puns, foreign terms, complex phrases and local usages.

5.5.2.6 Cultural Setting

As the workplace attracts people from diverse cultures and regions, it becomes difficult for them to understand and response to a communication in the same way. While working as a group in an office, professionals should be attentive listeners and sensitive enough to accommodate such cultural and regional differences for harmonious co-existence and improved compatibility.

> *Any problem, big or small, within a family, always seems to start with bad communication. Someone isn't listening.*
>
> — Emma Thompson

5.6 FUNDAMENTALS OF GOOD LISTENING

Listening is a skill that can be developed and mastered with patience and preparation. Dianne Schilling (writer, editor, graphic artist and instructional designer) laments in her article in Forbes that how genuine listening has become a rare gift–the gift of time. It helps build relationships, solves problems, ensures understanding, resolves conflicts and improves accuracy. At work, effective listening means fewer errors and less wasted time. At home, it helps develop resourceful, self-reliant kids who can solve their own problems. Listening builds friendships and careers. It saves money and marriages. In pursuit of improving your listening skills, you may practice the fundamentals explained in the following sections.

Good listening skills come with patience.

5.6.1 Be Open-minded

An open mind helps you listen to a speaker objectively. You should avoid making judgments and try to understand the speaker's perspective. It makes you a poor listener if you come to conclusions without comprehending the real message of the speaker.

5.6.2 Be Focused

The best thing you can do for your speaker is to give them your undivided attention. Never do anything distracting while listening to the speaker. Put aside your important papers, hold your calls stop looking out of the window and indulge in other physical distractions. Do not give any impression that you are uninterested or distracted.

5.6.3 Be Empathetic

Empathy is an integral part of good listening. Try to put yourself in the speaker's shoes and understand his/her intent. Try your best to make the speaker comfortable and composed. Do not interrupt at any stage. Allow him/her to express his/her views freely. You can nod or signal your positive feedback with proper facial expressions.

5.6.4 Be Sincere and Silent

One major problem often encountered in the communication process is that everyone wants to speak and no one wants to listen. To be a good listener, you must remain silent while listening to the speaker. Train yourself to listen to someone sincerely without disturbance and wait for your chance to speak.

5.6.5 Be Sensitive

In your efforts to improve listening, keep your senses alert to engage actively in any given situation. Your active senses help you grasp a message in its totality.

5.6.6 Be Observant

An active listener will not only observe what is being communicated but also notice what is not being communicated. Good listening demands a clear observation and assimilation of verbal and non-verbal aspects of a message.

5.7 NATURE OF NON-VERBAL COMMUNICATION

Non-verbal communication refers to the body signals that we use in our communication every day. It is also known as 'communication without speech or writing' or 'communication in silence'. A non-verbal message has a unique quality that it is not said or written but still it communicates the desired sense meaningfully. Communication experts believe that non-verbal signals make up a huge part of our daily communication. From eyes to lips and from hands to legs, there are umpteen ways in which we naturally use our bodily movements to communicate what is not probably possible to convey with words. Without saying anything, non-verbal cues can convey volumes of information. Many research studies conclude that non-verbal part accounts for between 50% and 70% of all communication.

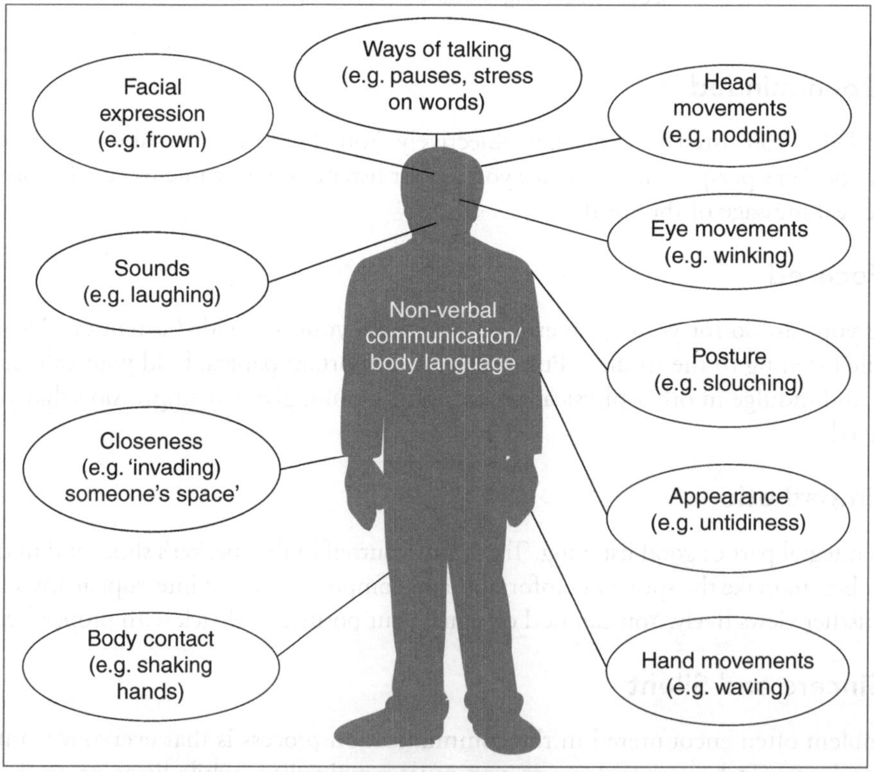

Non-verbal communication model.

The most widely practised forms of non-verbal communication are mentioned in the following sections.

Ways of non-verbal communication.

5.7.1 Body Movement

Facial expressions (eye contact and lip movements), gestures and body stances including various postures can speak a lot about a person and further help him to reinforce his/her verbal message.

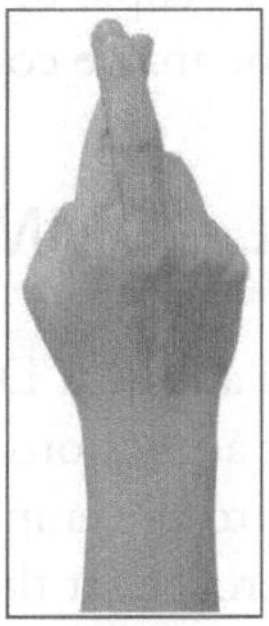

5.7.2 Physical Appearance

As the saying goes, a beautiful face is a silent recommendation. It is apparent that a smart well-dressed person is bound to look more attractive, credible and intelligent than a dull shabbily dressed man. Our appearance includes grooming, dressing and wearing accessories, which strongly communicate the various shades of our personality and professionalism. To a large extent, these things help us create our first impression on strangers.

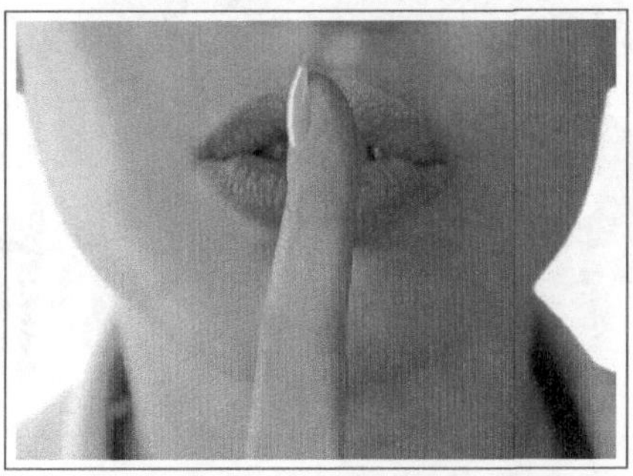

5.7.3 Verbal Sounds

The type of voice and its attributes, such as tone, speed, volume and accent, can greatly affect the delivery of a verbal message. The way we conduct our voice represents our mood, personality and authority in a given situation. It is easy to understand by the tone of a person's voice whether he/she is sarcastic, humorous, loving, confident or irritated.

5.7.4 Physical Distance or Closeness

Our proximity to or physical distance from a person determines our relationship and the space that we share with that person. Psychologists have suggested four space zones (intimate, personal, social and public) that describe our relationship and space-sharing with other persons. Many non-verbal messages are delivered through distance or proximity to indicate bonding, animosity, admiration or dominance.

5.7.5 Time

Time is an interesting non-verbal cue to judge a person's attitude, position and commitment. The way people use time also highlights their cultural values and the status that they have acquired in the society/organisation.

Non-verbal cues are natural and they provide strong indications of what is going on in our mind or body. But the meanings of these cues vary from people to people and culture to culture. So, one must be careful while deciphering a particular meaning of an eye contact or hand movements.

5.8 NEED FOR INTERCULTURAL COMMUNICATION

In today's globalised world, diverse workforce is a reality. Diversity requires a type of organisational culture which helps each employee pursue his/her career aspirations without being inhibited by gender, race, nationality, religion or other factors that are irrelevant to the employee's performance. It is becoming increasingly important for businesses to bridge cultural differences at the workplace and provide equitable work culture where everyone has his/her identity and space for growth.

Intercultural communicative competence, or ICC, refers to the ability to understand cultures, including your own, and use this understanding to communicate with people from other cultures successfully. Intercultural communication has become a critical skill desired most when we work with the multicultural

population worldwide. Familiarity of intercultural communication is the essential need of global workstations. ICC enhances our capability when we are dealing with international business partners, planning global acquisitions and mergers and pursuing new development projects globally. In fact, international businesses will not exist without intercultural communication. The following guidelines may help you prepare for adapting to cultural diversity at the workplace.

1. Take interest and spend time learning the new diverse workforce. Be keen on developing relations with people from different cultural backgrounds.
2. Be sensitive to their values and beliefs and show respect for them.
3. Be receptive to new ideas and improve your understanding about new and unfamiliar fields. Try to adapt to new change.
4. Be flexible to adjust with new social and cultural situations. Try to learn the right behaviour from the people who are the most acceptable and successful while working in diverse settings.
5. Be resilient enough to take risks as a way of learning.
6. Try to overcome the culture shock. Be strong to learn from any embarrassment or criticism in a new environment.
7. Be a quick observant. Initially reading non-verbal cues helps you more understand the people and their behaviours.
8. Be clear and direct with diverse groups. Do not work on assumptions and express yourself clearly by paraphrasing the words that they understand.
9. Be able to build trust and generate warmth by conducting yourself positively and making your intentions clear.

> In order to bridge cultural differences at the workplace and provide equitable work culture where everyone has his/her identity and space for growth, there is a need for intercultural communication.

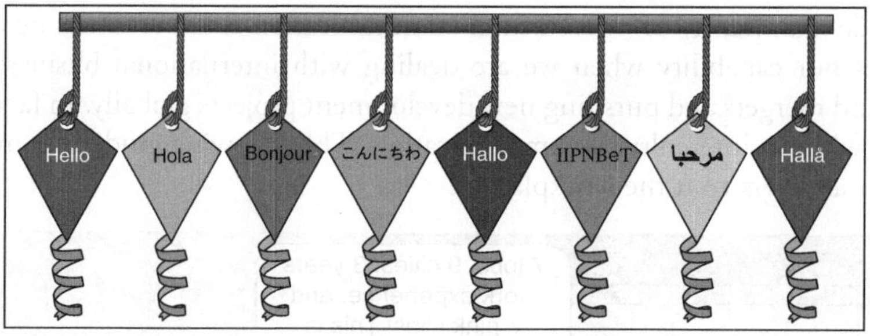

Saying "Hello" in different languages.

5.9 COMMUNICATION IN A DIGITAL WORLD

Today communication technology is one of the essential elements needed for running businesses. Everything is online and the way market communicates with the customer has changed forever. Organisations are now using communication technology to communicate faster, facilitate decision-making, train employees and promote business. We cannot imagine a business activity that is devoid of the use of communication technology. It has played the role of a powerful enabler for young corporate India that is ambitious and tech-savvy and eagerly waiting to make a difference at the workplace. The modern workplace uses a host of new technologies to communicate to with consumers and general public. Professionals are quickly adapting to global practices with faster, smarter and easy applications and replacing their old communication methods. Emails, voice/video chat, newsletters, magazines, intranet, digital media and, not to forget, the latest sensation social media — all are being used increasingly for organisational communications. The digital age driven by online networks and computers has completely overtaken businesses and their communication practices. As shown in the figure below, many new technologies of communication have been developed in recent years. The following sections describe the use of some of these communication technologies.

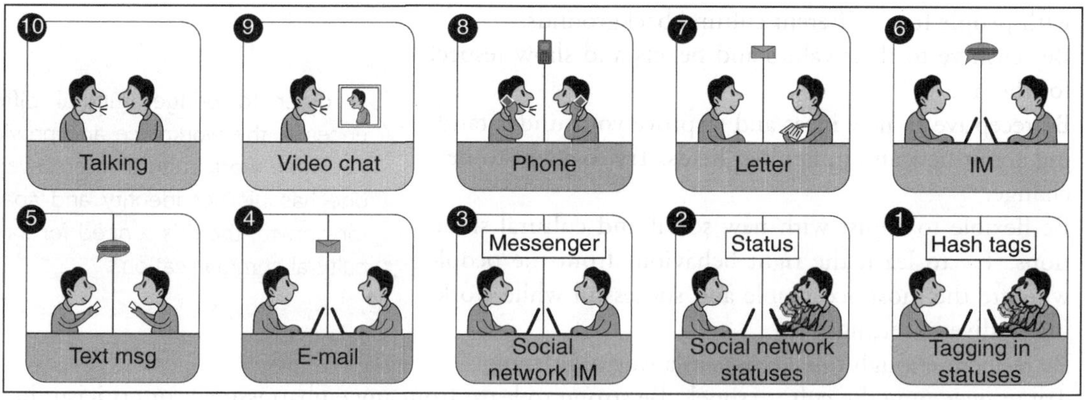

New ways of communication.

5.9.1 Email

It is a very quick and smart way of connecting to the outside world. Sending email messages is much quicker and easier than writing letters. Professionals rely on email technology for its effectiveness, as it has made presentation of traditional memos and letters paperless. The advantage of email lies in its cost and convenience.

Companies can send thousands or millions of emails each year with almost no incremental cost per piece. Email is easily archived to facilitate compliance in regulated industries for protecting precious data and improving credibility of the businesses.

5.9.2 Websites

Websites anchor public marketing for most small businesses. A well-designed website shares basic information like product and service lists and associated costs. Some companies go a step further and use their websites to host customer discussion forums, videos, documents and blog posts. With website interaction customers believe they are getting something of value, while businesses increase their goodwill among their target market.

5.9.3 Social Media

Today the hottest trend in business communication is social media marketing – that is, the careful use of social networking sites like Facebook, My Space, YouTube and Twitter to engage consumers within the context of their trusted circle of friends and family. Consumers create online profiles on social networking sites, and businesses create "fan pages" or Twitter accounts that customers may 'like' or otherwise associate with. Although some communication consultants oversell the promise of social media, it is truly becoming a new game changer for a corporate leader who wants to leverage the collective intelligence of its talent.

5.9.4 Video-conferencing

A video-conference is a live video connection between people placed in separate locations, established for the purpose of communication or interaction among them. Video-conferencing allows people to communicate visually from anywhere in the world. Groups see each other and interact in real time, although they may be worlds apart. Companies are using this communication technology regularly for business promotion and smart communication. It benefits immensely in terms of savings on travel time and communication expenses, and enhances the effectiveness of communication, productivity and collaboration.

5.9.5 Videophone

It is also called video telephone. It is a device that simultaneously transmits and receives both audio and video signals over telephone lines. To facilitate an effective audio-visual engagement between two partners, a computer or a television is not needed, and yet the video conferencing is possible through a videophone. Because of these qualities, videophone is widely preferred in business circles.

Every corporate is waking up to the reality that how best it can employ new-age communication tools to have greater bonding and effective management of its employees. If used correctly, new communication technology provides businesses various cost-effective ways to connect with their business partners and forge new bonds for efficiency and productivity. Real-time conversations, enabled by communication technology, energise the work place and speed up operations and decision making. To optimise the use of communication technology, it is important to leverage it strategically and treat it as an integral part of a company's overall strategy. The new media, based on communication technology, have tremendous power to save businesses' time, money and work force.

Summary

Communication skills are akin to life skills. Mastering them is essential to make our presence felt in this world. Communication skills enable us to be express ourselves confidently and communicate anything that we wish. Communication is principally a process of transmitting information from one place to another, from one group or individual to the other through vocal, written or non-verbal media. The communication process is meaningful and complete only when we try as clearly and accurately as we can to convey our ideas, intentions and objectives. It becomes successful when both the sender and the receiver understand the true meaning of a message. Our ability to transfer and receive information effectively determines how good our communication skills are. Good communication skills are an asset for any individual and can help him/her in every sphere of life — from the professional circle to the social world and everything in between. Genuine listening is a rare art. Listening takes place when we not only pay attention to the ideas, but how they are expressed, the type of words used, the voice and tone, and how the speaker uses his/ her movements. With companies focusing on diversity at the workplace, it has become increasingly important that we become more inter-culturally sensitive and competent in spite of our cultural differences. Having the desire to connect effectively with persons of different cultures is essential to enhance our ability to communicate inter-culturally. Businesses are becoming online and they expect their employees to be more digital-savvy. Everything is online and the way market communicates with the customer has changed forever. This new communication technology impels us to re-examine our abilities to communicate and redefine our notions of successful communication in terms of the digital world.

Chapter Review

1. What is communication?
2. What are the features of non-verbal communication?
3. Explain why listening is most important of all communication skills?
4. Why does the communication cycle need to be repeated?
5. How has technology affected workplace communication? Discuss the pros and cons of the same.
6. What measures will you suggest to improve the intercultural communication?

Direct Questions

1. Discuss GSC's3M model of communication?
2. What do you mean by the barriers to listening? Name some barriers to listening.

3. Why is feedback necessary for effective communication?
4. Why there is need for intercultural communication at the workplace? Justify your answer.
5. How technology has facilitated faster communication in the business world? Discuss some new communication technology tools that have been practised recently in the workplace.

Analytical Questions

1. As the saying goes that there is a difference between listening and hearing just as there is a difference between seeing and knowing. What can you infer from this saying? Justify the saying in the context of professional communication.
2. As a project manager of a team comprising members from different cultures and nationalities, how would you plan your cross-cultural communication strategies to avoid any confusion and achieve your business objectives with everyone's participation?
3. How can listening skills be a decisive factor in a workplace environment such as a business setting or a negotiation meeting? How can listening skills make or mar prospects of a significant business venture?

Resources for Further Reflections

1. Example of effective communication skills: video of President Obama's first public address after being elected as the president of the Unites States. https://www.youtube.com/watch?v=rPG-6g2AAWo.
2. A relationship between body language (non-verbal communication), communication and confidence. http://www.ted.com/talks/amy_cuddy_your_body_language_shapes_who_you_are?language=en#.
3. A guide to effective cross cultural communication. http://www.colorado.edu/conflict/peace/treatment/xcolcomm.htm.
4. Technology and workplace communication http://www.forbes.com/sites/unify/2013/12/10/how-technology-has-changed-workplace-communication/.
5. Effective communication for managers http://www.business.vic.gov.au/hiring-and-managing-staff/staff-management/communication-skills-in-the-workplace-for-managers.
6. Susan Adams. "The 10 skills employers most want in 20-somethingemployees." *Forbes*. http://www.forbes.com/sites/susanadams/2013/10/11/the-10-skills-employers-most-want-in-20-something-employees/.
7. Scot Ober. Contemporary business communication. Fifth edition. *Biztantra*; New Delhi 2004.
8. Dianne Schilling. "10 steps to effective listening." *Forbes*: http://www.forbes.com/sites/womensmedia/2012/11/09/10-steps-to-effective-listening/.
9. John H. Bryan. "The diversity imperative"*Executive Excellence*, 1999; Sage Publication: New Delhi. p. 6.
10. Intercultural communicative competence. http://www.teachingenglish.org.uk/knowledge-database/intercultural-communicative-competence.
11. Modern Means of Business Communication Jason Gillikin, Demand Media. http://smallbusiness.chron.com/modern-means-business-communication-2819.html.

Caselet 1

Communication Skills for Life

Arvind Bhattacharya was a big shot banker, serving as managing director of a big nationalised bank. In the year 2014, the year of his promotion to the post of managing director, Arvind recovered several bad debts and made a profit of nearly Rs 10 million for his regional branch. This profit was the highest in 15 years for the branch, a remarkable achievement for Arvind. He always dreamt of reaching this position and bringing a big change in the economics of the bank he had been working for almost two decades now.

However, looking at the way he developed as a person since his childhood, it was not easy for Arvind to reach this far in his career. When he was a child, his parents did not arrange better schooling for him. He was sent to an ordinary local school where no attention was paid to the personality development and communication skills of students. Consequently he could not communicate a full sentence in English without stammering. His body language was also pathetic.

However, serious drawbacks in his personality, Arvind being good at studies qualified for the best engineering institute in the country through a national entrance test. During his bachelor's course, he kept a good grade. But the good grade did not help him sail through placements. The reason was obvious – his lack of communication skills! Earlier he was simply ignorant about this stark reality of his personality, but now it stared him in the face, crushing him down.

Disappointed, Arvind he decided to go for a career in banking. He figured it out that it was easy for him to be a banker because it only required clearing an entrance test to get posted as a bank manager in a good government bank. His interpersonal communication skills were not going to be assessed in the test. Soon enough, Arvind passed one such test and was appointed as manager in a reputed bank. His joy knew no bounds. He thought he had escaped the need for communication skills for the rest of his life. But alas! He was wrong again.

While discharging the responsibility as bank manager, Arvind knew his facts and figures well. But he didn't know how to deal with customers. His body language, dressing and speaking and listening skills were never good enough. A bank gets all kinds of customers in a day: people speaking different languages, coming from different ethnicities and with different problems. Arvind failed to deal with them. His job was at stake. Then it dawned on him that he could never make a good career with bad communication skills. He needed to learn, develop these skills as soon as possible.

Ultimately, Arvind took admission in a part-time course for communication and interpersonal skills development. He would work at the bank in the day and attend the course class in the evening. The course coupled with intensive self-practice helped him change the way he spoke, improve his body language. His entire personality changed. By the end of the course, he emerged a different person, more confident and articulate. He felt he could deal with anyone, and that was, in fact, true. Days and years passed. The curve of this new improved banker saw an exponential growth, putting him in the managing director's post. And, this happened thanks to his perseverance to master communication skills!

Questions

1. Describe the important components of communication skills that Arvind lacked.
2. Why do you think it was necessary for Arvind to develop communication skills if he had to stay and grow in the corporate world?
3. Are good communication skills necessary only for progress in one's professional life? Justify your answer.

Chapter 6

EMPLOYMENT COMMUNICATION: RESUME AND JOB APPLICATION

Learning Roadmap

After reading this chapter you will be able to:

- Understand the necessity of job communication
- Differentiate between resume and curriculum vitae
- Familiarise with dos and don'ts of resume writing
- Structure the resume-length, format and content
- Choose the right format for resume writing
- Develop job application or cover letters

PERSPECTIVE

Writing a powerful resume is as valuable as having a good professional degree. Anyone who understands English language well cannot guarantee that he/she will write an extraordinary job application or resume. Apart from the command over English, one also needs to master the skill of resume writing to be able to draft a well-crafted resume with perfectly showcased cover letter. Most young job aspirants find it challenging to design a convincing resume using a persuasive language to express what qualities and qualifications they possess. As a young graduate or professional, you may have competence or experience but it may not fetch you a good job unless you are able to communicate your eligibility for the job convincingly through a well-written resume. Your resume serves two major objectives – first, it highlights what you can do for the company, and second, it tells your prospective employer why you are a better choice than the rest. To present yourself as an accomplished candidate through your resume, you must organise your ideas to highlight your virtues and present yourself as a versatile professional who is ready to take up challenges for building a good career. Doing this is essential because today companies look for versatile workforce to survive and grow in highly competitive global markets. World's best universities offer 'writing labs' for mastering job communication skills. Graduates are trained to write resume and job applications with in-depth explanations and step-by-step processes. There is a standard process that needs to be followed in order to design a resume which portrays correctly the capabilities and overall personality of a potential candidate.

"The supreme accomplishment is to blur the line between work and play."

— Arnold J. Toynbee

6.1 INTRODUCTION

You earn your degree and prepare yourself to embark on a rewarding journey as a professional. Young graduates like you dream to have a decent job. In your quest for better placement, one essential step that you have to take is designing a meaningful resume that may help you get the first interview call. To write a good resume you must be aware of the requirements of job markets and plan your career accordingly. You also need to assess your personality, identify your skills and set your goals to lead a successful professional life. Hence, resume writing and job application are two very vital segments of career management.

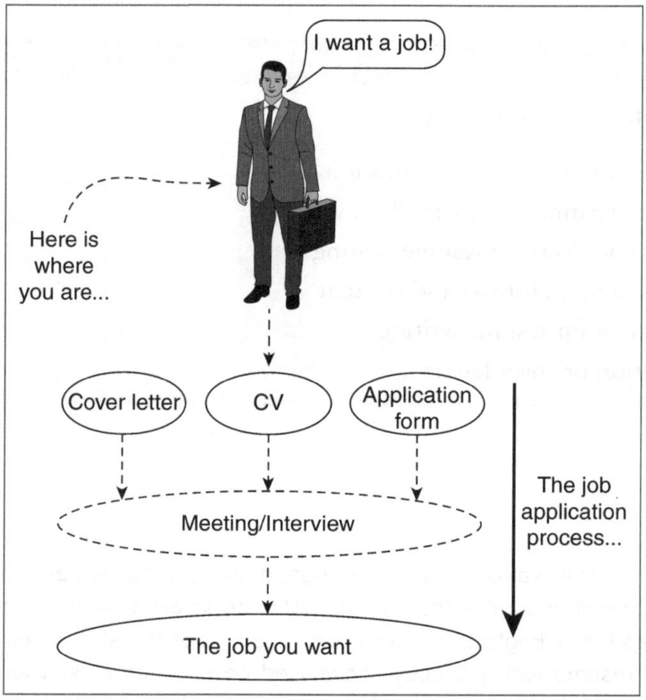

6.2 WHAT IS A RESUME?

A resume is a self-promotion summary that enables you to tell your story, express your personality and gain a competitive edge in the job market. In other words, your resume is a short and crisp written snapshot highlighting your education, skills and work experiences. It is a clear indicator of your past laurels and future aspirations. It is the passport to your dream job. Resume should be designed attractively so that it could immediately capture the attention of a prospective employer. A good resume is developed in a way that it can be skimmed quickly.

"You are not your resume, you are your work."

— Seth Godin.

A well-planned and well-written resume elucidates that you meet all the requirements for the position you are applying for and you deserve an interview call. The ultimate aim of any resume is to land an interview. The best resume is the one that enables prospective employers to know everything about the job applicant in the shortest possible time. Ideally, within 15–20 seconds of resume reading, your prospective employer should know who you are, what are your strengths, what are your future aspirations and how would you serve the company's interests. So, the real challenge in resume writing lies in presenting all the information, concerning a job aspirant through a neat, simple and concise resume.

A resume is like a sales statement in which you are promoting yourself. A clear, well written resume will cut through the competition and get you the much awaited job call.

I do wonders for my company or I can put any company in Forbes Top 100 companies.

6.3 WHAT IS A CURRICULUM VITAE?

A CV, also known as curriculum vitae or vita that means course of life in Latin, is a complete sketch of your accomplishments – education, employment, research projects and university engagement or community work. In the USA, CV is mostly used to present a person's academic status and achievements. What academic appointments you hold, which research projects you work on, where you publish, etc., are the main ingredients of your CV. CV is usually longer than the resume and it may run more than three pages depending on your profile. Broadly, a CV is a reflection of your scholarly identity while a resume constructs your professional identity.

Differences between resume and curriculum vitae

Parameter	Resume	Curriculum vitae
Length	Shorter	Longer
Format	Chronological, functional and hybrid	Varied by careers
Purpose	All-purpose	Mostly for academic and scientific positions
Experience	Professional	Scholarly

"Choose a job you love, and you will never have to work a day in your life."

— Confucius

6.4 WHAT IS A SCANNABLE RESUME?

A scannable resume is an electronic resume that is viewed using a scanning machine or document imaging technology to store it in a computer database. It is no different from the regular resume as the basic sections remain same in both. More and more employers are using image technology to manage and screen job applications. This technology saves time and resources for recruiters by automatically extracting key information from the resumes received from job aspirants. To ensure that important information about you gets extracted when your resume is scanned by prospective employers, you need to work on two aspects: keywords and formatting. The following points explain how to take care of these aspects:

> Your resume should be designed to match the job advertisement and complement the skills asked for.

1. Use most appropriate and job-related keywords, particularly nouns. For instance, a computer would scan for 'Human Resource Management', not 'manage human resources'. For example, 'team work' and 'interpersonal skills' are relevant keywords for a business professional.
2. Keep the resume format simple and font face consistent to avoid any misreading by the scanner.
3. Do not use fancy design with graphics and pictures. Avoid bullets, tables and visuals.

6.5 HOW TO DEVELOP AN IMPRESSIVE RESUME

The following are some useful tips to help you master resume writing so that you could write an impeccable and impressive resume and win an interview:

"The secret of success is making your vocation your vacation."

— Mark Twain

6.5.1 What to Do

1. Know your **purpose**. Be clear that your resume is to help you get an interview call, not the job.
2. Keep your resume **simple**, **direct** and **concise**.
3. Create short and meaningful sentences and use **Standard English**.
4. Make sure to use appropriate **keywords**. They are your identity and strength. By using the suitable keywords, you will attract more interview calls. Job ads will give you an idea what the hiring managers are searching for. For example, for the position of **accountant**, you could include **accountancy**, **finance**, **budget** and **firm** as keywords.
5. Get your resume proofread.
6. Make sure to use **bold type** or **bulleted points** to represent your credentials. Times and Arial fonts are advisable.
7. Use **action verbs**. Words such as '**pioneered**' or '**championed**' get more attention rather than '**commenced**' or '**initiated**'.
8. **Update** your resume on a regular basis with every new change in your position or experience.

Ensure that your resume is in a logical order, easy to skim, readable with clear layout and has a positive tone and action words.

Use spell-check while typing your resume, and run it through a friend to be sure.

6.5.2 What not to Do

The following should not be done:

1. Include **insignificant details** such as sexual, religious and political preferences.
2. **Bluff** and kill your candidature for good.
3. **Stretch** your resume **more than two pages**; the shorter the better.
4. Load your resume with **too many details** of your qualifications and experiences.
5. Use fancy **design**, coloured **graphics** and **photos**.
6. Include **personal pronouns** 'I' and 'we'.
7. Use of **CAPITAL letters** and **exclamation marks** is unnecessary. Avoid **jargon** and **slang** in resume.
8. Decorate your resume with **empty phrases** such as '**extremely creative**', '**noble hearted**' or '**problem solver**'. Try to connect with real-life experiences.
9. Mention people as **referees** without their prior consent.

> *"Your work is going to fill a large part of your life, and the only way to be truly satisfied is to do what you believe is great work. And the only way to do great work is to love what you do. If you haven't found it yet, keep looking. Don't settle. As with all matters of the heart, you'll know when you find it."*
>
> — Steve Jobs

6.5.3 What to Include

As stated earlier, your resume is a precise record of your qualifications, skills and qualities. To make a good first-time impression on a prospective employer, it should be written in a crisp language providing concise information about you through bullet lists rather than verbose sentences and paragraphs. It should help the employer skim the necessary information quickly and decide whether you deserve an interview call. You may design your resume to highlight your academic credentials and professional experiences. But remember, your resume should not be shorter than one page and longer than three pages unless it is required specifically for certain jobs.

A resume can have many sections but the basic information remains the same in every resume, such as personal details, work history, education, career objective and other additional information.
The following is a description of the basic sections that you must include in your resume:

1. Begin with your **personal details**, that is, your name, address, telephone number and email address. It would be handy for the hiring manager to contact you if needed. Do not include personal information such as marital status, family size and religion.
2. Mention a clear and concise **objective** focusing on how better would you help the company achieve its goals. Do not give the impression that you are using the company for your personal growth. For instance, you may state your objective as follows:
3. **Objective**: Enable Mudra Communications to become a market leader by adding new brands to its basket as a marketing consultant.
4. Describe your **employment history** meticulously by detailing key responsibilities and accomplishments that are relevant to your present job. You can include names and addresses of the companies where you have worked, date of employment, title and responsibilities.

In addition to the above basic sections, you may also include the following components in your resume. But their inclusion is **optional** – mention them if they are necessary to highlight your position and personality. These components are the following:

1. Achievements and awards
2. Professional memberships and affiliations
3. Voluntary and community service
4. International travel and experience
5. Special skills and languages
6. Interests and hobbies
7. Referees

There is no "one standard" format to organise your resume, so be sure to choose the style that will most effectively showcase your skills and abilities.

6.6 DIFFERENT FORMATS OF RESUME

Depending upon your experience and job for which you are applying, you can choose any one of the formats for designing your resume, introduced in the following sections.

6.6.1 Chronological Resume

The chronological resume format is the most widely used format. The following are some important features of a chronological resume:

1. It is effective for those with a steady employment history.
2. In it, your work history is showcased by job title with the most recent mentioned first.
3. It works well when your professional experience matches the desired job.

Vikas Vikram Bhalla

Local Address:	**Permanent Address:**
123 Manglam Apartment Kasturba Hospital Lane, Mumbai – 400011	Flat No. 100 Triveni Apartments New Delhi 110034

Mobile: +91 9786823464
Vkb1@gmail.com

OBJECTIVE

Public Relations position in a multinational company to enhance the global reputation and brand image of a corporate and its business. Resourceful marketing professional with a proven track record of effective people-management skills and a rich sales and public relations background.

EMPLOYMENT EXPERIENCE

Senior Manager, Corporate Communications, Tata Motors
December 2012 – current

- Initiated Social Media networking for major brands and garnered a new young consumer base.
- Coordinated all the operations of corporate communications including websites, newsletters and advertising.
- Launched a national public relations campaign focusing on better employee engagement and growth.

Project Manager, Publicity and Advertising, Vibgyor Communications

January 2010–November 2012

- Led marketing strategic plans including recruiting, training and managing six zonal areas.
- Implemented a comprehensive marketing plan to increase brand awareness and brand image.
- Created integrated web-based marketing strategy.

Copywriter and Marketing Consultant, Ogilvy & Mather

August 2008–December 2010

- Assisted the creative team in brainstorming and developing the copy for top brands.
- Analyzed the advertising case studies and came out with new creative plans.

EDUCATION

August 2008 Melbourne Business School, Australia

Master of Business Administration
Distinguished Student Program
May 2006 IIIT Allahabad, India

Bachelor of Technology
Graduated with Gold Medal

SPECIAL SKILLS

- Strong and persuasive interpersonal skills
- Strategic thinking and team building competencies
- Proficient in handling latest graphic design software
- Wide international exposure and fluent in French and Spanish

AFFILIATIONS AND ASSOCIATIONS

- Honorary Member, Federation of Indian Asian Marketing Association.
- Founding Member, Global Media Planning.
- Joint Secretary, Press Council of India.

INTERESTS

Scuba diving, Elizabethan theatre, Travelling, Beatles

REFERENCES

Available upon request

A sample chronological resume.

6.6.2 Functional Resume

The functional resume format is important for people who have varied job experiences. The following are some important features of a functional resume:

1. It features your skills without mentioning the dates associated with your work.
2. It includes those skills that are most relevant to job you are trying to get regardless of dates of employment.
3. It is suitable for applying a job even when you have gaps in your employment history.

Vikas Vikram Bhalla
Vkb1@gmail.com

Flat No. 100 Triveni Apartments New Delhi 110034 Mobile: +91 9786823464

OBJECTIVE Public Relations position in a multinational company to enhance the global reputation and brand image of a corporate and its business. Resourceful marketing professional with a proven track record of effective people-management skills and rich sales and public relations background.

SKILLS

CORPORATE COMMUNICATIONS
- Worked extensively on Social Media for brand awareness and consumer preference at Tata Motors.
- Initiated award winning CSR campaigns for many top companies.
- Was 'Corporate Student Manager' in the final year of MBA.

PUBLICITY and BRANDING
- Assisted the Indian Culture Fest at the United Nations as a PR consultant.
- Developed branding manuals for top three English newspapers in India.
- Created integrated web-based marketing strategy at Vibgyor Communications.

PEOPLE MANAGEMENT
- Launched a nationwide public relations campaign focusing on better employee engagement and growth at Tata Motors.
- Supervised human resource development programmes for Jet Airways.

SPECIAL SKILL
- Trained Copywriter
- Web Content Designer
- Strong and persuasive interpersonal skills
- Proficient in handling latest graphic design software
- Strategic planning and team building competencies
- Fluent in French and Spanish
- Well versed in corporate laws and practices
- Extraordinary PR and negotiation skills

EDUCATION
- **Master of Business Administration**
  August 2008 Melbourne Business School, Australia

- **Bachelor of Technology**
  May 2006 IIIT Allahabad, India

EMPLOYMENT EXPERIENCE

- **Senior Manager,** Corporate Communications, Tata Motors
  December 2012 – current
- **Project Manager,** Publicity and Advertising, Vibgyor Communications
  January 2010–November 2012
- **Copywriter and Marketing Consultant,** Ogilvy & Mather
  August 2008–December 2010

AFFILIATIONS AND ASSOCIATIONS

- Honorary Member, Association of Indian Asian Marketing Federation
- Founding Member, Global Media Planning
- Joint Secretary, Press Council of India

INTERESTS

- Scuba diving, Elizabethan theatre, Travelling, Beatles

REFERENCES

- Available upon request

A sample functional resume.

6.6.3 Hybrid Resume

A hybrid resume:

1. Suits most to the students who have acquired valuable experience by performing many unrelated projects, courses and jobs.
2. Combines the best features of the chronological and functional resume formats.

6.7 JOB APPLICATION OR COVER LETTER

Your job application, also known as cover letter, is your first interface with hiring managers. It expresses your objective or goal for joining a particular organisation. A job application is duly supported by a well written resume. It covers or communicates the most promising features of your professional life for the prospective employer. It can be of two types – one, the solicited application letter, which is designed in response to an advertised post, and two, the unsolicited application letter, through which an aspirant makes his/her own efforts to secure a job that has not been advertised.

> The cover letter is the first contact point between you and the potential employer. It gives you an edge to make you stand out from the crowd and get you the desired call for the next round.

6.7.1 Need for Cover Letter

You need to write a cover letter:

1. To emphasise why you are the best choice for a particular job or office
2. To assure that you have done homework about the department you are applying to work in
3. To demonstrate how you can help the company grow with your addition

6.7.2 How to Develop a Cover Letter

Resumes and cover letters go hand in hand. An impressive resume needs an equally great cover letter. Like a formal business letter, a cover letter provides a preview of your resume. It prepares the prospective employer to decide whether to look at your resume or not. A cover letter is developed in full block business letter format, where the text is left-aligned. A sample cover letter for the resumes, presented in the figures above, is shown here.

Flat No. 100
Triveni Apartments
New Delhi 110034

January 15, 2014

Ms Shalini Verma
Human Resource Manager
Hindustan Unilever Ltd.
Empire Building
Mumbai

Dear Ms Shalini,

VACANCY FOR CHIEF MANAGER, CORPORATE COMMUNICATIONS

My extensive corporate experience in public relations and marketing, coupled with my management and engineering degrees, has better prepared me to apply for the position of Chief Manager, Corporate Communications, HUL as advertised in Times Ascent on Wednesday, January 1, 2014.

HUL is a company of particular interest to me. My homework of the organisation gives me a clear understanding about its business philosophy to work ethically as a team and to serve the clients best and solve their business problems. This professionalism builds lasting relationship with the customers and the employees and inspires me further to practise my communication and human resource skills that I have acquired over the years from companies and academia for your organisation.

In my current position as a Senior Manager with Tata Motors, I coordinated all the operations of corporate communications including websites, newsletters, and advertising. Further, I mobilised the company business by putting all the major brands on Social Media and garnered a new younger consumer base for the company. By working collaboratively with senior management, I have honed my HR skills in planning, goal setting, recruiting and training.

I have excellent PR skills and as a Public Relations consultant, I have initiated community education programmes to raise awareness of consumer rights and formed consumer forums to strengthen the movement. Throughout my professional life, I have served my clients and organisations exceptionally in meeting their objectives and expectations.

I have great interest in learning and excelling new technologies relating to my career. Promotion through Social Media and Content Web Designing are two core technical skills that make me a desirable choice for this position.

I believe that my experiences and credentials match the requirements you have outlined in the job advertisement. To support my candidature, I enclose my resume for more details about me. I can be reached anytime on my Mobile phone (+91 9786823464) or at my email (Vkb1@gmail.com). I am excited to speak with you about this employment opportunity.

Thank you for your time and consideration.
Sincerely

(sign here)
Vikas Vikram Bhalla
Enclosure: Resume

A sample cover letter.

You may have noticed in the sample cover letter that apart from introduction, it has three essential parts: opening, body and closing. The following sections explain the contents and objectives of these parts.

6.7.2.1 Opening

In the opening of your cover letter, you:

1. Include the job name and vacancy reference
2. Mention how you came to know about the job vacancy
3. Explain that you have done enough homework about the organisation by including the relevant information

6.7.2.2 Body

In the body of your cover letter, you

1. Sell your skills and experiences the way expected by the employer
2. Tell how company can be benefited by hiring you
3. Highlight your prominent job-related accomplishments that make you stand out as the only choice for the job

6.7.2.3 Closing

In the closing of your cover letter, you

1. Reaffirm how your candidature aligns with the organisation's goals
2. Restate how your professionalism will help the organisation
3. Request for an interview or meeting
4. Thank them for their time and consideration

A cover letter demonstrates that you know about the organisation and are curious in its businesses. You should explain why you chose this organisation.

The sample format of a cover letter, listing all its parts, is shown below.

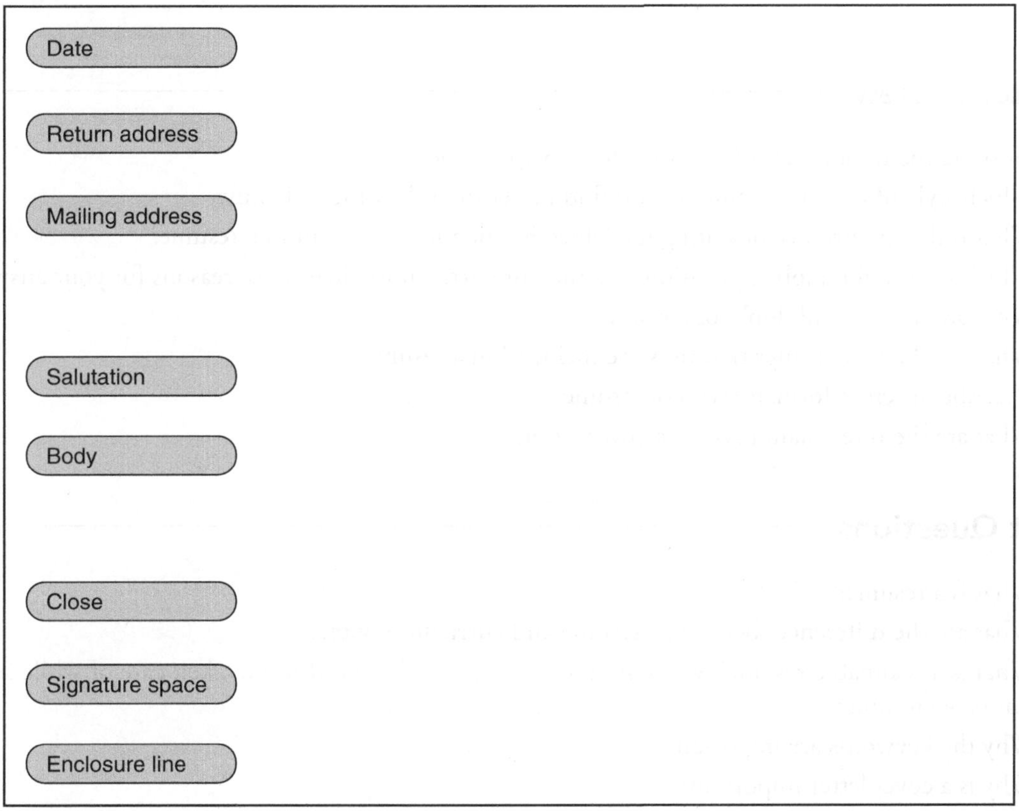

Parts of a cover letter.

Summary

A résumé is a small document that captures your professional experience. It is a well-organised summary of your education, employment history and experiences that are relevant to the job you are applying for. The main objective of any resume is to procure an interview call. A resume may have sections containing information about the applicant such as contact details, education qualifications, experiences relating to the job and honours and distinctions. It should not be lengthy and include everything precisely so that it becomes easy for the recruiters to skim the desired information immediately. Resumes are prepared in three main formats: functional, chronological and hybrid. To make the desired impression on prospective employers, you need to do a lot of homework before designing your resume. You should gather valuable information about the company you are aspiring. You also need to collect information about the people who are going to recruit you and the nature of job you are going to handle. This homework would help you align your resume with the mission and expectations of the organisation you are applying to work in. Your objectives must be clearly stated, explaining how you can be useful to the organisation. A powerful resume will create a positive impact and bring the expected outcome. It can go a long way in leading you to greater heights in your career.

Chapter Review

1. Illustrate the importance of a resume for job applications.
2. Which style of resume writing do you find better than the others? Justify.
3. What is the importance of stating the 'objective' of a job applicant in a resume?
4. Which is ideal for a job application – resume or curriculum vitae? Give reasons for your answer.
5. What are the dos and don'ts of a resume?
6. What are the basic things that must be included in a resume?
7. Describe different formats styles of resume.
8. What are the three main parts of a cover letter?

Direct Questions

1. What is a resume?
2. What are the differences between a resume and curriculum vitae?
3. What is a scannable resume? What are the two aspects that need to be taken care of while making a scannable resume?
4. Why the keywords are important?
5. Why is a cover letter important?

Analytical Questions

1. Why do you think bluffing is not advisable in a resume?
2. Is it advisable to summarise all your skills, listed in your resume, in a cover letter as well? Justify your answer.
3. Imagine you were a part of five major academic projects. You were also a member of a sports team that had represented your institute in various tournaments. You can accommodate only five points in your resume. What would you do? (Either you mention five projects or mention four projects along with a sporting achievement?) Explain your reasons.

Resources for Further Reflections

1. Cover letters that makes hiring managers smile http://www.forbes.com/sites/dailymuse/2014/02/06/the-cover-letters-that-make-hiring-managers-smile-then-call-you/.
2. How to tailor your resume and cover letter for different posts http://www.huffingtonpost.com/her-campus/how-to-tailor-your-cover_b_5034837.html?ir=India&adsSiteOverride=in.

3. Tips to write a perfect CV and cover letter http://www.theguardian.com/careers/careers-blog/cv-cover-letter-tips-how-to-write-perfect.
4. NE speaker stresses on resume http://collegian.tccd.edu/?p=25555.
5. What an employer wants in a cover letter http://jobs.theguardian.com/article/what-an-employer-wants-from-your-covering-letter/.
6. The only resume advice you will ever need http://www.forbes.com/sites/trudysteinfeld/2012/06/06/the-only-resume-advice-youll-ever-need/.
7. Importance of resume https://www.youtube.com/watch?v=Who2Xax1GX8.
8. Resume Questions: http://career-advice.monster.ca/resumes-cover-letters/resume-samples/top-resume-questions/article.aspx.
9. Resume Templates: https://www.themuse.com/advice/the-41-best-resume-templates-ever.

Caselet 1

Placement Puzzle

Venkat was among the hundreds of students about to graduate from an engineering college. It was his final semester and he was, just like others, preparing his job applications. The placement session in his college had begun and the companies kept pouring in for interviews. Venkat was graduating with a degree in computer sciences, one of the highest ranked and highest paid technical programmes in his institute. So, he was sure about grabbing a package worth millions per annum. Each time a company visit was announced, Venkat prepared himself for technical tests and the technical and HR rounds of interviews.

Venkat's is grades were good so he was always screened for preliminary round of written technical tests. Of all the tests he gave during the placement proceedings, he cleared 99% tests, getting selected for the technical round of interview. Most of the time, he cleared the technical interview as well. But he never managed to get through the final HR round of interview. He had appeared for 10 companies during the first month of the placement season. His confidence started to shatter because of his repeated failure in HR interviews. He asked his friends who had been selected about what could possibly be the best answers to the common personality-based questions and prepared according to their feedback. He practised before the mirror to speak confidently and dress appropriately. He tried to fix each weak link that he thought could possibly obstruct his selection. But nothing worked out.

Slowly, time was passing by. The inflow of good companies to the campus was decreasing, so was the package that they offered. The pressure on Venkat and his parents was increasing. Another company came by and Venkat was chosen for the HR round of interview. In the interview, he answered every question carefully and tried to be watchful about his posture and body language. Suddenly, the HR manager asked him a question about his resume: 'When exactly did you do this internship at CDAC that you have mentioned in your resume?' Venkat replied, 'Two years back' and tried to be as subtle and polite as possible. 'Great. And what about the one you have listed over the CDAC one? The one at IISER?' again asked the HR manager. 'Just after my first year of college', replied Venkat. 'OK, I was just asking because you haven't mentioned the period during which you worked. HR manager pointed out. Venkat was numb and embarrassed at the poor designing of his resume and omission of this vital information that caused him loss of many lucrative jobs. Although he had the credentials of a powerful candidate, his lack of resume planning and writing skills made his job prospects gloomy. Later, while going through his resume, Venkat also realised that it was lengthy, disorganised and poorly written with some spellings and grammar errors. Not it reflects the personality and skills that Venkat actually possessed.

Questions

1. Why do you think a resume holds special importance in job applications even when the technical skills and qualifications are up to the mark?
2. What are the ideal points that you should follow while formulating a resume?

Chapter 7

PROFESSIONAL PRESENTATION

Learning Roadmap

After reading this chapter you will be able to:

- Understand the importance of professional presentations
- Plan the initial steps for preparing presentations
- Explain the complete procedure of planning and presentation
- Discuss the types of visual aids and their utilities
- Explain how to manage stage fright and anxiety
- Suggest how to rehearse and deliver

PERSPECTIVE

Leaders are communicators. Whether they sit in the corner office of a corporate or preside over the Raisina Hill, the seat of power of the Government of India. Among the contemporary political leaders, Barrack Obama and Narendra Modi have greatly impressed the masses and media by their extraordinary public speaking acumen. They represent two different worlds, but as far as their mastery of the art of public speaking is concerned, they both are impeccable orators and enjoy public discourse. They are media-savvy and people-friendly and this gives them an edge over their competitors. When we listen to their election speeches, we understand that they are great strategists; they know their purpose and audience; and they just deliver what people want to listen from them. Both the leaders are very popular among the young people and always connect and communicate to them through social media. Further, Modi is a master craftsman who does good homework before his speech and never forgets to discuss local stories related to his audience, combining them with humour or seriousness as per their context. These two leaders should serve as a valuable learning source for budding presenters who must analyse their craft of public speaking to derive some important lessons. This learning would help budding presenters a lot in their planning of presentations and people management.

Great stories happen to those who can tell them.

— Ira Glass

7.1 NATURE OF ORAL PRESENTATION

No professional can think of rising in his/her career without acquiring the ability to make good presentations. Quite often professionals or employees are required to make formal presentations regarding some proposal or project or the work they are doing. Presentations may be defined as a well-prepared short discussion or talk on a specified theme mainly delivered to a select audience to generate their interest or to share something new and informative. Good presentations help professionals excel at workplace and build strong bonds with the people around them. Presentation skills are an asset for an individual and help him/her reach the upper echelons of an organisation. Presentations can be planned for various reasons – students throwing light on their qualities during placements, executives projecting sales growth, teachers discussing novel concepts, leaders planning new businesses etc. So, a presentation depending on the objective of its presenter can have various purposes – entertainment, educational, business and social.

Today, in the highly competitive, information-driven world, job aspirants try to be good speakers or presenters to market themselves as good professionals. So, presentation skills are the most visible and game-changing skills. These are of equal significance for men and women and strongly desirable for a bright future. Despite our shyness or stage fear, we can develop excellent presentation skills that will prepare us to express our views in a convincing way. Planning and practising go hand in hand for acquiring presentation skills and establishing ourselves as confident and competent presenters. We need a systematic approach to plan our presentations: selecting the right topic, identifying the target audience, developing the topic and delivering the presentation.

Any presentation is meant to inform, influence and motivate action.

7.2 PLANNING A PRESENTATION

Planning a presentation is like a writing a well-crafted message. It demands purpose, selects audience, outlines a main topic and plans the duration and occasion. Your planning of a presentation decides what you want to get or communicate to your audience. The harder you prepare, the better you deliver.

7.2.1 Deciding the Purpose of Presentation

Purpose drives any communication. There are various purposes for which you can do a presentation. Your presentation cannot be effective unless you are clear about what do you want to convey to the target audience. It is the purpose that decides whether you want to educate, entertain or sell something to your audience. Professional presentations primarily aim to inform, update, persuade and inspire the audience at the workplace. While planning these presentations, you must answer these questions to decide the presentation purpose – Do you want to make a sales presentation? Do you want to persuade the employees in your company to accept a change in the promotion policy? Do you want to convey the company's new initiatives for sustainable green work culture?

7.2.2 Identifying and Analysing the Audience

A successful presenter does a great a deal of homework to understand who is his/her target audience. So, while planning a presentation, you must be aware of the demographics of your audience – age, gender, occupation, religion, language, cultural lineage etc. What type of content you would choose for your presentation depends on your audience; how much are they familiar with the topic; and what they expect from the presentation. There are many other audience-related critical variables that you must consider while planning your presentation. These are –local issues, social and political mood, work culture and motivational level of the audience. A skilled presenter could easily analyse these issues to have a better understanding of his/ her audience and prepare the presentation accordingly. It is also essential for the presenter to have a good grasp of the values, attitudes and beliefs of the target audience. It would help him get an idea of their expected participation, interest and reaction during the presentation.

7.2.3 Determining the Occasion and Time

Knowing the occasion and time of presentation is important for planning an effective presentation. A smart presenter may like to work out the following while determining the occasion and time of his/her presentation:

1. Time and duration of presentation
2. Significance of the occasion
3. Venue and arrangement of the presentation
4. Strength and mood of the audience

> The most important aspect to remember during audience analysis is to know them thoroughly and deliver what they expect most from any presentation.

Taking care of the above issues in advance will give you enough time to research your topic, organise your information, work on your visual aids and finally deliver an effective presentation. It is expected of you after having understood the nature of occasion and the mood of the audience you will formulate appropriate strategies to make your views appear convincing to the audience.

> *If you have brilliant ideas, but if you can't get them across, your ideas won't get you anywhere.*
> — Lee Iacocca

7.2.4 Selecting the Topic

While planning your presentation alone or in a group, it is pertinent that you develop a list of issues which may help you to decide the topic clearly. It covers the main theme that you can generalise in a single sentence your purpose to the audience. The topic should feature the big picture, for example,

The New retirement benefit scheme for employees

Considering the following issues and coming out with right explanations give you an edge over others:

1. Is the topic relevant to the people and place?
2. Is the topic interesting?
3. Is the topic impactful?
4. Is enough information available about the topic?
5. Is the topic leading to serve the purpose?

> The presenter must have the clarity about the purpose of presentation. The audience should carry a clear message that you want them to remember.

Answering these questions would make your task of choosing a topic much easier. It is to be understood that selection of a topic should be commensurate with time available, audience chosen and place provided.

7.3 PREPARING THE PRESENTATION

Good preparation helps your audience understand your purpose and gets the desired response from them. Preparing for a presentation involves researching the topic, outlining the content, using if visual aids, and finally selecting the formats for presentation.

7.3.1 Researching the Topic

Researching the topic chosen for your presentation is an arduous task. Because you need to approach the topic meticulously by presenting relevant facts and convincing arguments in your effort to achieve the presentation objective. For this, you need to explore the various aspects of the topic to make its presentation meaningful. To begin with, you can organize a brainstorm on the topic and arrive at a rough outline including everything you find informative and interesting about the topic. Then would begin your search for relevant and authentic sources of information, statistical facts, testimonials, pictures, views of experts, etc. As it is applicable with other research, you may like to include primary as well as secondary sources of information in your presentation. The topic outline may further help you in selecting the sources of information such as library online catalogues, reference works, social media networks, search engines, e-magazines and newspapers. Apart from online sources, you can also use the primary research data that is possible to obtain from personal observations, interviews and questionnaire-based surveys. Remember, you may try to explore and include the best possible information to make your presentation impressive, but never forget that you have limited

> Research your topic. Your sound understanding of the main points of your topic may help you develop a plan and execute it timely.

time for the presentation. So, do not overload your presentation with information; only opt for crisp information that adds real value to the presentation.

7.3.2 Developing the Topic

Research leads you to a plethora of information related to the presentation topic. But it also poses the challenge of organising the desired information systematically for its easy understanding by the audience. If the information is not organised properly, the presentation looks incoherent and the audience loses interest in it. You may divide the information to be presented into three parts: introduction, body and ending. This is one of the best arrangements to design a presentation. The three main parts of the presentation are described below.

How to Keep the Audience Engaged with Yourself

- Describe a scene or a character
- Tell a story
- Share a personal experience
- Relate to a recent event
- Piggyback on a previous speaker's remark or theme
- Point out something important about the audience or the current setting
- Show a compelling visual image
- Ask a provocative question
- State a fact that is troubling, amusing or remarkable
- Spell out what is at stake for your listeners
- Offer a humorous observation or anecdote
- Explain your own interest in the topic
- Tell listeners what the topic has to do with them

If you're not comfortable with public speaking - and nobody starts out comfortable; you have to learn how to be comfortable - practice. I cannot overstate the importance of practicing. Get some close friends or family members to help evaluate you, or somebody at work that you trust.

— Hillary Clinton

7.3.2.1 Introduction

In this part of your presentation, you present yourself to the audience. It is the moment when you come face to face with the audience. You try to capture the mood of the audience while explaining the objective or topic of your presentation. After initial greetings to the audience, you may state the presentation purpose by asking a relevant question, sharing a short anecdote, interesting facts or something that is very central to the topic and engrossing to the audience. When establishing initially engagement with the audience, you may introduce yourself and establish your credibility and authority about the presentation topic.

Your introduction is the main glue to engage them further in the presentation. If you hold their attention early, they may be with you until you finish.

You may state your purpose in the following way:

'I'm going to speak about...'
'This morning I'm here to talk about...'

You may also provide a short preview of what comes next in the presentation, for example:

'In the next 20 minutes, I'll discuss three major options: first ... then'

7.3.2.2 Body

Body is the soul of your presentation and it offers everything about the purpose and topic of the presentation to the audience. It contains key points of your topic, specific observations, clear visualisations, challenges and rewards, results and other useful supporting information. While delivering the body part, you should focus on key points one by one in a systematic way. You should be able to emphasise the important aspects with proper supporting information. Your audience should be convinced why a particular point is so important. While highlighting the main points, take pauses after each point, giving the audience time to understand what you are saying.

Verbal signposts can be useful to engage your audience with you throughout the presentation.

It helps in many ways specially when a main idea may have another sub idea. For example,

(*'Another issue is ...'*) or

A contrasting view may be given to stress a point. For example,

(*'A different or opposite view to this is...'*).

You may give a vivid and colourful account of your information by transitional phrases such as

First... Second...or Finally
The next point is that...
Moreover, it is significant to...
The first reason is that...

> The body of your presentation helps you establish the key issues with appropriate examples and cases.

You should make sure you provide clear links between main points, explanations and examples.

7.3.2.3 Ending

It is your chance to deliver the crux of your presentation. When you come to this stage, your audience is through to your complete presentation and you have a sense of completion or accomplishment. How you finish your talk is important because people usually remember what you say in the last. The closing should sum up the highlights of the presentation. Be aware that you are going to introduce nothing new at this stage. Just restate the key ideas, thank the audience and invite questions.

You may conclude your presentation with similar phrases and sentences

So, to restate the central ideas...
In support of my topic, I have presented three main issues
I'd just like to sum up by saying...
Thank you everyone. Is there any question?

7.3.3 Using Visual Aids

Visual aids make a presentation interesting and keep the audience engaged. They enhance the comprehension of the intended message and improve the retention of information. They make the presenter confident and comfortable by allowing him or her to present visually important points or facts to the audience.

Technology offers many visual aids to make a presentation colourful and exciting. The following visual aids are available to the presenter to express his or her ideas more effectively along with the text.

1. Objects and models
2. Graphs, maps, pictures
3. Samples
4. Handouts
5. Interesting videos
6. Animated images
7. Soundtracks
8. Whiteboards
9. Computer-assisted slides

> Visual aids can improve the understanding of your idea and add spice to your presentation. They would simplify the complex ideas and illustrate something dry in a more colourful manner.

Good visual aids enhance the presentation and audience interest.

Visual aids are the accessories to decorate a presentation, but too much of them make the presentation flashy and distract the audience from the presentation. They should be used only when essential and should be simple, expressive and interesting.

7.3.4 Selecting Presentation Organisation Format

The information in the body of a presentation needs to be properly arranged. Keeping in mind your purpose and audience; you may select a suitable organisation plan for your presentation. Some of the widely practised presentation organisation formats are ideas as follows:

1. Chronological
2. Sequential
3. Simple to specific
4. Specific to simple
5. Spatial
6. Cause/Effect/Problem/Solution
7. Categorical

> Effective presentations are organised in patterns: chronology to geography, comparison/contrast to problem/solution, function to importance etc. Use pattern that is relevant to the content and suitable to the audience.

7.4 DELIVERING THE PRESENTATION

Your planning and preparation come to culmination when you are ready to deliver your presentation. In delivering your presentation, you learn to cope with stage fright, rehearse repeatedly, work on the delivery modes, give your presentation and do the self-analysis of your performance.

7.4.1 Coping with Stage Fright and Anxiety

> *I used to be incredibly afraid of public speaking. I started with five people, then I'd speak to 10 people. I made it up to 75 people, up to 100, and now I can speak to a very large group, and it feels similar to speaking to you one-on-one.*
>
> — Robin S. Sharma

Now you have organised your speech with your available research information. Your day of presentation has arrived and you visualise your imminent interaction with the audience. You get anxious and worried. The fear of facing the audience during presentation delivery gets so overpowering that you feel like not getting onto the stage. You are not the first one who encounters such bouts of fear and depression before speaking. However, you can overcome anxiety by knowing its causes, planning strategies to handle both physical and mental nervousness and rehearsing your presentation thoroughly. There could be umpteen reasons for being nervous: feeling incapable, fear of uncertainty, fear of being evaluated/judged/refused or fear of consequences/failures. A well-structured presentation with systematic approach may help you overcome stage fright and boost your morale before the audience.

The following are some useful techniques that may help you control fear and perform well during presentation delivery:

1. Keep smiling. Your audience will positively react to your smile and make you comfortable.
2. Visualise your audience and venue during rehearsal. Imagine yourself approaching the podium, delivering the talk and being applauded by the audience.
3. Deep breathing is a real solace. Inhaling and exhaling will calm you down and improve your posture and voice.
4. Practise, practise and practise. If you are well prepared, your chance of getting nervous is quite less.
5. Be organised. Keep your notes and visual aids handy. It may avoid the last minute rush.
6. Avoid worrying about small mistakes. It is okay to make an occasional mistake. Do not feel bad about it and keep going.
7. Stand relaxed in a balanced way. Look for friendly faces in the crowd and draw energy from them initially.

> Anxious speakers tend to speed up, so try to pace yourself. Speak clearly with moderate tone and slow down to emphasise key points.

Experts believe that little nervousness is a healthy stimulant. It gets the adrenaline going, keeping you alert and allowing the complete check on your presentation plan.

7.4.2 Rehearsing Presentation Delivery

All great speakers properly plan their presentation delivery and rehearse it well. Corporate leaders, presidents of nations and actors spend hours rehearsing and revising their presentations before they come to the podium. Rehearsing helps lift the presenter's mood and confidence to face the public boldly. The following tips may help you do a good rehearsal of presentation delivery:

1. Rehearse your presentation thoroughly. Keep your outline, note cards and PowerPoint slides' print-outs ready. Speak naturally glancing at your notes occasionally.
2. Familiarise yourself with the visual aids so that they may not fail/work at the last minute.
3. Keep your language simple and conversational. Develop the habit of using regular previews, summaries, transitions and repetitions to facilitate your audience to understand your speech. Use short and direct sentences and avoid using words with complex pronunciations.
4. Speak steadily but in a firm voice. Project your voice clearly with the right pitch and tone.
5. You may rehearse alone or with friends and family members. Be impressive with your body language. Stand straight and hold your head high. Get feedback from your friends or look into a mirror to correct your postures.
6. Videotaping of your rehearsal is also helpful in guiding you to improve yourvoice, gestures, timing and presentation scheme.
7. Always adhere to the announced presentation plan. Finish your talk within allocated time. You can time your speech during rehearsal by using a timer.

> The way you conduct your body reflects your confidence and character. Stand straight and relaxed. Look around and make eye-contact with people in the audience.

7.4.3 Working on Delivery Modes

Selecting an appropriate delivery mode or method is a critical task that the presenter has to do before the final day and master the selected mode by rehearsal. There are four presentation delivery modes to choose from: he can read it, memorise it, opt for an impromptu speech or deliver using notes. Each of these modes have been explained below.

1. **Memorisation:** In this mode, a presentation is delivered by memorising a speech manuscript. Presenting a word-by-word speech from memory is a risky and challenging task. It exerts unnecessary stress on the presenter and makes his/her speech dull and unimaginative. First-timers usually feel that it is easy and comfortable to memorise their speeches and give presentation. But finally it does not work. However hard you may try to memorise the presentation speech, chances are that you may forget some portions of the speech. You may face some embarrassing moments when you fail to recall some portion of the speech. A few lines of the speech, especially the beginning and the conclusion, may be delivered based on sheer memorisation. Overall, memorisation may not be a preferred mode for giving routine business presentations.
2. **Reading:** In this mode, the speech manuscript is read aloud before the audience. Again reading a written speech is not a good mode of presentation. Unless it is essential to state some specific facts, numbers and words in a particular way, the reading mode is not a natural choice for the public speaking. Some situations like presentation of an annual report by a CEO or a country's budget by its finance minister may be appropriate for using this mode, as they deal with a large database of information with high impact. A major drawback of the reading mode is that the presenter is confined to reading the script and he/she does not feel connected to the audience. Presidents and ministers of external affairs usually read their speeches as every word they utter is of high speculation and sensitivity to other countries and the global media. If you have a plan to read your speech, it is important to rehearse it through a tape recorder. It will help you a lot in sounding natural.
3. **Impromptu:** This mode of delivery is used when you are supposed to speak spontaneously without any prior plan or practice. It is the right method for someone who is a seasoned public speaker. Such speakers can deliver good impromptu speeches. You may also face a situation when you are asked to share something unexpectedly. In such situation, keeping in mind the purpose of your presentation, you should quickly work out a speech pattern with a decent beginning, a proper middle and an a good end to address the audience impromptu.
4. **Speaking from notes:** This mode is considered as the much favoured method for professional presenters in business circles. This mode allows you to design your notes as per your presentation scheme. With this mode, you are in better control of your presentation plan and can have a regular eye contact and feel confident as a presenter. You can also easily change your pace of speaking or make use of visual aids. While preparing the notes, you should precisely mention your ideas and thoughts that you want to share with the audience. Write everything essential in a proper order with simple and complete sentences on the notes. With rehearsal, you can keep tab on the presentation sections and sub-sections while maintaining the desired eye contact with the audience.

The modes of delivery include memorisation, reading, impromptu and notes. Speaking from the notes is considered more natural and convincing than any other modes.

7.4.4 Giving the Presentation

After all the planning and preparation, you are ready to give the presentation. The following suggestions may help you win your audience and achieve the objective of your presentation:

1. Dress like a professional. It gives you confidence and makes you acceptable to the audience. Always wear formals in business presentations as this attire projects a high level of professionalism and competence.
2. Take time to settle down and ensure that everything is perfect. Walk confidently, look around, develop eye contact, arrange your notes and begin your presentation.
3. Greet your audience and deliver the first line from the memory. It energises you and exhibits your mastery over the topic.
4. Avoid reading from the slides. Try to talk as much as possible.
5. Do not be in hurry to finish the talk. Speak with a moderate pace. Go slow to highlight your key ideas.
6. Show your energy and authority in your body language/bodily movements. Let the audience admire that you are committed and passionate about your talk.
7. Go for the final impression. Summarise your main points and complete the presentation.

7.4.5 Analysing Your Performance Post-presentation

After giving the presentation, it is a rewarding exercise to know how you have justified your talk– introducing the topic, taking it forward to the level of the audience's acceptance and expectation, handling visual aids, managing your anxiety, adhering to the presentation duration, handling questions etc. Such exercise of evaluating yourself is quite beneficial for your next presentation as you come to know about your strengths and weaknesses.

Summary

Effective presentations are based on a clear analysis of their objectives and their audience. Planning of a presentation involves a decent beginning, a proper middle and a good ending. While preparing a presentation, it has to be ensured that the beginning defines the topic, provides a preview and captures the audience's attention. The body or middle of the presentation focuses on the key points with explanations and verbal signposts to engage your audience throughout the presentation strengthen the issues. The conclusion or ending recapitulates the main points and leaves the presentation open for questions. The presenter plans certain visual aids to make his/her objectives clear, convincing and memorable for the audience. Be clear about of the mode of presentation delivery – whether you are going to speak impromptu or with help of notes. It helps a lot to plan and rehearse the presentation before the final day. Dressing, adhering to the announced duration, eye contact, and handling of visual aids are some of things that are crucial to make your presentation successful and acceptable. Everyone feels some kind of nervousness or anxiety while facing the audience, but thorough preparation and stress reduction techniques can help overcome the stage fright.

Chapter Review

1. Explain various reasons why presentations are an effective tool of communication in organisations and institutions.
2. Discuss the ways through which you can research to develop a topic for a presentation at the workplace using an example.
3. Do you think using visual aids in the presentation makes it effective? Give reasons for your answers with examples.
4. What are the various presentation organisation formats available for organising the presentation content?
5. Discuss the importance of rehearsal before a presentation. What points should be followed during rehearsal to ensure that the presentation is delivered smoothly?
6. How important are the body language and dress code for an effective presentation? Justify your answer with examples.

Direct Questions

1. What are verbal signposts?
2. Explain the format of an ideal presentation.
3. What are the types of visual aids that could be used in presentations and how?
4. Discuss ways to combat stage fright and deliver a perfect presentation at the workplace.
5. Describe the modes of delivering an effective presentation. Discuss the pros and cons of each mode.
6. Discuss the importance of summarizing the presentation properly.

Analytical Questions

1. How to make PowerPoint presentations lively and informative? Why is using too many visual aids considered a wrong designing plan? Give reasons for your answers with examples.
2. As a first-time presenter, how would you cope with stage fright and what would be your strategy to handle the audience.

Resources for Further Reflections

1. How to give the best presentation http://www.huffingtonpost.com/karl-gude/how-to-give-the-best-pres_b_3932280.html?ir=India&adsSiteOverride=in.
2. 5 important questions to ask before your next presentation http://www.huffingtonpost.com/ellevate/frozen-in-translation ooc_b_6024058.html?ir=India&adsSiteOverride=in.
3. Interview presentation http://www.theguardian.com/careers/careers-blog/eight-tips-how-make-interview-presentation-shine-job-offer.
4. 10 tips to move your audience through presentation http://www.theguardian.com/small-business-network/2014/nov/04/how-to-give-a-presentation-10-tips.
5. Appearances count! http://www.forbes.com/sites/cherylsnappconner/2013/01/14/appearances-count-in-business-presentation-is-everything/.
6. Cisco's obsession with presentation skills: real life example http://www.forbes.com/sites/carmine-gallo/2014/08/13/ciscos-obsession-with-presentation-skills-makes-managers-better-leaders/.

Caselet 1

Crusader of Women Empowerment

Manika was a crusader of woman education and empowerment. She was against young girls being forced to marry without giving them opportunity to complete their education. She had closely observed the lives of girls around her – the maid's daughters, Sharmaji's niece, Mr. Chowdhury's granddaughter and herself. All these girls and many more suffer the ignominy of being illiterate and be treated as uneducated puppets for the rest of their lives. But Manika was brave enough to be different. She wanted to study, be a doctor. She also wanted the maid's daughter to study and be whatever she wanted to be. So she raised her voice against her parents will and against the society's wishes. She would go to people and ask them to let their daughters study. She would tell them why it would be better to not get their daughters married early and let them study. Some parents did get convinced by looking at the spark in Manika's eyes, her zeal and her desperation for education. Others did not. But Manika never gave up.

Gradually, her efforts started giving fruitful results. She became a well-known figure among the activists working for women education. The word about her contribution to the society's progress by enabling several thousand girls to study had spread far and wide. One day, in a meeting, while Manika was trying to convince a couple about the social advantages of women education, she received a call from the office of the chief minister of her state. The chief minister's secretary informed her that she was selected to be honoured by the chief minister himself at the Republic Day function. The secretary wanted to know whether she would come to the function to receive the honour and would like to deliver a speech to enlighten the people about her activism. He insisted that it would be a great opportunity for her to influence people from such a large platform and convince them about the necessity of girl education for the country's progress. Manika's joy knew no bounds and she accepted the invitation. She couldn't wait for the Republic Day function. She had prepared her best soul searching speech.

Finally the big day arrived! Manika reached the Republic Day function venue dressed formally and walked confidently with her head held high. When the chief minister called her on the stage, she knew it was her time. She had to utilize those 10 minutes to impress upon thousands of people to let their daughters get educated. She slowly moved to the stage, but with each step her confidence seemed to melt down. When she reached the podium and faced such a large audience, she suddenly felt numb. All her senses gave up. Her thoughts started to fade away as she felt people's curious eyes penetrating her. She could feel her blood pressure and heart rate pounding and if she did not get off the podium immediately, she could collapse in a heap.

The speech, which she considered to be highly impressive and influential, vanished from her mind in a second. All she could utter was a big frightened 'thank you' and then she instantly got down the stage. Every one kept staring at her and a few managed to applaud. Months later, Manika could still see those penetrating eyes in her dreams and the embarrassment she had to face just because she could not speak. She thought it was time she conquered her fear and worked upon her public speaking skills, otherwise in her goal of women education and empowerment could be harder to achieve.

Questions

1. Why do you think despite having such a confident motive and a goal, Manika failed to speak at the Republic Day function?
2. Elaborate the plan and enlist the stages that you should have followed for such an event. How could have you overcome anxiety?

Chapter 8

JOB INTERVIEWS

Learning Roadmap

After reading this chapter you will be able to:

- Know about the importance of job interviews
- Understand how a well-written resume leads to interview calls
- Know about the company before giving interview for a job in it
- Distinguish between different types of interviews
- Know the preparatory steps to face a job interview
- Learn positive traits
- Know the tips to crack a job interview

PERSPECTIVE

Sunil Rawat, after graduating from a well-known engineering institute, was sure that succeeding in a job interview would be a cakewalk for him. The reason was that he was excellent in academics and had also led many teams during his student life. Soon he got an interview call from a reputed company. He prepared well for the interview and on the interview day his confidence level was very high. When his turn came for the interview, he entered the room of the company director with élan. The director interviewed him for almost two hours. As his interview was taking too long, the candidates sitting outside the director's room started feeling that Sunil would surely come out after getting selected. But, ironically, just the opposite happened with Sunil. He failed to impress the director who told him that he was arrogant and less flexible. Having strong academic excellence is no guarantee the person will gel well with the team. Basically the company wanted a person with good soft skills which Sunil lacked. The interview failure was a great setback for Sunil who felt very dejected. But after some days he started working on his lacunae. He joined a personality development course to improve his soft skills. After completing the course, he felt confident of doing well in any interview. When Sunil faced the interview next time, he took care of his demeanour, posture, gestures and eye contact. Overall, he carried a positive attitude. He replied to the interviewers' questions after a pause, understanding them well. He did not reflect the know-it-all attitude but showed as if he was still on the learning curve. His amicable smile and polite tone fascinated the interview panel. They appreciated his academic achievements and his humility in answering the questions. He was taken in.

"You can do anything if you have enthusiasm"

— Henry Ford

8.1 INTRODUCTION

Whether these were the interviews conducted in good old times or the ones which are conducted today, they resemble in their basic purpose, which is— to find more and more about the candidate being interviewed and judge how appropriate is he/she for the job advertised. So if the interviewer is an expert, he/she will easily judge a candidate's suitability for a job position or promotion or for some other responsibility. With the passage of time, job interviews have become very structured and professional, facilitating the proper evaluation of the candidate's talent and other qualities. Though there are other candidate screening methods such as written test, group discussion and presentation, the personal interview is the best way to closely observe and evaluate a candidate's personal traits, communication skills, knowledge, maturity level and inclination for teamwork. However, selecting the candidate through an interview depends a lot on the quality of questions asked by the interviewer. So, right questions must be asked to select the right candidate. The interviewer can be a single person or a panel of experienced professionals, both men and women. Interviews can be taken face to face, on telephone or through teleconferencing.

Placement interviews often become a student's nightmare. It happens because the student is under great stress to get into a good company with a decent compensation and a respectable position to prove his worth to his parents and friends. It is truly said that during campus recruitments, the interview is the only process through which the student gets selected rather than getting eliminated which is the case with the tests and group discussions (GDs). The expression used of success after the interview is "I am selected" and the rejection doesn't talk about elimination.

Interview is the purposeful conversation where both the parties are equally interested.

These days job interviews have become complicated because of use of technology. When the interviews are held on telephone or Skype, they tend to put the candidate under stress. They may look simple at the surface level but the truth is they are more challenging. Companies are spending extraordinary efforts and resources on organising interviews because the challenge before them is to be able to do the right evaluation of job aspirants while interviewing them. Each company has its own demands and needs to fulfil which they search for the right fit among the candidates who knock at their doors. You can imagine how difficult it would be for them to make judgement based on just a half hour interaction with the candidate. The interviewing techniques are improving every day and are getting more sophisticated. And, to achieve perfection in their interviewing techniques, some organisations conduct preliminary interviews before the final interview. Facing preliminary and final interviews put a lot of pressure on the candidate.

Some organisations have a separate department for recruitment. Others hire external agencies that specialise in conducting interviews and recruiting candidates. These agencies have competent human resource experts who devise effective techniques and strategies to conduct the recruitment process in a highly professional manner.

The recruitment process may differ, depending on the size and composition of the company — whether the company is an established concern or a new one started by a young entrepreneur. These days the number of the latter type of companies is swelling. The established companies conduct more structured interviews than the newly-formed companies.

8.2 IMPORTANCE OF RESUME

Resume should be meticulously prepared and regularly updated.

You may have already learnt about resume writing in Chapter 7 which is the first step for getting in the interview. The interview is said to be the second meeting between a job aspirant and the company representatives. The first is resume of the job aspirant on the basis of which he/she has got the interview call. Thus it is very important to have a resume which catches the attention of the company's interview panel. A resume with details of doing some interesting internships, handling projects or working on positions of responsibility will make the panel eager to meet the job aspirant in person. But remember you as a job aspirant should be able to explain confidently each and every thing written in your resume. It will not be acceptable to the panel that you fumble on a question asked about a point in the resume.

It is recommended to keep separate resumes for core and non-core companies. A core resume should highlight any technical projects done as well as achievements in your core field. A non-core resume should contain information about work done outside your core field and any remarkable breakthroughs in them.

"Emphasize your strengths on your resume, in your cover letters and in your interviews. It may sound obvious, but you'd be surprised how many people simply list everything they've ever done. Convey your passion and link your strengths to measurable results. Employers and interviewers love concrete data."

— Marcus Buckingham

8.3 DEFINITION OF INTERVIEW

The term interview refers to typical purposeful conversation between two entities, of which one is the person seeking a job and the other is the interviewer or a panel of interviewers. The interview method could be of a highly structured format or very creative or unstructured. The last type would be freewheeling conversations between the job aspirant and the hiring person(s). But for conducting proper and more meaningful interviews, it is better to go for structured interviews. The word interview has its origin in the French word 'intrevue' which means to see each other. Of course, in modern times, the sight between two persons can be through video conferencing or over telephone. The outcome of interviews can never be predicted as the course of an interview may change depending on the response of the interviewee. Whenever you face the interview, start collecting the information about the company you have applied in.

Interviewing is an art and a challenge for both interviewer and interviewee.

8.4 BACKGROUND INFORMATION

The first step is to gather information about the company to which you have applied for a job. Be ready with the company's data beforehand so that the interview becomes easy for you to handle. You must know everything about the company, like its past performance, its turnover, the number of people it employs, the nature of job, etc. To know about the company, go to its website. You can also request appropriate people in the company to provide you the company literature. There are a few questions which are usually asked during the interview, like "Why do you want to join our company?" "How well are you aware of our job requirement?" "How do you rate our company vis-à-vis other competitors?" "Our company was in the headlines a few days back, why?" If you have done enough research on the company, it would be easy for you to answer these questions.

The information which you need to collect about the company includes the following:

1. Work culture
2. Services provided/product manufactured
3. External liaison
4. Growth rate
5. The hierarchal structure – tall/flat?
6. Financial status
7. New policies
8. Communication channels
9. Board members

> You are already ahead of others if you know the details of the company beforehand.

Basically, you must be curious to know about the organisation of which you wish to become a part. Apply in the organisation if you are really interested to join, or else it will not add to your experience. If possible, do talk to people who are part of the organisation to get a real feel of it.

8.5 TYPES OF INTERVIEWS

Organisations select employees for various jobs through a variety of interviews. Some of these interviews are described in the following sections.

8.5.1 Screening or Telephone Interview

This is type of interview helps in shortlisting the number of candidates in the initial stage of the recruitment process. The company incurs nominal cost and devotes less time in conducting this interview. A telephone interview usually lasts only 30 minutes. While giving interview on telephone, you must keep your resume in front of you and also have easy access to the information you have gathered about the company. Remember, you are communicating vibes through the telephone, so have vibrancy and positivity in your voice. Your energetic tone and inflection play an important role in getting you shortlisted for the main interview.

8.5.2 Informational Interview

The main objective of this interview is to know about the career field, employer or the prospective job. If you are not sure of your career goals, this interview will help you decide your career path. Basically, the objective of the informational interview is to know whether the job is a fit for you. Does the job you are applying for match your skillset, values, abilities and interest? This interview is a highly focused session with networking contact design to choose the appropriate career path by considering insider views. The areas discussed in this interview are: industrial trends, lifestyle, work environment, required qualification, typical compensation, rewards and challenges, career growth. This interview works better when it is conducted face to face in the same organisation where you want to work. You can alternately have it on telephone, email chat group, Facebook or internet. Never ask for a job during an informational interview. To find appropriate contacts for the informational interview ask family friends, colleagues, faculty members and former employers for a referral to a candidate for an information interview. Prepare well for the informational interview by:

1. Reading about the organisation
2. Knowing about the career area in which the interviewee is affiliated
3. Working on the opening statement that gives a brief profile and your interest in the field
4. Developing well thought questions to have stimulating discussion
5. Dressing well to give good first impression if it is a face-to-face interview

8.5.3 Individual Interview

Also called personal interview, this interview is the most common for selecting employees. In this interview the individual job aspirant faces the interviewer in the latter's office. It is one-to-one gruelling which lasts 30 to 90 minutes. While giving this type of interview, you should be succinct and precise with your answers. Do not beat around the bush, as each word you utter is a reflection of your personality. Following are the guidelines to face the individual interview with confidence:

1. Be polite and courteous
2. Greet with zeal
3. Prepare to respond behavioural questions
4. Be assertive and not aggressive
5. Listen attentively and reflect that you understand their needs
6. Show interest in what you are saying by smiling.

Build positive support of the interviewer during the individual interview by behaving in the following way:

1. Making proper eye contact as it demonstrates honesty and confidence.
2. Smiling which shows you are comfortable and interested; it also reflects your positive attitude.
3. Emulating the interviewer's style by following his posture, speech pattern and mannerism. Do not mimic exactly as it will look like mockery.
4. Address the interviewer appropriately as that gives him/her importance.

8.5.4 Small Group or Committee Interview

In this type of interview, you face two or more people constituting the interview panel. Every member of the panel will interpret the answers given by you in his/her own way. Therefore be prepared to face several decision makers simultaneously. Ensure to make eye contact with everyone, no matter who asks the question. You should also be audible to each member. If possible, know the names and designations of the people sitting across the table.

8.5.5 Second or On-site Interview

Once you have cleared the first-round interview, the interviewer calls you for the second or on-site interview to ensure that you are the right choice.. In the second interview, your goal is to receive an offer of employment from the company. So you have to take care of all those things which you did for the first round. Follow the tips given below to do well in the second interview:

1. Make sure you are appropriately dressed.
2. Take care of your personal grooming–clean nail, short hair, shining shoes. Keep the use of perfumes and jewellery to the minimum.
3. Have enough copies of resume.
4. Show up at the interview place 15 minutes earlier than the scheduled time.
5. Take care of your body language.
6. Keep good eye contact, smile, speak confidently and maintain the right tone.
7. Be truthful and positive when you speak.
8. Be enthusiastic and do not get irritated to answer the same question if it is asked more than once.
9. Reiterate your interest in the position and the company.
10. Establish a follow-up time-frame.

8.5.6 Behaviour-based Interview

This interview is conducted by HR professionals to identify your suitability for the job. HR professionals go by the assumption that your past behaviour will have an important impact on your future behaviour. The interviewer checks out whether you have skills and competencies to perform the role you have applied for, by asking subjective questions on your past experience and actions. It enables him/her to judge your qualities. Therefore you should be able to articulate your abilities properly. You may be asked, "If someone in the team is not cooperating, how you would make him work?", to evaluate your ability to work in a team. You must answer the question in a way which presents you as a team player. Do corroborate your abilities with real-life examples to strengthen your claim for the position you want to be hired for.

> If you have good memory, it will be an asset if you remember the names and designations of the interviewers.

8.5.7 Stress Interview

Stress interviews are conducted to find out how the candidate behaves in stressful situations. If you do not have skills to handle stressful situations, you may ruin a few projects. It has no connection with your personality as this trait is unique in the individual. The interviewer may ask irritating questions like "Why are you wearing this shirt on this hot day?" Or, "You look awkward with this frame of your specs. Why have you opted for this frame?" Handle such situations with a cool mind as there is a purpose behind asking such preposterous questions. Do not get perturbed and answer rudely. For example, you can answer the shirt question saying that it is a gift given by your mom so it is very special rather than telling the interviewer that he/she had no business asking such personal questions. There is no right or wrong answer to such questions but the interviewer wants to see how you deal with them. Stress interviews are mostly conducted by sales and marketing companies for positions which deal with a lot of deadlines. These are conducted to see the candidate's behaviour

> Real life examples strengthen the stand of the candidate for the position!

when he/she is operating out of his/her comfort zone. These are usually many-on-one kind of interviews where one of the panellists might remain quiet the entire time giving different expressions to the answers. The purpose of the stress interview is to put pressure on the candidate so to test him/her further the vague expressions are reflected by the interviewers.

8.5.8 Case Interview

In this interview, the candidate is given a case study involving a problem which needs to be solved in the given time. The interviewer looks for the problem solving skills of the candidate and the procedure followed to solve the problem. While judging the candidate's effort, a lot of importance is given to the question he/ she asks while solving the problem. This gives the interview panel an idea whether the student will fit into the team where the position is available or will it cause a disruption in the team. Management consultancy firms, such as BAIN Compatibility Centre and Zinnov, are famous for conducting such interviews.

8.5.9 Analytic Interview

This type of interview is usually taken by analytics and marketing companies. Puzzles and guesstimates form the major line of questioning. These interviews test of student's attention to detail as an analytics job in requires handling huge amounts of data and even a small mistake could cost the company a lot. Companies like Tata Analytics conduct analytic interviews.

8.5.10 Technical Interview

Generally, technical interviews are conducted after HR interviews. Preparation for this interview cannot be done at the last minute. The technical interview judges your technical capability as well as the depth of your technical knowledge. So you must revise extensively the subjects of your technical expertise related with the job you have applied for. Questions are mainly asked on the basics of technical subjects related with the job. When you are asked a question which needs pen and paper to solve, then solve the question. Remember the objective behind asking such questions is to assess the depth of your technical knowledge. If you do not know the answer of question, it is better to accept the fact and not beat around the bush. It shows your ability to accept mistakes and work on them. Technical interviews are usually conducted by core companies.

8.6 PREPARATORY STEPS FOR JOB INTERVIEWS

Most job aspirants get unnerved as soon as they get interview calls. Their foremost fear is: "What if I got rejected! My friend will again ridicule me that I could not make it." Even when you are confident and knowledgeable, you tend to get nervous before and during the interview. To control your nervousness, you must tell yourself, 'What worst can happen?' At the most you would be rejected for the job! You also need to get aware of the complete interview process and then get ready to face it. There is no substitute to good preparation. You have to be prepared for any type of interview– face-to-face, telephonic or video conferencing. Facing the interview becomes easier if you are well prepared.

> *Be so good they can't ignore you.*
>
> — Steve Martin

During the interview be as systematic as possible and try to be your natural self. If you want this job, they are also on the lookout of an appropriate candidate. You should try your best to establish a rapport with the members of the interview panel in just half an hour. Before facing the interview, do the following:

> Do brush up your technical knowledge as the core companies focus the most on it.

1. Know about the organisation.
2. Understand the requirements of the organisation.
3. How your skillset matches with the need of the organisation.
4. Research the latest trends in the market about company's market share, advertising strategies, etc.
5. Know the interview format.
6. Anticipate the interviewer's questions and keep your answers ready.

Apart from following the above mentioned guidelines, you should also work on the following tips:

1. Start much before the interview time to reach the interview venue. If possible, visit the interview venue the previous day as a rehearsal to see whether there are any travel hassles.
2. Finalise the dress you are going to wear. It may not be a new dress but a suitable dress for the interview.
3. Sleep well for better performance.

While preparing for the interview, you must introspect, analyse your background and achievements and identify your extracurricular activities and your skills.

8.6.1 Introspect

You must introspect what are your strengths and weaknesses and what are you able to achieve so far. Actually we never give a thought about our accomplishments. So you must think that based on your accomplishments and strengths what value addition you can make by taking up this job.

8.6.2 Analyse Your Background

If you analyse your background, it will prepare you for questions like "Tell about yourself". So critically examine your educational and family background. What have you learnt in the process of growing up? What was the influence of your friends and family on your life? When you are asked to describe yourself in a few sentences, narrate the best of you to the interviewer. You may be well aware of your qualifications but keep in mind what the organisation is looking for. So match your background according to the need of the organisation. If you have a degree in civil engineering and you are sitting for a placement in computer science, then highlight your interest in computer science, not in civil engineering; speak about the relevant course you have done in computer science; and how much you enjoyed doing it.

> Do not memorise so hard that you appear to have memorised. Sound natural!

8.6.3 Highlight Your Achievements/Accomplishments

Remember, achievements are different from accomplishments. Accomplishments reflect your different skills which you use for some specific job while achievements refer to your academic or professional achievements. You must present your achievements and accomplishments in such a way that the prospective employer is convinced that you are best fit for the job. Remember all certificates, awards, prizes, fellowships and praises you had received for your achievements. When you are asked "What are your achievements?" you should enumerate them at one go. Accomplishments are those skills which you display while leading a project, organising an event, conducting a cultural programme, etc. Gather information about all your accomplishments. You can talk about them with past instances, maybe in school or college.

8.6.4 Know Your Extracurricular Activities

Apart from your academics you must have participated in other activities. Recollect what have you mentioned in your resume. Do not write fake hobbies as it is very embarrassing when you are caught on the wrong foot. If you have mentioned you play basketball, it is expected of you that you know how many players are there in a basketball team. Also, you may be asked about the dimensions of a basketball court. Your involvement in extracurricular activities shows your overall development.

8.6.5 Analyse Your Skills

The basic attributes that a company looks for in job aspirants are the skills and knowledge needed to carry out specific jobs of the company. Do analyse your skills and match them with the ones needed for the desired job before you set out for the interview. Use impressive adjectives to describe your skills. The interviewer may ask the following questions related to your skills:

1. Why do you think we should hire you?
2. What makes you fit for the position?
3. What is your greatest strength?
4. Why only you and not others?

Keep your things properly organised the previous day!

While narrating your skills, use the adjectives such as creative, pleasant, amicable, reliable, sincere, energetic, enthusiastic, reasonable, tactful, resourceful, friendly, successful, zealous, etc. to describe yourself. These adjectives have positive connotations, so use them lavishly.

8.6.6 Pre-interview Preparation

You must do your homework properly before facing the interview. One of the most common mistakes is to not know about the company where you have applied. When you are asked the question "Tell about the company you have applied for", you will start on a bad note if you have not done enough research on the company. As mentioned earlier, you must research about the company properly. You must also know about the competitors of the company. The following tips about the pre-interview stage preparation will make you confident:

1. Do not forget to keep all your certificates and important document in a file.
2. Plan appropriate dress code.
3. Polish your shoes and have matching accessories.
4. Scan newspaper headlines without fail.
5. Get up early to reach the interview venue in time.
6. Prepare and review the main topics and areas.
7. Cultivate the right attitude.
8. Show relaxed expression.

8.6.7 Behaviour During the Interview

The following tips will help you show decent behaviour during the interview:

1. Control your nervousness.
2. Seek permission to enter the room.
3. Greet politely.
4. Sit only when asked by the interviewer.
5. Carry yourself smartly.
6. Remain cool and calm while answering the questions.
7. Listen attentively.
8. Take time to think.
9. Accept if you don't know the answer.
10. Don't grin, you can smile.
11. Sit smart, don't slouch.
12. Accept tea/coffee if offered.
13. Maintain eye contact.
14. Reflect zeal and enthusiasm.
15. Create good impression by your pleasant disposition.

16. If given a chance to ask anything about the company, you may ask whatever you want politely.
17. Keep your answers short between 1.5–2 minutes and to-the-point.
18. Structure your answers in 3-4 points.
19. Explain your answers with personal experience.
20. Use positive tone.
21. Use active verbs and power verbs to describe yourself.

8.6.8 Post-interview Behaviour

After your interview is over, do not hang around. Send a thanking note to the company and ask when you will be intimated of the results. Do not annoy the company recruitment staff by sending repeated messages. Be open to accept whatever the results may be. Once you have put your best efforts, do not think too hard. Remember you may be very good but the company may be looking for someone just average. So, you may not fit in the company's requirements. Do not let your spirits down.

- Computer skills
- Mathematical skills
- Problem solving skills
- Analytical skills
- Communication skills
- Listening skills

8.7 INTERVIEW SKILL TIPS

You must appear very positive and confident in the interview. Sometimes you become overzealous and then over-react which makes you appear supercilious, leading to your rejection. Some of the techniques, described in the following sections, will help you in improving your interview skills and present yourself as a competent candidate.

8.7.1 Body Language in the Interview

You have already learnt about body language in Chapter 2. You must be highly cautious about your body language during the interview. Your posture, gesture, eye contact and facial expressions communicate more than your words. If you are not truthful about what you are saying, it will be reflected through your non-verbal cues. Your first impression is created by the way you dress and behave. Through your dress and body language, you will be subconsciously making the interviewer form opinion about you. To leave an indelible good impression on the interviewer, you must demonstrate the appropriate body.

8.7.2 Opt for the Best Position

If the interview room is big and you can choose a place to sit, then opt for the chair which enables you to see every member of the interview panel. They should also be able to see clearly. Also see if the light is falling on the chair you have chosen.

8.7.3 Right Posture

If you have a table in front of you do not sit very close to it. Do not bend too much on the table, but let your arms be on the table with elbow slightly outside the table. The ideal distance between the chest and the table is around 4 inches. Your feet should be grounded properly on the floor. Bend slightly forward to reflect you are listening. Avoid slouching if you do not have a table in front of you. Then keep your hand on your lap.

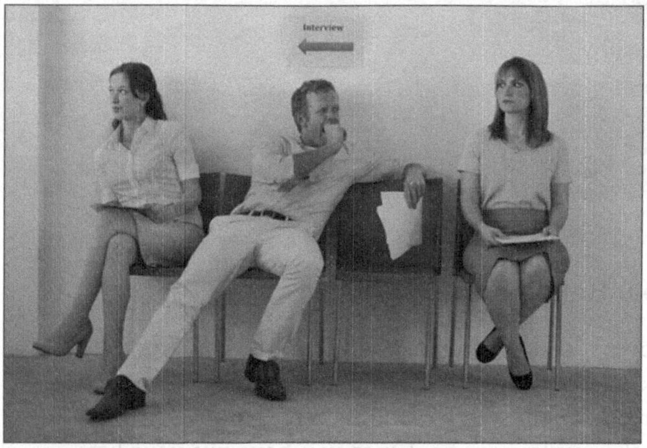

The right posture should be maintained in an interview.

8.7.4 Respect Your Own Space

Do not be conscious of the fact that you are under scrutiny so that you have to manage sitting in an uncomfortable place. Relax a bit as it shows confidence. Do not be too tight with any posture.

8.7.5 Control Your Hand and Arm Movements

Let your hand and arm movements be natural but too much of these movements can distract the attention of the interviewer. Be your natural self. Avoid fidgeting with your hands or break the knuckles. Never cross your arms as it reflects you are close to ideas.

8.7.6 Smile

No one likes a sullen-looking person. So, make it a point to smile after entering the interview room. Smile can put you and the interviewer in a receptive mood. But if you have a nervous smile, the interviewer will know it. Unnecessary laugh must be avoided. It's not acceptable that you crack a joke just because you have to smile.

8.7.7 Eye Contact

Eye contact assures that the candidate is confident and lack of it shows evasiveness and insecurity. Do not stare at the interviewer as that can make him/her uneasy. If you are facing many people, maintain eye contact with all of them while answering questions as that involves everyone in the interaction.

8.7.8 Emulate the Interviewer Behaviour

Behave or act almost in the same way as the interviewer so that you can connect with him/her through his/her body language. If the interviewer is sitting upright you may too adopt that posture. If he leans forward, you too lean but make sure not to overdo it. If it is noticed that you are emulating the interviewer, it might put him/her off.

8.7.9 Relax

Just be yourself. Don't think too hard about anything. If you are answering well, you will automatically demonstrate appropriate body language. Your body language is a barometer of your confidence. So, if your preparation for the interview is good, all will go well and spontaneously.

8.8 CHANGES IN THE INTERVIEW PROCESS

There have been some changes in the idea behind taking campus interviews. This development can be related to the different business concepts that have risen in today's market. For example, the self-managing team concept where a team has no overhead manager and the team as a whole manages itself and is responsible for its tasks and results. This new trend of introducing self-managing teams at entry-level positions has resulted in a change in the objective of a campus interview. To recruit members of self-managing teams, the interview panel mainly looks for students with excellent communication skills, leadership qualities, ability to work in a diversified team and willingness to take up challenges. Questions for such positions focus on the projects and the positions of responsibility handled by students. Another example can be taken of companies which are into developing blue ocean strategies. For filling positions in such companies, interviewers look for students with creative and innovative minds. The students who have handled projects with unique and interesting ideas have an edge for such positions.

Interviews with the companies following new interview processes usually last about an hour per student. These interviews can be very tiring. It is important to remain calm in while giving these interviews and answer every question with confidence, maintaining a proper eye contact at all times.

8.9 FREQUENTLY ASKED QUESTIONS DURING INTERVIEWS

Here are some of the frequently asked questions (FAQs), which are common in any interview with tips on how to answer them. It is recommended to have answers to these questions prepared and rehearsed before the interview. But during the interview the answers should not sound like well-rehearsed answers.

1. **Tell me something about yourself?** It is one of the most common questions asked at the beginning of the interview. It is advised to keep answer to question professional rather than making it personal. An effective way to start answering is by listing out one's objectives in life and any work done till now to achieve them. Also list out the internships and projects which have helped in moving on the path towards the objective. This gives the interview panel an idea of the student's expectations from the job and helps in assessing whether the student will be the right fit.
2. **Why would you like to work for our company? Or, why would you like a job in this field?** The answer to this question requires an extensive research beforehand on the company's profile as well as the job description of the position offered. It is best to make the requirements for the need of the job and prepare answers accordingly. It is important to make the panel believe that they are recruiting a student who will be adding value to the company.
3. **Where do you see yourself in 5 years? Don't you want to pursue a degree in Management?** This question is asked to confirm whether the student will be staying in the company for an appropriate period of time. The company invests a lot of money and resource in the training of a new employee and the panel does not want to see this money go waste. This is a tricky question and the answer to

it must be prepared carefully. Some safe answers to this question – "I have not yet planned for higher education", "I see myself managing a team of my own in the next 4 years", "My plan is to pursue MBA after getting a corporate experience of 4-5 years".

4. **Tell me about an instance where you handled a difficult situation?** The answer expected for this question usually changes from company to company depending on what they are looking for. If the position in the company requires leadership skills, narrate a situation where you solved a group's problem by effective communication and integrity. If the panel is looking for technical skills, give the instance of a difficult situation encountered in a project and how an innovative idea helped solve it.

Even if you know how to answer some questions beforehand, it depends on your handling of the interview how best you answer them. So, maintain your composure and answer with a cool mind. Try to make the best of your abilities.

Summary

Interview is a purposeful talk between two people – one who wants the job and the other who wants to hire. In other words, the purpose of an interview is to find the right candidate for a job. Interviews have become very structured and companies' expectations from job aspirants have gone very high. These days job aspirants face heavy pressure as they have to prove their calibre in just a few minutes during the interview. Most of the big organisations have hired people who look after their recruitment process. Resume writing is the first step to be shortlisted for an interview. Knowing the profile of a company to you have applied for a job is very important. So get updated with the basic details about the company, like its turnover, the number of employees it has, its growth rate, its board members, the profile of the advertised job, etc. There are different types of interviews – screening, informational, individual, behavioural, stress, case, analytic and technical. Each one is dealt with in a different manner. Before you face the interview you must go through the preparatory steps of facing the interview. Introspect and analyse your background, highlight your achievements and analyse your skill-sets. During the interview maintain your composure and answer without getting perturbed. Do rehearse most commonly asked questions so that you are not taken by surprise when faced with these questions.

Chapter Review

1. What information should you collect in a company research before interview and why?
2. Describe an informational interview. How can you prepare well for an informational interview?
3. Describe some guidelines for a personal interview. How can you build a positive support from the interviewer in a personal interview?
4. How can you relate the changes in the interview process to self-managing team concept?
5. Describe in brief the preparatory steps for a job interview.
6. What is an ideal response to a question asking about your weaknesses?
7. What is a good strategy to respond to biographical questions?
8. Why is it important to consider your social media profile before an interview?

9. What is the importance of "questions for the interviewer" which is offered by the interviewer to the candidate to ask?
10. What are the ways to handle stress and pressure during a job interview?
11. Discuss the importance of locating the information about the interviewing organisation/company before the interview.
12. Write a brief statement describing why you think you are suitable for a particular post in a multinational company. Support your answer with your qualifications and experience. List your strengths and weaknesses and how you would contribute to the development of the organisation.

Direct Questions

1. What is the basic purpose of an interview?
2. What is the difference between achievements and accomplishments?
3. What is an analytic interview?
4. What is the purpose of a technical interview?
5. Which types of details and information about the interviewing company/organisation/post you should locate?
6. Explain the roles of the following in a job interview:
   a. Stress
   b. Motivation
   c. Self-confidence
   d. Body language
   e. Self-grooming
7. What is a virtual interview? Discuss the role of technology in job interviews.
8. What are the major focus areas of a job interview?
9. What are the types of employment interviews and how are they different from one another?
10. What are the non-verbal cues which can affect an interview? Discuss the ways in which non-verbal communication can be important in an interview?
11. What is a case interview and when is it used? How can a case interview be different from a normal job interview?

Analytical Questions

1. Imagine you are facing a technical interview. You are given a technical question along with a pen and paper to solve, but you do not have any idea how to solve it. What are you going to do? Justify your answer.
2. Assume that you are a student with degree in civil engineering but sitting for an IT placement. You are being asked to tell about yourself and why you have opted for a degree in civil engineering instead of computer science. What would be your answer?

3. Imagine you are just outside the interview room waiting for your call. On your turn, describe how your behaviour and body language would be – right from the moment of your entering the room to the moment of taking your seat.

Resources for Further Reflections

1. http://www.job-interview.net/: Guide to job interviews.
2. http://jobsearch.about.com/od/interviewquestionsanswers/a/top-50-job-interview-questions.htm: Top 50 questions regarding job interview.
3. http://www.kellyservices.com.au/AU/Careers/my-Career-Centre/Job-Interview-Questions-and-Interview-Tips/#.VSPdgPmUcus: Tips for an interview.
4. http://www.fourquarters.com.au/ckfinder/userfiles/files/FourQuarters%20Job%20Interview%20Essentials.pdf: Job interview information.
5. http://www.videojug.com/film/how-to-dress-for-a-job-interview-3: Job interview dressing.
6. http://www.forbes.com/sites/lizryan/2015/02/18/ten-interview-questions-to-ask-your-next-boss/: 15 interview questions to ask your future employer.
7. http://www.huffingtonpost.com/eileen-williams/tips-for-winning-job-interview_b_6654326.html?ir=India: 3 tips to win a job interview.
8. http://www.forbes.com/sites/learnvest/2015/02/20/how-to-handle-the-tricky-whats-your-weakness-job-interview-question/: How to handle "what's your weakness" question.
9. http://www.news.com.au/finance/executive-lounge/it-scares-off-a-lot-of-people-appsters-gruelling-22-hour-job-application-process/story-fng3e17m-1227225740967: Could you survive a 22 hour job interview?

Books

1. Marc P. Cosentino. *Case in Point-Complete case interview preparation.*
2. Charles J. Stewart and William B. Cash Jr. *Interviewing: Principles and Practices.*

Movies to Watch

1. Special 26
2. Slumdog millionaire

Caselet 1

Interview Plan

Mukesh, Vice President of Global Analytics Division, Reliance Jio, is taking interview of Samuels for the middle level manager. Samuels is a young graduate professional with an experience of eight months as business analyst in Syntel Inc. The Interview goes like this:

Samuels: Excuse me. May I get in, Sir?

Mukesh: Yes, come in Mr. Samuels.

Samuels: Thank you. (*Comes in*) Good Morning Sir!

Mukesh: Good Morning Samuels! Please take your seat.

Samuels: Thank you Sir. (*Sits in the chair and gives his resume and other details to Mukesh.*)

Mukesh: So, Samuels, I don't want to be an interviewer here. Rather I will have a discussion with you. Is that okay for you (*looks at Samuels' facial expression*)?

Samuels: Okay Sir!

Mukesh: Fine. So, tell me those things about yourself which I cannot know from these papers.

Samuels: Sure Sir. I am basically interested in football. I regularly watch and play football. I like to travel more than anything else. One day I would like to go on a world trip with my own money. I do sleep a bit late at night. But definitely I'll complete my work if I feel I need to do it. So, I'm kind of dedicated person when it comes to work. I like Carnatic music, Sir. I do listen to music whenever I have time. I go to fitness centre to keep my mind and body fit.

Mukesh (*Writes few points*)**:** Interesting. So why did you leave your company and want to join here?

Samuels: It is because they are offering me a position which is challenging but not of my domain. So I'm looking at something which is of real interest for me. And, I found this advertisement on your website.

Mukesh (*Constantly writing something without paying much attention to the speaker*)**:** So, would you like to travel or get relocated if you join us. Why or why not?

Samuels (*Peeping at the paper on which Mukesh is scribbling*)**:** Yes Sir, but not more than 25% of the work.

Mukesh: Samuels. Don't worry, I'm just evaluating your answers. You are not required to look at this paper.

Samuels: Sorry sir.

Mukesh: Keep your cool. Don't feel panicky. Drink water if you want.

Samuels (*Cleaning his fingers with kerchief*)**:** It's okay Sir (*in a low tone*).

Mukesh: I haven't given the result yet. Don't get upset. Be confident. What is that great in our company which made you feel interested?

Samuels: Actually, business analytics consists of finance and marketing analytics which are basically topics with conflicting interests. But after I went to that position I realised that it's not of my interest and hence searched for different positions before getting call for this interview luckily.

Mukesh: So where do you see yourself in the next 5 years?

Samuels: A manager in the field of Global Analytics, where I must be in a position to accurately measure the worth of a merger or an acquisition.

Mukesh (*Looks at Samuels because his words are not convincing*)**:** Okay then. You may leave for now. We will let you know about the result in two weeks. Do you have anything to say or ask?

Samuels: No Sir.

Mukesh: Okay. You can leave.

Samuels (*Feeling relieved*)**:** Thank you Sir.

Questions:

1. What are all the observations made by Mukesh?
2. What are the errors that were committed by Samuels which he could have avoided and how?

Chapter 9

GROUP DISCUSSION

Learning Roadmap

After reading this chapter you will be able to:

- Understand the definition and meaning of group discussion (GD)
- Know the difference between GD, panel discussion and debate
- Understand the dynamics of GD
- Know about the traits to be developed for successful GD
- Understand the reasons for failure in GD

PERSPECTIVE

A group of college students was sitting under the shade of a tree deeply immersed in a discussion on "The righteousness of Yudhishtar in accepting Duryadhan's invitation to play the game of dice." The group was a heterogeneous mix of boys and girls aged 18–22. While expressing their views on the topic, the students showed no inhibitions and constraints. They put forward their arguments and counter-arguments for the points that came up during the discussion. The situation related to the Mahabharata instance was also compared with many present-day incidents. After half an hour, they did repeat what they had discussed but could not reach a conclusion whether Yudhishtar did the right thing by accepting to play the game of dice. In fact, many issues, highlighted in the epic Mahabharata, are open-ended and one cannot forcefully pronounce a right or wrong verdict about them. Most of the issues in life need discussion to remove wrong notions about them and see them in clear perspective. Therefore the importance of group discussions is growing as they can resolve the issue which seems to be difficult to handle by an individual.

> *"In one case out of a hundred a point is excessively discussed because it is obscure; in the ninety-nine remaining it is obscure because it is excessively discussed."*
>
> — Edgar Allan Poe

9.1 INTRODUCTION

You as student cannot escape group discussion, therefore, leave your inhibition and don't let people label you as introvert – speak out your mind. Get into discussion wherever amidst the fellow friends. Listening is appreciated but unless you tell others what opinion you hold your presence cannot be felt. As against public speaking group discussion gives you more freedom as you are not exposed to public eye. Once your confidence develops through group discussion, presentation will also come to you as whiff of soft breeze.

The participation in group discussion can mould your personality-informal group discussion can pave your way to the formal discussion. Whenever you are participating in informal discussion, be a good observer noticing who is creating more impact and what is the reason. You can always adapt that strategy. It has been observed that students get jitters in the name of group discussion (GD)s. You can be more confident by using updated contemporary news and the information. Topics can vary from politics to general therefore with information; you should also have wit and humour. This can be inculcated over the period of time. It is one of the most difficult and but you can always prove your point with interlacing your opinion with wit and humour. Today GD has become an integral part of the recruitment process. It is considered an important method to assess the personality of a job aspirant. In social settings also, friends and relatives often do discussions on important issues of common interest before taking decisions on them. GD is defined as discussion in a gathering/conglomeration of people who have freedom to share their ideas, opinions, feelings and viewpoints without hurting the sentiments of any individual.

If participating in GD is challenging for a job aspirant, assessing his/her worthiness for a job through GD is also equally challenging for the evaluator who has to make his/her judgment in a few minutes. Generally, a group constituted for discussion consists of 7–15 members who express their views on a topic suggested by the evaluator. This topic could be anything under the sun – from a frivolous one to something profound. The group members have to compete among themselves for 20–30 minutes to prove their worthiness for the job at stake.

With the advent of technology it is not necessary for the individuals, taking part in a GD, to be physically face to face with each other. A GD among the people, placed at different distant locations, may also be conducted through video-conferencing or some other technological means. Facebook and 'WhatsApp' have also emerged as popular platforms of discussion among friends and relatives over social, professional and national issues.

> Group discussions are integral part of the organisations for decision making.

9.2 AMBIENCE/SEATING ARRANGEMENT FOR GROUP DISCUSSION

The most feasible seating arrangement for participants in a GD is that they should be visible to each other. They should be able to maintain eye contact with each other, not with the evaluator. If the audience is present in a GD, it remains a silent observer. The most popular seating arrangements for GD are: U shape, V shape, semi-circle and full circle.

In seating arrangement, if you have a choice for a seat, then go for a prominent place. It should make you adequately conspicuous to other participants as well as the evaluator. Let your friends and supporters sit close to you so that you can prove your point better. If you are asked to sit at a specific place, accept it and make the best use of it. Whatever the place, assume it to be the best place for you. Though seating arrangement is very important in a GD, generally as a participant you do not have much role in deciding it. It is for the organization to make the best possible arrangement. They must make a good arrangement. Otherwise, they may end up choosing wrong candidates. For example if the good student is sitting at inconspicuous position and he doesn't get noticed, he/she might not be selected.

The organisation must provide comfortable chairs to GD participants so that they do not feel restless. Another important factor is of light. The participants will not be able to see each other properly in the absence of a good light arrangement. So light should fall with equal intensity on all the participants.

Proper seating arrangements in group discussions help to zero in on the right candidate choice.

9.3 IMPORTANCE OF GROUP DISCUSSIONS

Today GD is most commonly used for selecting candidates for SSB, MBA, banks, airlines, call centres and research positions. You as a job aspirant cannot escape GD. Therefore, you must get rid of your inhibition and do not let people label you as introvert. Develop the habit of speaking out your mind. Participation in GD can mould your personality for the better. Get into discussion whenever there is an opportunity with friends or fellow students. Listening is appreciated but unless you tell others about your opinions on a topic being discussed, your presence cannot be noticed.

Informal GD can help you do well in formal discussions. Whenever you are participating in an informal discussion, be a good observer. Notice who is creating more impact and why? You can also adopt that person's strategy. To be more confident for a GD, keep yourself updated with contemporary news and other important information. GD topics can vary from politics to general; therefore, keeping yourself abreast with current affairs and happenings will be advantageous for you. Remember, you should also use wit and humour while putting your views on the GD topic. This will help you relieve your stress and also enable to have a laugh thus preventing GD turning into a serious affair.

> *"My belief is that during conversations, it's not so much what you say, it's how you say it that matters. What's being heard is secondary to what's being seen, as body language leads the discussion and dictates the mood."*
>
> —Jarod Kintz

As against public speaking, GD gives you more freedom as you are not exposed to public eye. You are more comfortable sitting with the peers and speaking in the group discussions.

To do better in a GD, go by the following tips:

1. Keep yourself abreast with the latest topics highlighted in the print and electronic media. Topics could range from economics, politics, science, management and social/ cultural issues.
2. Research well on the issues that are bothering the humankind. Be thorough with these issues.
3. Dress immaculately and professionally. If you smell foul, no one would like to sit near you. Even if you wear a strong perfume, someone may be allergic to it and would avoid sitting with you.
4. Occupy the most comfortable seat if you are given the freedom to choose.

9.4 DIFFERENCE BETWEEN GROUP DISCUSSION, PANEL DISCUSSION AND DEBATE

The following sections explain the distinction between three forms of discussion – group discussion, panel discussion and debate.

9.4.1 Group Discussion

In a GD nothing is decided prior to the discussion on a topic about the degree of involvement of the individual participant. GD is free flowing of ideas, opinion, knowledge and information about a given topic. The topic may be known or unknown to the participants. GD is usually not very systematic and you participate whenever you get an opportunity. A GD topic has two sides. You may have points to speak for both the sides but you may choose to support only one side of the topic. However, you should not have a closed mind not to change your stance when you get convinced by the arguments given in support of the other side of the topic. You are judged based on your performance during GD.

Newspapers are a great source of information; therefore, you must develop the habit to read them daily.

9.4.2 Panel Discussion

Panel discussions are organised for the benefit of the audience. Those participating in a panel discussion, that is, panellists, are experts on the topic of panel discussion. They throw light on different aspects of the topic of panel discussion. It would be preposterous to bring in someone for panel discussion who is not at all related to the discussion topic. For example, if we have a discussion on "Need for Commonwealth Games in Developing Countries", we will invite some prominent players representing various sports, some coaches, sports journalists and some stakeholders in sports. The judicious mix of these people would make the panel discussion fruitful. Usually in a panel discussion, the role of audience is also active, as they are invited to pose questions to the panellists on the any aspect of the topic or to clarify some points emerging from the discussion. The expertise of panelists enables them to answer these questions. Panel discussions are very popular on TV. A panel discussion usually has an anchor or a moderator to take it in the right direction. The responsibility for the success of panel discussion partially lies on the shoulders of the moderator as he/she is expected to elicit the relevant information or analysis on different aspects of the discussion topic from the panellists.

9.4.3 Debate

Debates or declamations started long back during the time of Socrates. The mode can be impromptu or extemporaneous. During a debate the participants take a stance either in favour of the given topic or against it. Debates are governed by certain rules. In a debate each speaker has to convincingly prove his/her point in the stipulated time. For better performance, the speaker must be convinced himself/herself about his/her stand on the topic. Otherwise, he/she will not be able to convince the audience about his/her views. In a debate, both the content and delivery method are important. The language, choice of words and phrases, tone, non-verbal cues and paralinguistic features play a significant role in making an impact on the audience Use of adages, anecdotes and personal experience can make your arguments stronger.

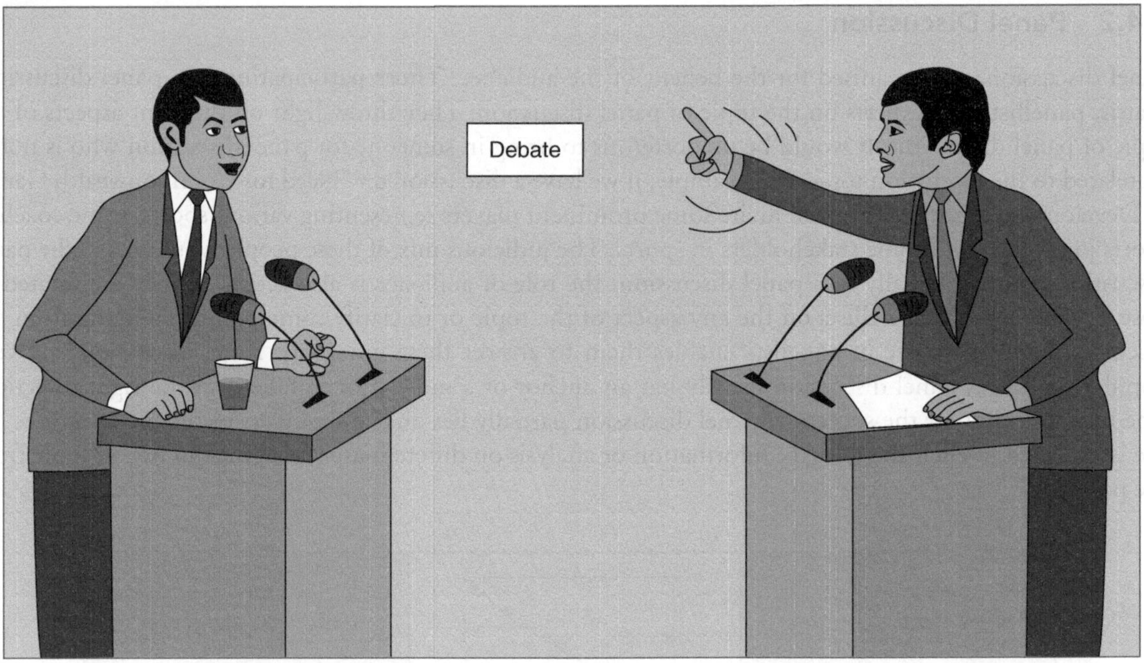

9.5 TRAITS EVALUATED IN GROUP DISCUSSIONS

GD is one of the popular methods through which personality traits of job aspirants are evaluated on the basis of their performance during 15–20 minutes. Traits like intellect, communication skills, leadership traits, ability to motivate others, socialization skills and listening of job aspirants are judged during a GD. The evaluator also closely observes whether or not the GD participants get perplexed about the topic. The participants' leadership abilities are gauged from their responses given to fellow participants' views and how they present their own views. The traits evaluated during a GD are:

1. Knowledge on the subject of the topic
2. Ability to work in a team
3. Communication skills
4. Ability to take initiative
5. Reasoning ability
6. Creativity and adaptability
7. Taking own stand
8. Assertiveness – power to prove one's point
9. Listening skills
10. Leadership qualities
11. Nonverbal cues

> *"The more we are able to engage in enthusiastic disagreement with each other, the more we will be able to uncover the best in ourselves and each other."*
>
> —Karen Kimsey-House

9.6 TYPES OF GROUP DISCUSSIONS

The most popular GDs are classified into two types – topic-based or case-based. Topic-based GDs can be further classified as factual topic-based, abstract topic-based and controversial topic-based. Let us discuss each one of them.

9.6.1 Topic-based Group Discussion

The following sections explain three types of topic-based GDs.

9.6.1.1 Factual Topic-based GD

As the name suggests, these GDs are about the factual topics which are related to individuals on the day-to-day basis. Whatever is contemporary news or information falls under factual topics. Factual topic-based GDs can be organised on something universal as well. For example, the issues related to the environment, education policy, women rights, etc. are universal and can be given for GD to observe how aware or sensitive the participants are to the environment and society.

9.6.1.2 Abstract Topic-based Group Discussion

Participating in a GD on an abstract topic is little tricky. It demands creativity on the part of the participant to form his/her views on abstract topics. Abstract topics are intangible and are rarely given for GD. Such topics could be — 'Zero is a number,' 'Grass is greener on the other side,' 'A is an alphabet,' etc. When you are tense and you face such topics, your ideas get blurred. You grope for words to express your ideas. When deliberating on an abstract topic, let your lateral thinking work on all directions to have several interpretations. There is nothing right or wrong about abstract topics, your success depends on how convincingly you put across your ideas. While expressing your views, open up new vistas so that other participants also get new threads for discussion. By doing so, you will be displaying your ability to take initiative and your leadership qualities. Give up hesitation and think positively. Avoid being aggressive because that can pull the participants and the evaluator away from your points. Being assertive is more fruitful.

9.6.1.3 Group Discussion on Controversial Topics

Controversial topics are argumentative in nature and can generate a lot of controversy. In fact, the participants discussing a controversial topic get charged up with emotions. Sometimes the discussion becomes a free for all, with everyone trying to put forth his/her opinion at the earliest. The participants become aggressive. The objective behind giving controversial topics for GD is to assess the maturity level of participants – whether they can keep a check on their temperament. While deliberating a controversial topic, the participant must be logical and rational rather than being emotional and personal. Keep a check on your temperament. You should be assertive, not aggressive. Most of the participants enjoy discussing controversial topics as they provide ample opportunity for expressing views freely. Some of the controversial topics given for GD are "Ragging should be banned completely," "Euthanasia is justifiable," and "Man and woman can never be equal."

> Be as creative as possible in GDs and you will be able to generate innumerable ideas.

9.6.2 Case-based Group Discussion

The case GDs are slightly different from topic-based GDs. One needs to understand the situation clearly and then provide an action plan so to that it is a win-win situation for both the parties. It should not be imaginative solution but a practical one which could be implemented effectively. Let us consider a situation. Your friend Sourabh has been a very intelligent student throughout his life. When he progresses to third year of his graduation course, suddenly he starts withdrawing from his social circle. His performance in studies drops and he starts feeling lethargic. You take him to the doctor who diagnoses that Sourabh is suffering from a psychological disorder. The doctor prescribes the medicine Trika for Sourabh in limited dose. Sourabh starts taking medicine and gradually starts behaving normally. He regains his interest in studies and also becomes socially active. However, with the passage of time, he becomes addicted to the drug. In the long run, this can prove to be harmful for his body and mind. Now as a good friend, how will you help Sourabh withdraw from this medicine to which he has become adamantly addicted.

When students take part in case-based GDs, they should thoroughly understand the given case and then give their suggestions discussing pros and cons. If they adopt the practical approach to the case of GD then it will enable them get a good score.

Some popular GD topics are as follows:

1. God is myth
2. Grass is greener on the other side
3. The goal and not the means is important
4. All roads lead to Rome
5. Women can become better managers
6. Home makers vs working women
7. There is no social justice in the world
8. Advertising is completely bilge
9. Women policy in India
10. Should bar dancing be legalized in India?
11. Indian economy — Where are we?
12. Should foreign universities come to India?
13. Brain drain?
14. Social Media: Pros & Cons
15. Ethics: Relevance in today's world

Take care of the following points which are to be followed and avoided in GD:

Do's	Don'ts
Sit alert	Be lethargic
Dress appropriately	Shabbily dressed
Start at the earliest	Be quiet for long
Make eye contact with everyone	Make eye contact with audience
Smile a while	Laugh
Listen carefully	Speak continuously
Nod sometimes	Nod too much
Have pleasant expression	Frown
Exude confidence	Be timid and shy
Have composed attitude	Shy attitude
Be assertive	Be aggressive
Show interest	Be lackadaisical

9.7 TIPS FOR SUCCESSFUL PARTICIPATION IN GROUP DISCUSSION

For making a good impression in GD, follow these tips:

1. Brush up your general awareness about contemporary issues and activities which have direct effect on our lives. These issues keep changing with time. For having a good grasp on contemporary issues, become an avid reader of newspapers and magazines on current affairs like Frontline, Business India and India Today. Films are also a rich source of information and they affect as more than anything else. Therefore watch films with full concentration. To prove your point on a GD topic, you can always corroborate with examples from films.
2. Once you are aware of the current happenings, jot down on a piece of paper your opinions and thoughts that you would develop from the premises given by experts on these happenings. Extensive reading will also enable you to make cross-references which would make your arguments strong. More you read, more knowledgeable you become.
3. The third important thing is to know what others think about your opinions. Form a habit to seek inputs from others. When seeking others' opinions, never argue with them but listen to them patiently. More you listen, more natural you become. Try to remove biases from your arguments. This can be done by basing your views on experts' opinions facts or your own experiences.
4. Controlling your temperament is very important. Inculcate the habit of respecting the opinions of others. They may be right, so do not close your mind to their opinions. Everyone has equal right to express themselves; therefore show maturity to accommodate others' thoughts. It is not necessary that you agree to everyone, but you must know how to defend and put forth your arguments. Train your mind to control emotions which is very important in GD.
5. You can speak well but also give the other participants opportunity to speak. Coax the reticent participant to speak out. Do not be rude but do it in a very polite manner so that the other person is tempted to speak. Request your senior who is a veteran to observe your GD and take his feedback, then work on his suggestion to improve your performance.

9.7.1 Group Discussion Proforma

The grid given below helps the evaluator to rate the candidates on give parameters:

Candidate Name	Initiative	Leadership	Knowledge	Communication Skills	Listening	Non-verbal	Total

9.8 INDIVIDUAL TRAITS

9.8.1 Creativity

While you are discussing a topic, be as creative as you can be, else the discussion will come to a standstill. Let your lateral thinking work. When discussing a topic like "All roads lead to Rome," try to interpret it from different angles. There is one obvious interpretation of this topic, but there can be other interpretations as well. Discuss the topic in the light of a different interpretation. This way you will prove yourself different from the other participants. This will also give clue to the other participants to pick the discussion.

9.8.2 Initiative

Non-verbal cues are less noticeable in GD but create a significant impression on the evaluator.

Start the discussion at the earliest; never think that someone else will help you to begin. The participant who broaches the topic is in an advantageous position. But never be in a haste to begin. If you have not understood the topic, take time to understand it. Give your opinion after fully understanding the topic. But you must not sit quiet for a very long time. You have to grab the opportunity to speak.

9.8.3 Listening

Everyone can be a good speaker but listening is an art. In GD if you do not listen properly, you will have no connectivity with the discussion threads started by the other participants. Whenever you are communicating your views, pick up from where the speaker preceding you has left, else that will show that you are a poor listener. To reflect that you are a good listener, keep nodding your head (not too much), tilt towards the side of the person who is speaking and show interest through your eyes.

9.8.4 Articulation

Lee Iacacco, America Automobile Executive has said, "if you have ideas and you don't put them in words you are nowhere". It is an apt advice to articulate your ideas effectively to make yourself counted in GD. After a GD, many participants say that they had been flooded with ideas but they could not express them. The reason of their inability could be hesitation on their part or dominance of GD by the other participants. But remember you are not going to be rewarded for keeping mum. So, if you have ideas then put them in words, say what have in your mind.

9.8.5 Non-verbal Cues

There is little scope for using nonverbal cues in GD. However, you must take care to use your hand gestures, postures and body movements properly. Do not overuse them because that shows you are restless. You must avoid shaking of legs rigorously, putting hands on your face or mouth, fidgeting with pencil or buttons, winking of eyes, etc.

Let us take an example to see how to reflect these traits during a GD. The following example will help you know how to participate in GD without hurting the sentiments of other participants and yet prove your point convincingly. The topic for discussion in the example GD is: "Euthanasia is justifiable". The discussion has seven participants. The evaluator announces the topic, gives two minutes to the participants to think over the topic and organise their thoughts. The participants can use notes if they want. The time duration is indicated at the start so that the participants can keep track of the time. The participants are: Snigda, Ketan, Madhu, Sandy, Tanu, Sanjeev and Ruchika. They all sit on the places assigned to them but they need not follow the order of their seating to speak in the discussion.

Ketan: Hello everyone! I am Ketan. Today we are given a very pertinent and interesting topic for the discussion. Let me first define what euthanasia is. This term is not as common as mercy killing. So euthanasia or mercy killing is the concept that allows a person or his/her close ones to decide to end the life of the person who is suffering from a terminal disease.

Madhu: I think we should consider the different cases and then decide.

Ruchika: If it was so easy, then I think this topic would have not emerged. Indeed, it is a very crucial decision and especially when you have someone in your blood relation, then to take the decision to take away the life is very tough.

Ketan: That is why we must ponder over this topic before getting into any conclusion.

Sandy: It is said that God has given life so we have no right to take it. Also doctors are not supposed to induce death as it is defined in their Hippocratic oath that they cannot take life of any individual consciously. So Ketan, do you think, it is justified?

Ketan: I shall stand by the fact that euthanasia is justified when a terminally ill patient is suffering for long time and has no hope to return to lead normal life. In such a case, it is better to put the person's pain to an end. Sometimes taking care of the terminally ill person becomes a monetary burden on his/her family members so it is better to end the suffering.

Snigda: I had been listening to all of you. I think euthanasia is allowed in a case where the person is terminally ill and it is facilitated by the doctors on the consent of the patient or his/her family members. Euthanasia is effected in two ways – active and passive. In active euthanasia, death is induced by administering drugs to the patient. In passive euthanasia, life-support systems, connected with the patient's body, are removed.

Tanu: Isn't it that both mean the same as both lead to death?

Snigda: Yes, the objective of both is same. But their ways are different. You see euthanasia in passive form is justified provided all factors are taken into consideration.

Tanu: What factors are you referring to? Can you please clarify?

Snigda: Yes I am referring to what has been stated by the Supreme Court in India that a person should approach the high court and a panel of expert doctors should scrutinise the case before giving the consent for euthanasia.

Sandy: But I haven't heard a single case in India where the Supreme Court had allowed mercy killing though many requests have been made by people.

Snigda: No, there are a few cases where it was allowed.

Madhu: That is why I have earlier said that it should be decided case by case. What is the point to stretch the suffering of the patient where hope is zero?

Tanu: But then I have heard about a terminally ill patient who could revive after 25 years. So human beings are always very hopeful, hence to take away life is not quite easy.

Madhu: These are rare cases. This doesn't mean that a patient should suffer endlessly just hoping that one day things will be fine.

Tanu: Why not? If there is one case out of hundred, it is worth taking a chance. Life is so precious and do you know in a country like UK, you may be put behind the bars if you pull the life plug?

Snigda: I reiterate passive euthanasia may be permitted with the help of law as giving complete freedom for euthanasia or legalising it may cause many fraud cases. Humans have the right to live, so inducing death through drugs may be considered a form of criminal death, whereas stopping treatment on justified grounds will mean simply not saving the life of a person who is in a vegetative state. There can be cases where a patient is in pain and there can also be patients not suffering pain. Deciding whether to take away a life has a major moral and ethical dilemma. Such sensitive situations need to be dealt with a lot of care. If conditions are such that mercy killing seems to be the only viable option, I would support only its passive form.

Ketan: I really wonder why Snigda is bent upon justifying that only mercy killing in the passive form is right. Whatever it may be, active or passive, voluntary or involuntary, mercy killing means taking away life. Sanjeev, I haven't heard anything from you. What do you say?

Sanjeev: Thank you Ketan for giving me an opportunity to voice my opinion. I almost agree with Snigda because active euthanasia leads to fraudulent cases as doctors have active role in decision making. In the Netherlands when euthanasia was legalised about 1000 people died the mercy death in a year. In these cases, doctors had decided that it would be justified to end the patient's life. Resultantly the laws were changed.

Ketan: Still I feel in the cases where the patient is suffering from excruciating pain for a very long time, the decision for euthanasia should be taken.

Sandy: So, let me conclude by saying that euthanasia should be handled with great sensitivity and the medical history of the patient should be convincing enough to allow euthanasia. Of course, every patient is different; the age also is one of the factors. So majority of us feel it is justified.

Summary

GD is a very old method of selecting a candidate for a job as it tests the competency and communication skills of job aspirants. In GD job aspirants are free to share their ideas, feelings and opinions without any inhibition. They are usually face-to-face but with the technological advancements social media is also used to conduct GD. There are different kinds of sitting arrangements — U-shape, V-shape, semicircle and full circle. The main objective of the sitting arrangement is to ensure that each participant is able to make eye contact with the other participants. To be an active participant in GD, you must be updated about the current topics and must have knowledge in the areas of human concerns. Be sure that you know the difference between panel discussion, debate and GD, as each is conducted in a different way. The traits of the participants, evaluated in GD, are: knowledge on subject of the GD topic, ability of work in team, communication skills, ability to take initiative, reasoning ability, creativity and adaptability, taking own stand, assertiveness – power to prove own point, listening skills, leadership qualities and nonverbal cues. There are two types of GDs – topic-based and case-based. The topic-based GDs are of three types – factual topic-based, abstract topic based and controversial topic-based. While participating in GD, take care of individual traits like creativity, ability to take initiative, listening, articulation and non-verbal cues. The participant must have confidence throughout the GD.

Chapter Review

1. What is a GD and its purpose?
2. What qualities in a person do you think a GD can test?
3. How is a GD different from a debate? Explain.
4. How does a friendly and cooperative ambience during GD help the evaluator as well as the candidates?
5. Describe the seating arrangement in a GD?
6. What points should you keep in mind during GD?
7. What are the traits for which candidates are evaluated in GD?
8. Describe and explain the types of GDs.
9. What is a controversial topic? What is the motive of giving a controversial topic in a GD? Give an example.
10. How does being assertive and not aggressive during GDs help a candidate to be successful?
11. Discuss the roles of panellists in a Panel Discussion. What are the benefits of panel discussion?
12. Discuss the importance of citation of quotes, statistics and live examples in a GD.

Direct Questions

1. What are the personality traits a candidate should possess to be successful in a GD?
2. Define GD?
3. What is the basic rule of conducting GD?
4. What is the main difference between a GD and panel discussion?
5. Discuss some GD summarization techniques.
6. What are the types of GDs?
7. What roles can a candidate play during a GD?

Analytical Questions

1. Imagine you are in a GD. The topic is decline of fresh water resources. If you were to initiate the discussion, what would you speak? Describe.
2. Imagine there are two friends of yours in your group for GD. How would you choose your positioning then? Describe why.
3. Assume you are in the middle of a GD. You identify that one of the group mates is discussing something which is irrelevant to the given topic. What would you say then? Describe.

Resources for Further Reflections

1. "Preparing for group discussion" http://www.uky.edu/~drlane/groups/ch07.htm.
2. Tips for group discussion https://www.youtube.com/watch?v=JREV7-ZkOCk.
3. Importance of group discussions http://www.thehindu.com/todays-paper/tp-features/tp-education-plus/the-importance-of-gd-in-interviews/article2507273.ece.
4. Group discussion notes http://www.sastra.edu/nptel/download/Prof%20GPRagini/pdf_New/Unit%2026.pdf.
5. http://www.freshersworld.com/interview/group-discussion : Group discussion tips and mock GD's.
6. http://www.indiabix.com/group-discussion/topics-with-answers/ : Some common group discussion topics with answers.
7. http://www.monstercollege.in/article/article_6.html: Some misconceptions about group discussions.

Caselet 1

Group Discussion

Assistant Commander Rajveer Singh is facilitating a group discussion (GD). There were nine people on the table and the topic is 'Facebook: Socialising Life or Creating a Virtual World.' The GD is as follows:

Rajveer Singh: Dear everybody, I would like to tell you few things before starting the GD. You have 15 minutes on the whole. Hence I would like to the time divide as: 1 minute for everybody to key in their point, 4 minutes for discussion and 2 minutes for conclusion.

Karan (*Looking for the first mover advantage*)**:** I think Facebook is creating a virtual world. After the invention of Facebook, people are hardly getting time to meet each other personally as they stick to this virtual world and continuously chat day and night. This is not socialising. And it is hazardous for the world too in near future.

(*Karan actually looks only at Rajveer Singh and most of the participants are just preparing for their turn.*)

Sakshi (*With a confident smile on her face*)**:** Looking at Karan, I don't think so Mr. Karan. Facebook is a social networking site and its aim itself is to socialise the lives of human beings. If few people do stick to it and don't make relations outside this virtual world, it is their mistake. And you cannot blame Facebook for it.

Tarun (*Trying to control the situation*)**:** Sakshi, it is better if you can give your opinion. There is time for discussion. Anyway let us move with another person to voice their views.

Komal: I feel it depends upon the perception of the individual. We cannot say that something is right and something is wrong. We have our own perceptions. If for somebody, accepting a new friend in the virtual world is better than accepting them as friend in the real life, it is simply socialising for them. But if somebody feels the opposite way, it is like creating a virtual world. Hence we cannot say Facebook is socialising or creating a virtual world. But for me it is socialising.

Tarun: Thank you komal. Mr. Shekhar, can we hear your point.

Shekhar: Yes. In my point of view, it is not really creating a virtual world because it has some barriers. And our parents can act as arbitrators if they feel their children are creating a virtual world.

Tarun: I also have the same opinion as Shekhar. It is the parents' responsibility to bring their child into the physical world and make them value real relations rather than virtual relations. As regards the purpose of Facebook, it is socialising life.

Priya: In my opinion, it is creating a virtual world wherein youth are behaving like as if they are in a shell. They should come out of it. If anything happens in the real world, everybody keeps it as a Facebook status for one day and forgets the very next day.

Shekhar: Very rightly said Priya, I appreciate you for that.

Lavanya: I don't think it is creating a virtual world. I have got enough of freedom right from my childhood and I didn't really live in Facebook. I use Facebook for an hour in a day and that too in my leisure time. So it is up to us to decide how to use it.

Neha: I feel it is creating a virtual world. My friends even when they are so near to communicate physically with each other, they text through Facebook for their interaction. They don't even feel that their health is getting spoiled by using Facebook very much.

Vishwanath: I want to share my opinion here. It is evident from the data that Facebook has the third highest population in the world next to China and India. It is clearly socialising the lives of individuals in this globalised busy world. But the extent of socialising has a thin line of separation between meeting the far ones and talking to each other virtually even when they are near.

Shekhar: It is already 9 minutes and let us discuss for 4 minutes before concluding.

Komal: As I have already told, it is in no way socialising or creating a virtual world. One situation can be socialising for someone while it is like creating a virtual world for another.

Shekhar (*Looking at Komal*)**:** If it is like creating a virtual world, parents can stop their children from using Facebook. Right?

Neha (*Explaining to all*)**:** Does anyone here expect the younger generation to listen to their parents on issues like Facebook?

Vishwanath: I agree Neha. Absolutely no! But there are ways to make them listen apart from telling them directly.

Lavanya (*With angry face*)**:** Why not, Neha? And how do you decide Mr. Viswanath. My parents talk to me directly only. They tell me everything what is good for me and what is not.

Tarun: Okay okay! Don't be angry Lavanya. It's just a discussion and they are sharing their opinions. That's all. I propose Priya to conclude this discussion.

Priya: Thank you, Tarun. I would conclude that Facebook is not creating a virtual world up to a certain extent. But few people who do forget their real lives should consider coming into the reality out of Facebook which otherwise will create problems for them and mankind in future.

Rajveer Singh: Thank you all. You can leave the hall.

(Rajveer Singh made notes of leadership qualities shown by Tarun, facilitation qualities by Shekhar, angry face of Lavanya and non-verbal communication of everybody before deciding on the result.)

Questions

1. Whom should Mr. Rajveer Singh select if he decides to select not more than four and why?
2. Behavioral aspects and non-verbal communication are tested the most in which type of GDs and why?

Caselet 2

Group Discussion

Rajesh Daliya, Head – Talent Acquisition at Flipkart is facilitating a group discussion (GD). There are eight people on the table and the topic is – 'Fast'. The GD is as follows:

Rajesh Daliya: Dear everybody, I would like to tell you few things before starting the GD. You have 15 minutes on the whole. Discuss and give few points about 'Fast'.

Sidharth (*Looking for the first mover advantage*)**:** I think we should speak about our generation. Ours is very fast generation when compared with our parents. All the facilities for living a fast life, which are available to us, weren't accessible to our parents when they were of our age.

(Siddharth while speaking actually looks only at Rajesh Daliya and most of the participants are just preparing for their turn.)

Nikitha (*With a sullen expression*)**:** I think fast is too dangerous for us. I was brought up saying slow and steady wins the race. So it's better to focus more and hit the target rather than hitting it without actually looking at the target.

Ashish: I think we need to be fast in this competitive world. It's not easy to compete in this world if you are slow. So, we have to be at a very fast pace to be in tandem with others.

Komal: When I heard the word 'fast', I thought about fasting for health. Fasting a day in a month will keep us fit and healthy. It's always better to stay fit, and to be fit, it's nice to fast.

Neelesh: Whenever I think of 'fast', I remember Shoaib Akthar. The Rawalpindi Express bowls so fast that most batsmen feel it's fine if we could at least defend his balls without giving him the wicket.

Abhinav: If I had to say about 'fast', I would remember the *Fast and Furious* movie series. I feel bad about Paul Walker who was life of the series. While watching the latest movie of the series, *Fast 7,* I did miss Paul Walker a lot.

Sirisha: I think of the speed of light when I think of 'fast'. The man has invented numerous things but still couldn't go beyond the speed of cheetah. I wonder when the man would travel at the speed of light, how the world would be.

Pavan: If I have to think about 'fast', I will remember Usain Bolt. He came into limelight like a tracer bullet. He is the fastest person on the planet.

Rajesh Daliya: Thank you all. Impressed with the information all the participants have provided today. We will communicate to you shortly about the results. Everyone can leave as of now.

Questions

1. Whom should Mr. Rajesh Daliya select if he decides to select not more than four and why?
2. The content and style of presentation is tested the most in which type of GD and why?

SECTION 3

PROFESSIONAL SKILLS (CAREER PLANNING)

Chapter 10

CREATIVITY AT WORKPLACE

Learning Roadmap

After reading this chapter you will be able to:

- Define creativity and its significance
- Know the importance of creativity in the workplace
- Find out how motivation can be increased through creativity
- Know the role of hobbies in nurturing creativity
- Learn about De Bono's Six Thinking Hats

PERSPECTIVE

Creativity is the ability to synthesise dots and experiences one has had to develop something new. On creativity, Steve Jobs said, "You can't connect the dots looking forward; you can only connect them looking backwards. So, you have to trust that the dots will somehow connect in your future. You have to trust in something–your gut, destiny, life, karma, whatever. This approach has never let me down, and it has made all the difference in my life".

Creativity is about thinking divergent and on different planes. Creativity gets stifled under the burden of wanting to be successful because this desire brings undesirable stress, burden and pressure to succeed. Thus, it is important to free oneself from this desire to induce novelty in thinking and bring lightness in the mind. Removing such load or pressure on the self helps individuals think afresh and become beginners.

Being creative is a subjective decision. One may choose to be creative if one wants. An individual could start being creative on everyday issues facing himself/herself, his/her family, organisation or society. It only needs the individual to come out of the groove or mental blocks which are big hindrances to creativity. One should be satisfied doing what one believes is a great work and the only way to do a great work is to love what one does. Also, one has to have great passion for what one does in life. One gives up easily if there is no passion in what one does; thus, creativity requires lots of perseverance.

Creative and innovative organisations do have a unique culture that runs through the veins of the whole organisation. Such organisations have open or declared policies towards experimentation, freedom on the job and acceptance for mistakes. The creative culture flows from the top leadership to down in these organisations. It is the top leadership that encourages and motivates their employees to think differently and experiment on new ideas.

There are painters who transform the sun to a yellow spot, but there are others who with the help of their art and their intelligence, transform a yellow spot into sun.

— Pablo Picasso

10.1 INTRODUCTION

Nowadays, creativity is a term that is used to define the end-result of any process that is done differently from other processes in a similar field. Some members of the modern generation think that creativity implies doing miracles and it is achieved by only a few people. It is hard to learn, as it is the quality of the gifted people. Another unfounded assumption is that creativity only belongs to the 'art' world and it is a matter of talent and nothing can be done about it.

Creativity is highly necessary in the monotonous world where you grapple with different kinds of problems every day. All people think differently, and to put the myriad thoughts in an organised manner requires a lot of creativity. Today the need for creativity has increased manifold as compared to the old days; earlier creativity was a mere hobby but now it is more of a necessity. To be able to face competition successfully, each organisation has to integrate creativity with its structure, working, building, infrastructure, etc.

Why are we 'creatively backward' culturally? The first and foremost reason is that everyone tries to build ideas from a logical base. Because chances are that any idea without a logical base would be deemed crazy and not given the consideration it deserves. If every creative idea has to be appreciated for the logic behind it, then it is only natural to suppose that the same idea could be reached by logic. So where is any scope for creativity to become important in this scenario?

Even the current education system does not emphasise the need to create an urge for creativity among learners, as it is considered that the very idea of teaching creativity is absurd. Very few educational organisations really believe that creativity can be taught to students. It is hindrance because students cannot take risk to be creative while answering as they are unsure of the evaluation.

Over the last few years, businesses have been focused on three major practices. One, restructuring which includes acquisition, leveraged buy-outs (LBOs), mergers, de-mergers etc. Two, growth means devising business strategies and cycle. Third, cost-cutting, which is still prevalent. With cost-cutting an organisation's profits may improve but there comes a time when all the fat (extra cost) is gone and further cost-cuts only remove the muscle of the organisation. New focus areas which are growing in importance for businesses are the quality and customer services. Excelling in these areas requires a great deal of creativity by businesses.

What happens when you have a lean and competent organisation and your competitors are just as lean and competent as you are? And, your traditional practices no longer provide a unique advantage. In this scenario, sooner or later, the more able senior executives in the organisation realise that creativity is the only way to compete successfully in the market.

Moving from organisations to governments, we find that few governments realise that change is as important as other aspects of their functioning. In fact, there is an urgent need for finding better ways of doing things and for introducing new concepts in government services. The public expects much more than traditional methods of governance.

However, there is a growing number of individuals in almost all walks of life who realise that to fulfil human needs and solve problems in future we need much more better thinking which would come only from creativity.

> There is a dire need for organisations to be creative else the survival is at stake.

10.2 CURRENT WORKPLACES

Today, workplaces in organisations have become drab and routine. Their focus is more on creating a better product than on enhancing the creativity of the minds whose role is crucial in creating a better product. Employees begin day in the office in a dull ambience, thinking that they are going to face the same people, behave in the same way and do the same activities. Consequently, their output declines. To create an environment which inspires employees to improve their productivity and work quality, creativity must be integrated in the work culture of the organisation. The question is how to do this and also will the organisation be able to sustain it for a very long time?

The workplace environment determines the behaviour of the average employee. With the dynamic nature of the current job market and rising career aspirations of employees, they are almost free to move between organisations for better prospects. Lesser the creative environment in an organisation's workplace, more the tendency of its employees to leave the organisation regardless of the salary or the comfort at the workplace.

Despite the importance of the creativity in the organisation only a few organisations have excelled in their creative initiatives. The rest aspires to have it in their organisation but they only talk about it, however, do not practice.

The necessity of creativity in organisational functioning has been realised quite late. Many organisations have started organising creativity workshops for their employees in the hope of increasing the creative output of the organisation. But in reality, only in few organisations these workshops succeed in inculcating a creative outlook among employees who strive to bring creativity in their work.

10.3 CREATIVITY

Creativity is related to coming out with completely new ideas and processes. We always think that a creative genius will come up with either artistic paintings like Michael Angelo or Pablo Picasso or amazingly great code like Mark Zuckerberg. But for the organisations it is not restricted to only that, as in many cases the employees can trigger great ideas which could be very creative and significant that can help in problem solving. So creativity is of two kinds: one is conceptual and the other is experimental. The conceptual creativity will have Eureka moment and there will be visibility. However, experimental creativity will be inert and it requires time to develop and evolve. The organisation must recognise both the creativity to have healthy environment.

Creativity is always rewarded.

It is a matter of choice to see creativity as a mystery or chance. When brilliant ideas are generated, one may not be aware of the behind-the-screen process which led to generation of these ideas. Generally, one is unaware of how or what triggered a brilliant idea.

There may be many entirely different definitions of 'creativity. Here we take a simple one: Creativity refers to bringing something new into being which is valuable. When creativity is regarded as a magic gift and if you are not lucky enough to have this gift, you would probably do nothing about it.

Imagination is everything. It is the preview of life's coming attractions.

— Albert Einstein

Creativity is the logic of being illogical. It is contrary to the traditional habits of vertical thinking. We have become used to the vertical thinking pattern, which is considered useful for its effectiveness in problem solving. However, to be creative, one needs to break out of the established vertical thinking pattern and look at things in a different way. But often, the fear of being proved wrong and the fear of making mistakes inhibit creativity.

However, De Bono believed that we can try to develop the type of thinking that encourages creativity rather than just being stuck in traditional ways thinking and doing things. Everyone can be creative, as creativity can be achieved by using lateral thinking. According to De Bono, creativity is a logically necessary outcome rather than some empirical gimmicks. This is different from 'brainstorming' which is admirable but actually is not the way to develop serious creative thinking skills. It represents a 'scatter-gun' approach. It is old fashioned and inefficient and only brings a mild level of creativity. Brainstorming cannot be done by an individual. Instead of brainstorming, lateral thinking skills like 'brain sailing', which is a liberating structure of thinking, bring creativity.

> To work on different solutions of a problem do not only involve in brainstorming but lateral thinking skill like brain sailing.

10.4 MOTIVATION

Most of the organisations are competing to survive in the modern day's fierce market. A performance assessment highlight the achievement and development of the organisation. The effectiveness of an organisation depends closely on the motivation being given to the employees by the organisation. The success of a company depends greatly on the motivation and development of its employees. Most of the companies today follow some "motivation planning". We as employees want management and leadership that we can look up to, not management that looks down on us. Hence companies are trying to cultivate strong skills in delegation in their employees. To be successful in motivating people a genuine recognition and respect is important. Having acknowledged this fact many policies like the rewarding policy and celebrating achievements are being introduced by companies. Satisfying employee needs is a major step in motivating employees.

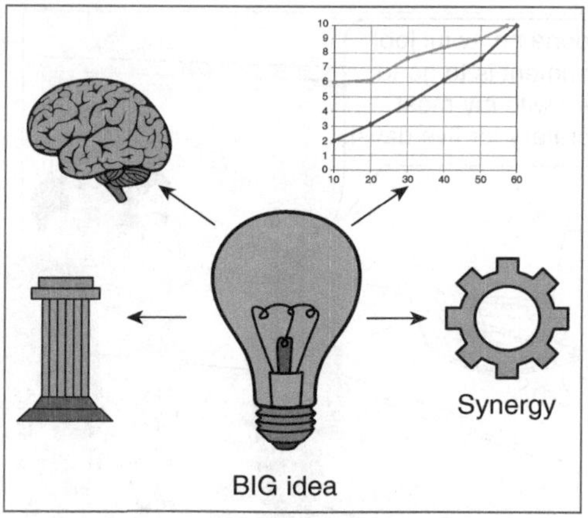

The tech giant, Google, hasn't just spent time and focus on new programs and inventions, it focused on people. Since its founding, it has grown its business from a two-man show operation to over 37,000 employees in 40 countries. Google makes employee happiness a priority. Google has a team of people whose job is primarily to monitor and execute employee perks and benefits.

Google, a leading organisation in the field of information technology didn't just spend time only on new programs, but also put quality focus on its people. This is the reason for the organisation to grow business from just two people to around 37,000 employees in 40 countries. The official one fifth of the work time organisation gives its employees to work on their own projects tells us how the management prioritises giving motivation to its employees.

In a talk about career choices, the CEO of Amazon said that the organisation covers up to 95% of the tuition for its employees for courses in various other fields like nursing, mechanics etc. irrespective of whether the skills gained would be advantageous to the company or not. The primary goal is to enable choices for its people.

Keeping employees motivated is a key challenge in environments such as retailing, call centres and other high-volume, low-pay workplaces. But the companies have made it a point to motivate their employees continually.

Creativity is often associated with the motivation of a person which is his/her willingness to pause and focus on some particular aspect of his/her work and make an attempt to think out of the box. It is indeed significant to pause and show willingness to think of new ideas and ways of doing things. This might not work out in all conditions, but in the long run it cuts through in many situations. Developing this thinking requires investment of time and effort for creating a new focus.

There are many stories about the important role motivation plays in creativity. One is of the case of the famous Red Telephone Company, Australia which was facing a problem due to its offer of limitless time for local calls on the payment of some initial cost. The problem was subscribers had been making full use of this offer and most of the lines of the Red Telephone Company were always occupied, leaving no room for the people willing to make short calls. Any idea of limiting the local call time or increasing the payment was totally ruled out as it would pull back the company in the competition. So, the CEO of the company came up with a novel idea of putting a lot of lead into their handset thus making the handset heavy for making long calls without getting tired. And, Red Telephones are famous for their weight till today!

> To keep the motivation of employees high, the companies keep launching new programmes on creativity.

What is the passion with which you start your day when you wake up in the morning? Is this the passion associated with your life when you work? This passion can be sustained if there is enough motivation to work. The triggers are different and unique for everyone when it comes to motivation. But regardless of your motivation and the things that bring out your peak performance, too much motivation in one area will weaken the other areas in your life.

For decades, motivation has been studied. Leaders in workplaces have used various standard assessments to determine their employees' personality types so that their behaviours and tendencies could be anticipated in a better way. In addition, motivation books are used to encourage employees to improve their performance.

Leaders should not only read the assessment scores of their employees but also try to understand the important features of their personality. This will help them in devising ways to help each employee achieve his/her goals, desires and aspirations. The main objective is to help one another, and to accomplish this objective leaders as well as employees need to identify things which motivate them in working together. For this to happen, leaders have to commit themselves for building a meaningful and purposeful relationship that really matters to their employees. This allows employees to better understand whom they are serving, just as it helps leaders to understand their employees.

First thing that boosts motivation is a trustworthy leadership. Leaders who support their employees wholeheartedly and take care of their best interest will surely win the trust of their employees, which in turn will make the employees motivated to achieve bigger targets. Trust for sure is a powerful motivational tool. Here is an example an employee who was motivated by the trust his manager reposed in him. The employee, who later turned an entrepreneur himself, says:

> *"I once had a department manager who always looked out for me. He was upfront in communicating his performance expectations and his feedback was direct. He never treated me like a subordinate and looked for ways to include me in senior management meetings. This opened my eyes to bright future prospects of my career and thus motivated me to reach the next level and in the process exceed the expectations of my boss."*
>
> — Glen Llopis

Being relevant is another factor that motivates employees. Today when everyone is in a race to be noticed and get recognition for their work, employees are motivated to achieve something to remain relevant. Hence, employees are in search of new ways for learning, improving their skills and investing in themselves. A help in increasing their relevance would help employees a lot in increasing their performance levels and enhancing their loyalty to the organisation.

A will to reach the pinnacle of success motivates employees, especially young professionals who seek to prove their calibre faster than the older generations in the workplace. The young lot at the workplace just does not want to be stereotyped or marginalised like their old colleagues. Organisational leaders should encourage their employees to exceed expectations by taking responsible risks. They should embrace diverse thinking and measure employees' ability to innovate. Also, an employee's ability to perform should never be underestimated until he/she has been properly evaluated by testing his/her abilities and potential.

The most important factor that encourages motivation is the craving to advance in career. Awaited advancement triggers extreme motivation in employees to achieve. Employees need to be mindful of every opportunity that lies around them regardless of whether it is below or above their expectations.

Trust is the key factor to keep the motivation of the employees high.

Many people get confused in today's workplace, especially about their future. But it is a reality that people only get a few real chances in their careers to reach their final goals. So, they would not like to lead a life with regrets by missing on these chances. To prevent employees from carrying this load of guilt, they need to be motivated to see things in proper perspectives. In fact, they themselves want to be motivated. Leaders can share with their employees, stories of their professional journeys and their successes and failures. Employees should be helped to embrace the unexpected and to navigate through uncertainty and change. Remember, an employee who does not believe in himself/herself will never achieve anything in life.

As per popular perceptions, security and safety are two important motivation factors. People want stability for their future, but they are worried about time passing by quickly and their inability to secure their future. As we can see, each and every one of us is in a race against time and hence motivated to achieve our goals as fast as possible. From the economic collapse in 2008, we have learnt that we can become victims of unexpected changes anytime. So, organisational leaders should be mindful of giving priority to providing security and stability of future to their employees. This eventually increases the motivational level of employees.

You can't use up creativity. The more you use, the more you have

— Maya Angelou

In the context of motivation an interesting factor is self-indulgence. Motivation focused on satisfying one's self-indulgence can be risky. There is no need to remind how some people's greed and selfishness contributed to economic hardships of some global giants in the field of finance. Regarding the downside of a motivational leader, Peter Drucker has said in his book *The Effective Executive*, every time you meet a person with great strengths, you are also meeting someone with great weaknesses. So, as a leader, one should ensure that employees' motivations are good and balanced intentions. Although self-indulgence brings tremendous short-term benefits, it leaves behind some adverse long-term repercussions.

These days, opportunities available to employees to create an impact through their work motivates them to become more and more achievement-oriented. One goal of their desire to perform excellently is to contribute in a way that enables them to secure from their organisation long-term benefits that are linked to certain achievements. So, in the work they perform, employees should be allowed to have a sustainable impact which recognises their performance as significant. Opportunities should be created for employees so that their achievements leave a long lasting impact on the people concerned and also reward the organisation by creating a good name for it.

Happiness is one of the most crucial factors that make people motivated. Desire to achieve happiness is one of the greatest motivations for scaling new heights in one's career. Happiness boosts one's self-esteem giving hope for a better future. Everyone is prone to feeling stressed out by taking work too seriously than it should be. For one's happiness, it is better to step back and enjoy one's professional without being stressed out. Actually, one must be motivated to earn a living that brings tremendous joy and happiness and also helps achieve one's goals. Leaders should always be aware whether their employees are satisfied with their work. They should deliberately talk to them to know the level of their satisfaction at the workplace. It is not unusual for employees to smile to save their jobs even if they are not satisfied with their work. So, it is the duty of leaders to motivate employees to achieve what makes them really happy.

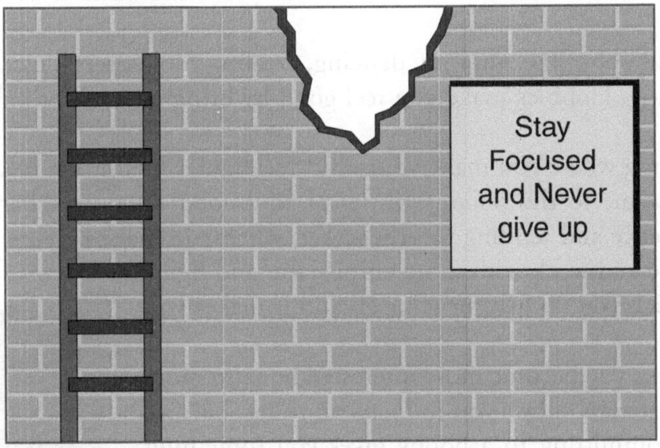

10.5 NURTURING HOBBIES AT WORK

There are many reasons why one should start nurturing a hobby. You cannot perform up to your real potential at your workplace if you focus only on work. Most working people, especially mothers, are interested in having a life that includes work but is not completely dominated by it. You would also like to be fully engaged in and feel passionate about all aspects of your life, although you often find it difficult to pursue interests, activities or hobbies outside your work life along with fulfilling your family obligations. You also might think that engaging in hobbies is too self-indulgent or not important, and this thinking prevents you from creating space for them in your life.

But when you take a hobby, like running, dancing, creating funky items, etc., you reap the benefits of inspirational self-nurturing. Hobbies make you feel good by bringing a better balance and more meaning in your life.

Take the case of playing where you make yourselves feel lighter by finding pleasure. As you grow older, you often lose your playtime to the responsibilities of adulthood – working hard and being productive, striving to make a difference and tending to others. Yet, when you make playing a priority in the form of a hobby, you can face life and work with more enthusiasm and lightness. It is something which you do just for yourself and it makes you feel good physically.

Hobbies not only make you become more interested but also more interesting. Expanding interests allows you to focus on things beyond your normal routine. Committing to a hobby gives you something to look forward to and spur on to achieve greater goals. When you participate in an activity and become highly engaged in it, your passion and enthusiasm become more contagious and make you more interesting to others.

Hobbies also enhance your self-esteem by providing an opportunity to gain new skills which give you a sense of accomplishment and confidence, making you feel better about yourself. Creative hobbies fuel your imagination and rid you of that 'something is missing' feeling. Instead, you feel satisfied.

"All work and no play makes Jack a dull boy".

Many companies today acknowledge the fact that "You can't be really first-rate at your work if your work is all you are."

Several companies today lay emphasis on cultivating hobby groups to energise their employees and rejuvenate them. They have embraced the idea of motivating the employees to interact constantly because they believe that good ideas come out of speaking with each other – be it about cricket, work or politics. It is important to cultivate hobbies not only for the benefit of the company but helps to rediscover ourselves on an individual basis. We want a life that include work but not completely taken over by it. But in today's world we forget to give ourselves permission to pursue our interests. It helps us to play and feel lighter and become more interesting and interested. Pursuing hobbies enhances self-esteem because it helps in our personal growth. Companies today are making an effort to engage people in their hobbies so that it helps people develop and ultimately leading to the increase in the growth rate of the company. Apart from picnics and parties, Cartwheel Creative Consultancy firm has Carom board, guitars and drum kits kept in the organization and the employees try their hands during the breaks. Table tennis and carom had been popular for a long time. The Uco bank employees are given freedom to play cards /carom so that they break monotony of work and increasing their work efficiency. Even in teaching institutes cricket matches, sports, drawing competition are organized at regular basis. Fun and frolic at the workplace develop sense of confidence and teamwork is encouraged creating a deep bond amongst the employees.

Varieties of hobbies are added to rejuvenate the employees.

Several companies are now encouraging formation of activity and hobby groups as part of their schedule, apart from routine picnics and excursions. For instance, a carom board, few guitars and a drum kit form an integral part of the Cartwheel Creative Consultancy Private Limited, a city-based consulting firm. The idea, says D Ramakrishna, the founder of the company, is to motivate the members of the company to interact constantly. Good ideas come out of speaking with each other, be it about music, movies, games, politics or work. Most of these groups are planned at the beginning of the year and are run effectively. Outbursts of spontaneity could include kite-flying, jamming and playing carom, apart from the planned cricket matches.

Such special interest groups not only facilitate bonding, but also help bail out a sinking morale. "If an employee wants time out to write a book, do a course, pen a screenplay, record an album, go backpacking, or just get sorted, we try not to stand in the way. Our employees have done all this and returned hopefully in a better frame of mind," tells Ramakrishna.

Music elevates your mood and affects your emotions. Pradeep Guha of 9X Media made a changeover to give a face-lift to the company. Guha's company has an in-house musical set-up where the staff practices together for their annual musical concerts. Employees are free to play musical instruments, at will, during office hours.

Starting the day with a non-work routine is relaxing and helps improve focus. A couple of companies carry out 15-minute activities every morning, including light exercises. These are creative as well as educative, and the experiences offer significant life lessons.

Several companies encourage teammate trivia – trivia about each worker. The idea is to let staffers assimilate and absorb themselves in the work culture. While some companies have a dedicated section on employee trivia in their newsletters, others send official mails introducing new joiners by mentioning their qualifications, experience and the value they bring to the organisation.

10.6 THE SIX THINKING HAT METHOD

Among the methods, developed by Edward De Bono to teach lateral thinking, the Six Hats Thinking Method is famous. This method consists of six hats of different colours representing different roles for people in of different situations. Wearing a hat of a certain colour means that we would like to think in a certain way suiting a particular situation.

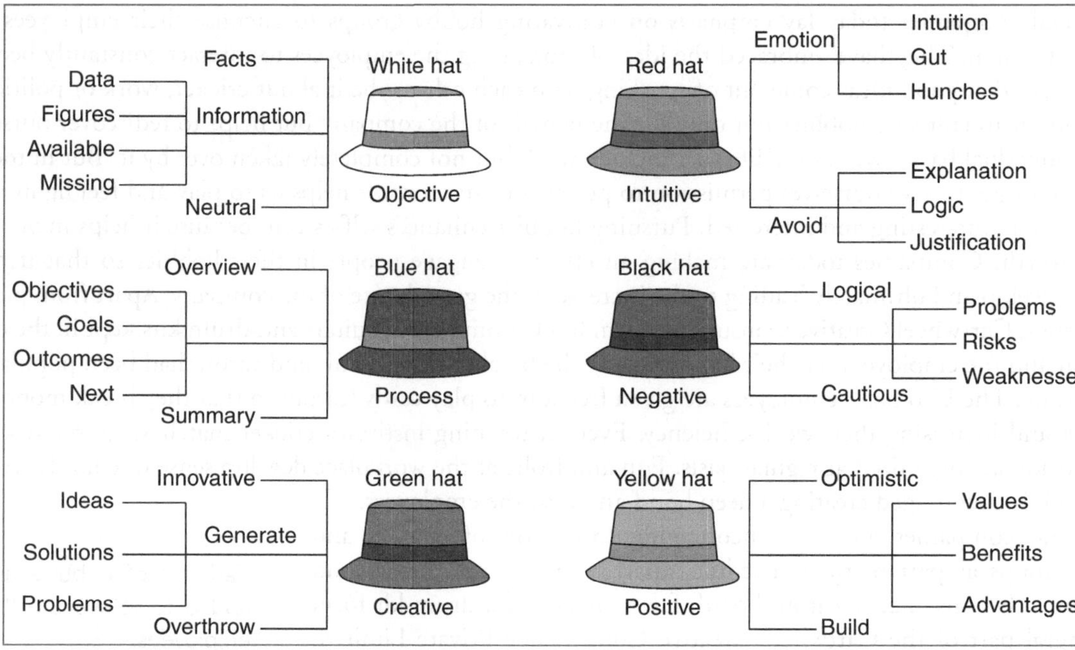

Edward de Bono's six thinking hats.

1. **White hat:** Information – what information do we need? Do we have it? If not, how to get it?
2. **Red hat:** Feelings, intuition, hunches, emotions, need not be apologetic, explanation, justification.
3. **Black hat:** Exercising caution; preventing mistakes; being critical; assessing potential danger?
4. **Yellow hat:** Benefits and feasibility which are logically based.
5. **Green hat:** Creativity, alternatives, new ideas, thought provoking.
6. **Blue hat:** Process-control, overview, agenda of thinking steps, summaries, conclusions, decisions.

A great virtue of the Six Hat Method is that you can switch thinking immediately without any offence and/or defence. Too often in real life, people are interested in winning or losing an argument rather than in exploring the subject. But, the Six Hats Method provides a way of productive discussions by separating ego from performance and the thinker is freed from the limitation of sticking to one position.

De Bono tried to put his techniques within a practical format, even for parents. He tried to make them simple and interesting. However, it is doubtful whether parents and teachers can understand and translate those ideas into a format which the young kids can understand. Therefore, the success of these thinking tools heavily relies on teaching.

Some real life effective outputs of the Six Thinking Hats Method include the reduction of multinational project discussions from 30 days down to two days for the ABB group-Automation and power technologies. The principal Healthy Indiana Plan members came from several different cultures – France, Germany, Sweden, Finland and USA. The employees of ABB group attended de Bono workshop which focused on improving performance in internal meetings, communication and market assessment by using six thinking hats. After this workshop decision making time reduced by 60%. The Six Thinking Hats methodology served to break through these cultural communication barriers. Corporate Research Director Juhani Pylkk, who participated in the workshop, was pleased with the power of the tool and remarked, "With Six Thinking Hats we gain results in two days, which with old methods would have taken at least a month." Effective communication was realised in minutes, and consensus reached quickly.

There are countless examples where this technique made a change in the way discussions were held – from matters of high importance, like strategy planning in multi-national companies, to general debates and discussions in a workplace. Even the Australian cricket team quoted the importance of the Six Hats technique for their victory in the 2003 World Cup.

This technique reduces confusion as one cannot do too much at once. Emotions, information, logic, hope and creativity all crowd in on us. Doing these different types of thinking, one at a time, is the essence of this technique. It also paves way for parallel thinking where everyone sees the same situation with their own different perspectives. De Bono used the 'thinking hat' metaphor because of the familiar expressions such as 'putting on your hat', and it removes 'ego' from the discussion process.

> Applying six thinking hats method to the problems faced in the organisation can solve them really fast.

With this technique, each situation or problem is explored and alternatives are generated that go beyond obvious solutions. This increases the constructive output from meetings and decreases meeting time. Thus, the Six Thinking Hats technique can pave way for creativity in the workplace of an organisation.

Summary

Creativity is to do anything in a different way to reach the end result. People usually do not attempt to be creative because of fear of failure. Many people also think creativity is gifted and cannot be learned, but that is actually not true. Creativity is very necessary in this monotonous world. People have realised the importance of creativity in all walks of life – be it education, medicine, advertising, cinema, etc. Being creative is just not restricted to the artist. Today, creativity has become an integral part of an organisation in terms of structure, working, building, infrastructure, etc. In education system also creativity is important, as once students have it in them, they can apply it in a professional setting. Creativity and motivation are interrelated as they force people to think out of the box. Workplaces without creativity appear drab and routine. Their output has come down. To improve the environment for better productivity in an organisation, its creativity bar must be raised. Creativity today is not a luxury but is necessity. That is why more and more organisations are now thinking of taking steps to incorporate creativity in their working. Creativity is helpful in problem solving. De Bono has used the concept of lateral thinking which forces people to generate a lot of new ideas. His Six Thinking Hats Method helps organisations come up with creative products.

Chapter Review

1. How can you define creativity and why do you think creativity is necessary in today's organisations?
2. Describe the role of a leader in nurturing the creativity of an employee.
3. Explain briefly the Six Thinking Hats technique.
4. How can you nurture hobbies at work? Give some examples.
5. How can creativity be employed to solve workplace conflicts and problems?
6. How can hobbies help in relieving stress and encouraging creativity? What kinds of hobbies are more suited for the development of creativity?

7. What roles does creativity play in entrepreneurship?
8. How are diversity among employees and creativity related?
9. Creativity and innovation go hand in hand. Explain.

Direct Questions

1. What were the major practices of business in the recent years?
2. What do you understand by the dynamic nature of current organisations?
3. Do you think creativity is teachable or learnable? Justify.
4. What are the different thinking roles identified by the six colours of the Thinking Hats?
5. How can you define a creative environment?
6. What are the ways to promote creativity in the workplace?
7. Discuss the factors in the workplace environment and people who discourage creativity? How can these factors be rectified to promote creativity at workplace?
8. How do confidence and motivation promote creativity? List some ways to improve self-confidence and enhance motivation of employees to make a workplace more creative.

Analytical Questions

1. Google is famous for providing an enjoyable workspace with many facilities for its employees like unlimited availability of chocolates, game room, etc. Do you think this has something to do with Google being one of the world's best corporates? Justify your answer.
2. Many people and books nowadays use the phrase 'thinking out of the box'. What do you infer from this phrase? Give an example of the out of the box thinking.
3. Assume you were asked to provide some ideas to improve the creative environment at your workplace. What idea would you suggest? Explain in detail.

Resources for Further Reflections

1. How to think out of the box. http://www.wikihow.com/Think-'Outside-of-the-Box'.
2. Example for use of lateral thinking solutions in business. http://debonoforbusiness.com/.
3. Some idea for a creative workplace. http://youearnedit.com/blog/25-ways-to-keep-ideas-flowing-in-your-workplaces/.
4. Six thinking hats. http://www.debonogroup.com/six_thinking_hats.php.
5. Look at decisions from many points of view. https://www.youtube.com/watch?feature=player_embedded&v=PqmCUAGcsnI.
6. Role of creativity in entrepreneurship. http://www.worldscientific.com/doi/abs/10.1142/S0218495810000501.

7. Stress and creativity. http://www.huffingtonpost.com/2014/05/29/want-to-be-more-creative-_0_n_5367423.html?ir=India.
8. Hobbies: personal path to creativity. https://www.psychologytoday.com/blog/imagine/200812/hobbies-the-personal-path-creativity.
9. Ways to unleash creativity at workplace. http://www.hongkiat.com/blog/unleash-creativity-workplace/.

Books to Read

1. Khandawala P. *Fourth Eye*. A.H. Wheeler & Co; 1984.
2. De Bono E. *Lateral Thinking*. Penguin; 2009.
3. Robinson K. *Out of Our Minds: Learning to Be Creative*. Capstone; 2011.
4. Kelley T, Kelley D. *Creative confidence: Unleashing the creative potential within us all.* William Collins; 2013.

Movies to Watch

1. Office space
2. Three idiots

Caselet 1

Development of Accompli – by Motorola

Motorola is a well-known global company in the area of communication technologies. It focuses on the product for the people whose priority is time management. Another product they manufacture is of course for people who give top priority to stay in contact with close ones. And the last one is for the opulent and bigwigs whose top priority is conspicuous consumption. It was in 2002 that Motorola changed the focus as it wanted to create a product for future.

The company wanted to involve people in the decision-making for developing a sleek high-tech, easy-to-hold device for those who wanted cutting edge technology but still did not want to spend heavily the new product. So, it organised a three-day event with product manager to plan the designing of the new product. At the event, master trainer Jay Wenberg was invited to give his best inputs for fruitful discussions.

The first day of the event was spent in developing consumer profiles based on extensive research with the main focus on the existing products. The presentations were made on the existing products with the regional perspective. The product manager tried to understand each product's target market. During discussions up to the complete profiles of consumers including their age, marital status, buying traits, education, cultural beliefs, likings, etc. were analysed. The product manager understood the behaviour pattern of Motorola customers.

On the second day, the focus was on 'technology soak', which means knowing good points and limitations of the present technology. Then trainer

Jay Wenberg talked about Six Thinking Hats and Lateral Thinking, which basically focused on creativity. The group gave a thought on the Green Hat to come up with innumerable ideas for the 'product of for the future'.

During the Green Hat session the members used the Lateral Thinking technique of counter argument to challenge the practical drawbacks of the technology. Jay started the exercise by passing on trinkets to carry on the Random Objects exercise. At the end of After the Green Hat session, ideas were offered, and each idea was evaluated separately by applying the Yellow and Black Hat thinking. The best idea was shortlisted by applying the Red Hat thinking.

The outcome of applying the Green Hat thinking was development of the final product called Accompli which was technologically advanced. This product functioned as a mobile which was like virtual office with full keyboard. The advantage of Accompli is its wireless network connection with fast Internet access from anywhere in the world. It is consumer-friendly, as extra business applications can also be installed on it and one can even play assorted games on it.

Finally, the group also did the White Hat task of accumulating information on 'a day in the life' of an Accompli owner. They wanted to see the duration for which the consumer used this new device and for what purposes. By doing this the team also noted what additional features the consumer is looking for to consider it more beneficial for himself/herself. For example, alarm, MP3 music files, greeting sounds, recorded reminders, etc. The group worked on the consumer's activities on an hourly basis to ensure Accompli was the right product for the target market. At the end the product manager was elated at the end result of the hard work and people who were not part of the three-day event were happy to know of the success story. Later Motorola launched Accompli in North America, Asia and Europe.

Questions

1. How could Motorola create the low-priced product Accompli?
2. Explain how the White Hat thinking was used in Motorola case to come up with the final product.

Chapter 11

ETHICAL VALUES

Learning Roadmap

After reading this chapter you will be able to:

- Understand the best ethical practices
- Know the definition and correlation of ethics and society
- Suggest ways to inculcate good ethical practices at the workplace
- Tell why ethics are important for organisations
- Know what problems organisations face due to lack of ethics

PERSPECTIVE

In a reputed institute, two students, Ameya and Sahil, were selected for the award of gold medal for scoring the highest marks in their academics. They were very intelligent and hardworking students. Other students looked up to them because of their sharp mind and good behaviour. They were also involved in other extracurricular activities of the institute and were very popular among girls and boys alike. Faculty members of the institute were happy that these two boys were getting the award from Mr. Kailash Satyarthi, the Nobel Prize winner for peace.

But just a day before the award function, it came to the notice of a teacher that the report for the project course submitted by Ameya had plagiarised parts and could not be accepted as per the rules of the institute. It was also revealed that the other student selected for the award, Sahil, had marked proxy attendance. An inquiry panel was constituted and when once its report indicated that both the students are guilty of compromising the institute's ethics, it was decided not to give them awards. Taking such a decision is not an easy task but this sends a message to all other students about what is ethical and what is unethical. They get a warning not to indulge in malpractices of any sort. The fact that this decision was taken for otherwise good students was a message in itself. It was easy for the faculty members to ignore the fault of Ameya and Sahil but by doing that they would have set a wrong example.

> *Educating the mind without educating the heart is no education at all.*
>
> — Aristotle

11.1 INTRODUCTION

We are governed by rules and regulations which we have to follow to be acceptable in our society and in the world at large. Sans these regulations the world would become an unruly place and people would go berserk. In such an unruly world, individuals will behave in their own ways without bothering whether their behaviour would cause problems to others. This can have disastrous consequences. Just to put the organisation functions in order, each organisation has its own set of ethics which are supposed to be followed by its employees. Few organisational ethics are unwritten but most of them are properly coded. Once you become part of an organisation, you realise what is expected from you in terms of adhering to its ethics. An organisation can work smoothly if the workplace behaviour of its managers and staff is strongly embedded in its ethics. It has been observed that employees will be more efficient if they behave ethically. If we analyse the success of great companies, we will find in it a reflection of the observance of a decent code of conduct by its employees.

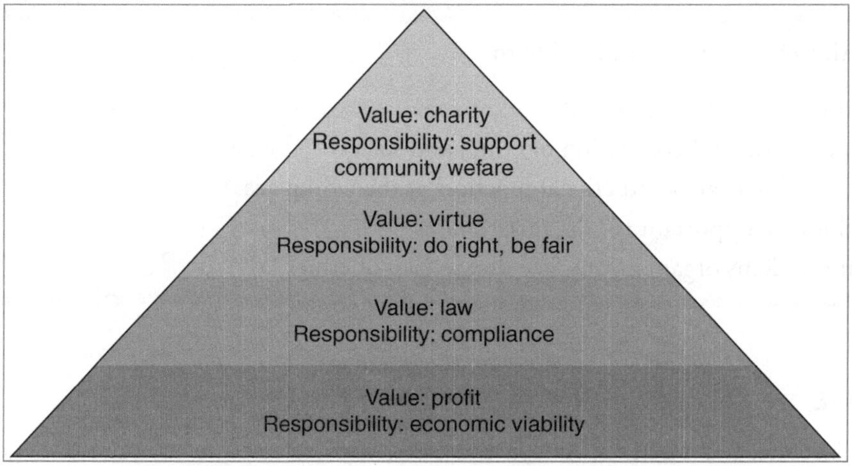

Whenever managers or staff loosen their adherence to organisational ethics, it adversely affects the work environment. So nowadays organisations take it as their priority to ensure adherence to ethics by their managers and staff. They view lack of ethics quite seriously.

In the fast-growing technological world, where there is constant pressure to perform well for maximum output, adhering to ethics poses a serious challenge. In January 2009, a prominent IT company of India – Satyam computers – was hit by a big scam. The scam caused a colossus loss of Rs. 14,162 crores to investors. Satyam CEO, Byrraju Ramalinga Raju, who was admired for his rags-to-riches story, ended up with a sullied image because of this scam. Not long ago, his name was taken with respect due to his good initiatives for the society. The root cause of the Satyam scam was Raju's unquenchable thirst for more and more money and power. As an astute businessman, he took care of all business functions but kept finance secret. Of course you cannot hide issues from public for very long as the key to ethical conduct is openness. Had Satyam deals been fair and ethical, the scam would not have occurred.

Organisational ethics are the standards and principles which companies follow and keep them as reference points in their business dealings. These include fairness, honour, compassionate, integrity and responsibility. In an organisation, it is the duty of leaders to ensure that their employees understand the importance of ethics and follow them in their work.

Youngsters who join companies immediately after completing their education may not be strict followers of ethics. Moreover, these youngsters may have a perception of ethics that could be entirely different what companies expect from them in terms of ethical behaviour. The youngsters may also be under the wrong notion that what they believe is always right. This type of thinking is highly subjective and unethical. Companies must organise workshops to teach them ethical practices and make them aware of the companies' expectations from them about their ethical behaviour. This will help to avoid the pratfalls.

> Following ethics can keep the employees satisfied and the chances of the progress of the organisation increases multifolds.

Organisations need to adhere to the following ethical practices while doing their business:

1. **Consideration and compassion:** Organisations must take care of illness, both mental and physical, of their employees. The sick employees must be allowed sufficient leave to recoup. If some employees are found to be addicted to drugs or alcohol, the organisation must initiate some advisory programmes to help them get rid of their addictions and live a life of hope and enthusiasm. The employees of this kind should be treated with care and helped to go for rehabilitation.
2. **Social responsibility:** For their progress, organisations and their employees are dependent on the environment and communities or the society in which they operate. So, it is their responsibility to protect the environment and the communities living in their vicinity. Organisations must maintain safety standards, keep their surroundings clean and provide potable water. If a company is making extensive use of natural resources, then it must take steps to minimize its use of those resources by looking for alternative production methods.
3. **Financial ethics:** Economy is the backbone of an organisation. Trust and confidence in terms of financial affairs become the building blocks of cordial relationships among peers. The society cannot flourish unless people do not trust financial institutions. The credibility of an organisation is lost if any financial scandal involving the organisation is unravelled. With the finance sector gaining increasing importance in the global economy, adherence to ethics has become essential to formalise creation of wealth honestly.

So ethics are the moral principles that govern a person's behaviour of the conducting of the activity.

> *Education without values, as useful as it is, seems rather to make man a more clever devil.*
>
> — C.S. Lewis

11.2 ETHICS AND SOCIETY

Ethics is explained in different way by different people. For some it is the gut feeling which indicates what is right and what is wrong. Others opine that their religious beliefs tell them ethics. Basically, it is the standard of behaviour your society accepts. No society remains permanent, and therefore society and ethical practices both change with time and place. In fact, religion can set high ethical standard but ethics is not just confined to religion. Atheists also behave in ethical manner, although they are not follower of any religion. Ethics are properly founded standards which provide guideline to humans what is right and what is wrong to do in terms of obligation, rights, benefits to society, virtues, etc. Of course it also indicates to refrain from rape, murder, fraud, slander,

> Be compassionate to employees' problem and their well being. They will work more sincerely for the organisation.

assault, etc. The virtues of honest, compassion and loyalty also fall under the umbrella of ethics. Ethical standards include right to life, freedom, privacy and speech. These are supported by well-founded reasons and therefore justified. There lies a gap between ethics observed within the four walls of a home and those followed in an organisation. But an individual needs to be in discipline at both the places. He/she has to work in consonance with the demands and expectations of the society in terms truth and justice.

Our behaviour and reactions are guided by values; therefore, if we have firm guidelines to be followed then we will be sure of our action. In an organisation, leaders must set examples by their ethical behaviour for their staff to emulate. They should act like torch-bearers and take up the responsibility of creating and sustaining ethical culture at the workplace. What they say, their action, behaviour, etc. should set standards for ethics in their organisations.

11.3 THEORIES OF ETHICS

There are three major theories whose basis is the competition among employees for influence, resources and information. So, it is very important that norms or criteria for righteous path should have been set by following employees can work efficiently. The first theory – the utilitarian theory – emphasises that the consequences will guide the plan and action. The underlying objective is more production in less time, that is, benefit should be maximum. The second theory is based on rights, that is, all people are entitled to exercise certain fundamental rights, for example, right to speech and expression, right to religion, right to education, etc. The third is the theory of justice which states that decision makers should be fair and unbiased while taking decisions. This right assumes importance during the time of promotions. If decisions about promotions are without fairness, the employees' trust in management dwindles.

11.4 CORRELATION BETWEEN VALUES AND BEHAVIOUR

Values are inculcated in the individual by whatever he/she learns from his/her surroundings. For example, elders and teachers influence a great deal the values children learn. In schools, teachers guide their students by telling what is wrong and right. Values exert control over our attitudes and attitudes in turn influence our behaviour. Remember your reaction to your friends' behaviour and activities is solely dependent on your attitude. If you have a positive attitude, you will surely disseminate positive energy. Good values align with the right ethical behaviour. The values which can contribute to inculcating and following ethics in life are as follows:

"Make sure things are done ethically and reasonably".

11.4.1 Probity and Righteousness

The righteous people in any organisation will refuse individual benefits if they are not aligned with the goals of their organisation. One must not give in to unethical luring for selfish motives. Of course, it requires a high degree of self-control to avoid these temptations but that is the right path.

11.4.2 Knowledge and Wisdom

Wisdom refers to your ability to convert the available information into something useful. Wisdom is derived from the individual experience of exploring information intelligently to come to a wise decision. Many times you may come across options which pose an ethical dilemma. In such situations, you must use your knowledge to distinguish between right and wrong.

11.4.3 Love and Empathy

Your love and empathy for someone is reflected through your caring words. In the context of an organisation, 'love' refers to profound positive reaction of employees to their colleagues in a given situation. The love, empathy and kindness expressed by employees for each other create positive vibes in the organisation, which enable them to behave ethically correct in all situations.

11.4.4 Fairness and Justice

All individuals must be treated equally by leaders in an organisation. In the leaders' behaviour towards employees objectivity and fairness must be keywords. They must not show biases towards any individual or group. All employees must receive positive and fair return for the energy and efforts they put in their work. Leaders must be just in allocation of funds and organisational resources.

11.4.5 Courage and Integrity

You must be courageous to be ethical in all situations without compromising your integrity. You should be able to recognise the difference between right and wrong and act accordingly. You must consistently follow the right path without bothering about consequences even when the path is not smooth.

> Follow the right path without bothering about the consequences, you will surely be successful.

All the values described above are interrelated. For example if the allocation of the funds in the academic institute is done by following the guidelines, no one objects. Sometimes because of personal interest or favours there are aberrations in the decision making which dissatisfies the employees. If the top authorities maintain integrity and stay by their words the environment will be cordial and faculty members will be satisfied.

> *Until he extends the circle of his compassion to all living things, man will not himself find peace.*
>
> — Albert Schweitzer

11.5 HOW TO NURTURE ETHICS

Inculcating organisational ethics in employees is the responsibility of the leaders of the organisation. The success of the organisation solely depends on the ethical practices followed by its employees.

Leaders should be polite to juniors.

The organisation should nurture the following ethical practices among its employees:

1. Leaders must reduce the gap between their knowledge and their real actions. Often leaders say they know what is right but they fail to practise themselves what is right. Sometimes they justify their wrong decisions/choices but the simple reason is that they failed to do the right thing. Despite their knowledge, they failed to act with wisdom. For inculcating ethics among their employees, leaders should not preach but set examples by their actions.
2. While taking new recruits, the organisation must assess their ethical behaviour. It should give equal importance to ethical values of the new recruits and their knowledge and skillset. Long-term success of the organisation depends on those people among its staff who give importance to ethical values. Therefore, the organisation must recruit the people with virtuous values as are the key for building ethical work culture in the organisation for its long-term success.
3. The organisation must ensure that the new recruits are part of its social gatherings where they would learn about organisational ethics and try to align their values with those of the organisation. At the orientation programmes, leaders should give effective talks to promote and influence the new recruits' ethical behaviour, and leaders must also affirm their ethical values through their actions. If there is no congruence in leaders' words and actions, it is difficult to propagate ethical values to employees.
4. The organization system should be strong and in place that by following the written procedures the employees know they are progressing in the right direction. However to ensure that the superiors should frequently applaud and appreciate their work as the kind words bolster the confidence and motivate them to work efficiently.
5. Leaders can make a positive impact on employees by fair allocation of organisational resources and linking them properly for better production. The five important resources are: people, money, information, time and capital assets. Leaders should adhere to justice and fairness while taking decisions. Consistency in just and fair decision-making can help in promoting ethical behaviour.

Leaders should be role models for the employees – they can set the things right without much conscious efforts.

11.6 IMPORTANCE OF WORK ETHICS

The healthy and positive work culture improves the enthusiasm and eagerness of employees to perform better as it boosts their morale. It results in increasing their productivity and also improves the employee retention rate of the organisation. Hence it benefits the organisation in the long run. When leaders, known for their impeccable ethical behaviour, become role models for workers, the latter are encouraged to emulate them. If employees succeed in their efforts then thus enhance their own goodwill as well the reputation of the company. The ethics-based reputation of the company and integrity of its employees attract talented hands to join the company thus improving the company's business. The following are some of the advantages enjoyed by the company due to its ethics-based work culture.

Following good ethical practices bring positivity and enthusiasm in the organisation, bringing the efficiency high.

11.6.1 Teamwork and Productivity

The cohesiveness among the employees of a company increases because of the positivity in the workplace environment, generated by adhering to ethics. It surely enables the alignment of the company's business values with the employees' values. It nurtures openness, encouraging consistency and communication regarding values of the company's business and strengthens integrity of leadership and employees. If keeping employees loyal to the company is part of the company's business values then it results in the increased productivity and motivation of employees.

11.6.2 Wealth Protection

If the organisation is immersed in ethical culture then it helps in safeguarding its assets. The employees, who abide by the ethics of the organisation, will safeguard its business assets. They will never spend the organisation money to make personal long-distance calls or use office supplies or equipment for personal use. Ethics demand the employees should take care of the company's property and they certainly would if they are treated with respect and dignity. They should be proud to work in the organisation which is well known for following high ethical standards.

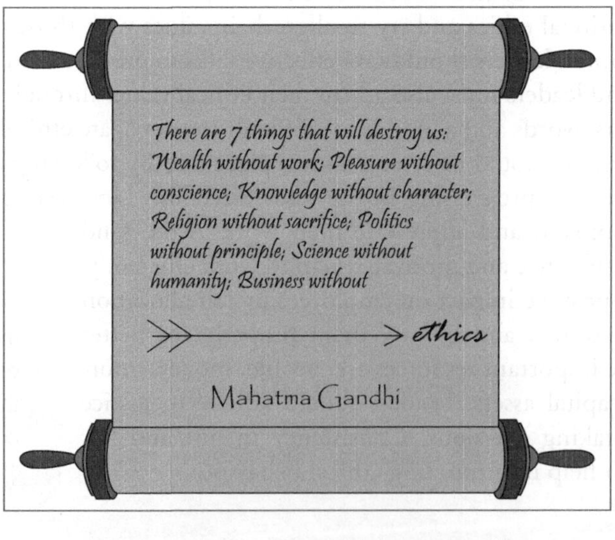

11.6.3 Positive Image

By following ethical choices, the organisation's management and its employees create a positive image of their organisation in the public domain. On such ethical choice could be proper discharge of the waste, generated by the organisation, as part of its social responsibility. This will disseminate positive vibes about the organisation among outsiders who will see it as company with strong integrity. Building positive public image will automatically attract more clients and the organisation's business will grow multi-fold.

Biases should be completely removed to build integrity in the organisations.

11.6.4 Decision-making

If the decisions, taken in the organisation, are unbiased and based on ethics, the organisation will survive in tough times. Ethical practice encourages righteous decision making in the organisation. It also paves the way for conflict resolution without much turbulence and difficulty. Even the employees do not object to sudden changes in the organisation if they have a strong faith that the organisation management takes decisions in the righteous way. The employees are sensitised by adherence to ethical practices and, therefore, they act in the ethical way even in difficult times.

11.7 PROBLEMS IN THE ABSENCE OF WORK ETHICS

Described below are some problems caused by the lack of ethics in an organisation.

11.7.1 Adverse Impact of Company Credibility

If the codes not follow robust work ethics, and people public get to know about its malpractices, then the organisation will lose credibility among people who will not patronise its business. It is a myth that the information about malpractices in the organisation does not reach the outside world. You cannot conceal it through advertising or other business gimmicks. Sooner or later media will smell the rot within your organisation and will let people know of your malpractices. Even if months later your organisation will not be in the news, its tarnished image will stay in the mind of people for a long time. It takes a lot of money and time to restore the image of the organisation, and sometimes it is never restored.

11.7.2 Lack of Cohesiveness among Employees

When the leader of the organisation displays a lack of ethical behaviour, it spells disaster for the employees as well as the organisation. First, he/she loses respect among the employees and then his/her unethical behaviour generate animosity and lack of trust among the employees. This environment is detrimental for the progress of the company as it deters the employees from collaborating to achieve business goals.

11.7.3 Performance Deterioration

The lack of ethics in the organisation's functioning leaves a negative effect on its employees' performance. They tend to make quick money by flouting rules and regulations. The honest employees, who are ethical in their behaviour, get demotivated by seeing their colleagues making progress through wrong means. This lack of motivation is reflected in their performance which adversely affects the organisation's progress.

11.7.4 Discouraging Unethical Behaviour

Generally, unethical practices crop up because of poor planning or loopholes in the business conduct of the organisation. Therefore, the organisation must not set unrealistic goals for its employees to achieve which they may indulge in unethical practices. While monitoring the employees' performance, they should be given practical suggestions and tips so that they could achieve their goals. Workshops should be organised to train employees and they should also be given credit for their good performance. Transparency in the functioning of the organisation will nurture trust, cooperation and positivity.

Summary

Lack of ethics can generate a lot of negativity and animosity among the workers.

Ethics have become very crucial in today's business world, which aided by technology is growing at a fast pace. Without rules and regulations which are the base of an ethical work culture, organisations go berserk blindly following their goals. Organisations need to adhere to ethical practices to have a good reputation. Their success is very much dependent on the ethical practices they adhere to. Considerations and compassion, social responsibility and financial ethics play a key role in an organisation's functioning. People's approach to ethics is very subjective and they keep learning them at every stage of their life. Ethics are the moral principles that govern a person's behaviour or the conduct of his/her activities. There is a correlation between values and behaviour. Values exert control over our attitudes and attitudes control our behaviour. Ethics should be nurtured in the organisation by reducing the gap between knowledge and real action. The new recruits must be assessed for their ethical values. They must be part of social gatherings organised by the organisation so that could learn about the organisational ethics and align their values with those of the organisation. The organisation must have a robust system to fix accountability. Leaders can impact positively the ethics learning of their employees by fair allocation of organisational resources and linking them correctly with organisational goals. Ethics is very important for the growth of the organisation as following them gives the employees positive energy.

Chapter Review

1. How do you think employee cohesiveness affects an organisation?
2. There is a woman employee who due to her close relations with the top management gets favours. This affects other employees who get demotivated. What can you do in such a situation?
3. Is it morally incorrect to use the stationery of your organisation for your personal purpose? Support your answer with appropriate citations.
4. Discuss ethical theories with reference to the practices followed in your organisation.
5. Why should an organisation be socially responsible? Do cite some important CSR initiatives of your organisation.
6. How can an organisation nurture ethics?
7. Describe the importance of work ethics. Is it equally important for the employees at all the levels?

Direct Questions

1. How can an organisation cultivate a strong and positive image?
2. Should new recruits be allowed to take part in the social gatherings of an organisation? Justify your answer.
3. If an employee in your organisation is wasting time watching objectionable pictures in the office, how will you convey to this person that he/she is committing a wrong?
4. Define ethics. Write five ways to nurture ethics.
5. Why an ethical organisation has more productivity?

Analytical Questions

1. Why is ethical behaviour an important value? What are the ways to inculcate these in an individual?
2. Mr. Satypal is a hardworking and silent worker who does not talk about his work with everyone. He suffers in terms of promotion every year. In the light of Mr Satypal's case compare smart work with hard work.
3. Mahatma Gandhi said, "The greatness of a nation and its moral progress can be judged by the way its animals are treated." Justify the statement.
4. You had written a research paper and your supervisor after making some minor changes get it published in her/his name. How do you deal with such a situation? Justify.
5. Unethical practices have spread to all spheres of life. What measures can you take to remove them from medical profession?

Resources for Further Reflections

1. Business Ethics: Concepts and cases by Manuel G. Velasquesz. Pearson Education.
2. http://www.teachwithmovies.org/standard-ethics-questions.htm.
3. Film: Corporate.

Caselet 1

Alpha Chocolate Pvt. Ltd.

Yash Vardhan is the Senior Accounting Manager at Alpha Chocolate Pvt. Ltd. Alpha Chocolate, a chocolate manufacturer of India, has a turnover of about Rs. 20 crores. Its products include different flavoured wafers, chocolates, candies and cakes.

As a Senior Accounting Manager at Alpha Chocolate, Yash Vardhan with eight years of experience looks after the company's finance. Murthy, one of the Senior Associates, has around nine years of experience in the company and is close to Yash. Ravinder is junior to Yash and works under him. He has over five years of experience in the company.

In the festive season of December 2013, the actual demand for cakes and chocolates was extremely high than the estimated forecast. The workforce at Alpha Chocolate in its existing strength was not capable to fulfil this sudden high in the demand. The company's CEO asked the HR department to recruit 10 temporary chefs to meet the demand. Since the demand for cakes and chocolates was very high than the expected, the company raised the price of its products by 10–14% based upon the cost incurred on their production. Due to extra production and hiked product prices, the company earned good profit and the CEO appreciated the whole team for this achievement. He rewarded Yash with a holiday package along with his family. When Yash went on the vacation for two weeks, Murthy looked after his work temporarily. He was assisted by Ravinder.

Murthy holds a technical position in the company. So, actually, it was Ravinder who under Murthy's guidance took charge of the accounting division of the company. One day while looking at few reports, Ravinder got to know that the temporary chefs appointed to meet the extra demand for the company's products were given higher salaries than his own salary. Ravinder was not supposed to look at those files but due to some reason he saw those files and he felt that the company was not giving due credit to his work. After this realisation, he was not able to concentrate on his work properly. He thought the company was exploiting him and he should complain regarding this to the CEO.

Questions

1. Explain what are the ethical issues involved in this case?
2. If you were Ravinder, would you complain about the issue? Why or why not?

Caselet 2

Satyam Computer Services Limited

Satyam Computer Services Limited (SCSL) was an information technology company founded by Byrraju Ramalinga Raju in 1987 in Hyderabad. It offered IT and ITES services to different companies. It was among Fortune 500 companies. In October 2008, the company claimed to have 53,000 employees. When Satyam Computer Services came under scanner, Price water house cooper were the statutory auditor for the company. S Gopala Krishnan and Talluri Srinivas were the auditors from PWC while V Srinivas was the Chief Financial Officer of SCSL. Maytas Group was an infrastructure and real estate company founded by B Rama Raju, brother of Byrraju Rama Linga Raju.

In order to increase his own share in SCSL, Byrraju floated two other companies – SCSL without permission of SCSL shareholders. Because of this, the SCSL balance sheet in September 2008 showed a non-existent cash and bank balance of Rs. 5040 crores with an accrued interest of Rs. 376 crores. Also there was an understated liability of Rs. 1230 crores on account of funds arranged by B Rama Raju. He did it in order to overcome the competition of any acquisitions or buy-outs. Because of the mistake of fudging the accounts committed by Byrraju, the deficit in the balance sheet was at its maximum and he felt it cannot be filled in the near future. The additional 13,000 employees with the existing 40,000 employees could not be retained.

On January 9, 2009, Byrraju confessed to media, "It was like riding a tiger, not knowing how to get off without being eaten. Since about 7 years, we wanted to show more income in accounts to avoid others from involving in the company affairs and any possible hostile acquisition".

Because of his confession, the Bombay stock market(BSE) fell down 7.41%. The then existing executive board of Satyam was barred by the Company Law Board. Insurance companies like Bank of America and State Farm Insurance terminated their services to Satyam. Credit Suisse suspended its investment in Satyam. GDP of India fell down by 0.4%.Jobs of more than 40,000 technocrats were at risk. Satyam owner Byrraju, Maytas owner B Rama Raju, Satyam CFO and PWC auditors were arrested and a charge sheet was filed by CBI.

Questions

1. Explain which factors made Byrraju go unethical.
2. What was the role of Pricewaterhousecoopers in bringing down the image of Satyam? Mention how PWC's role was unethical.

Chapter 12

CAPACITY BUILDING: LEARN, UNLEARN AND RELEARN

Learning Roadmap

After reading this chapter you will be able to:

- Know what is capacity building
- Understand why capacity building is essential for life
- Know the various zones of learning available to a professional
- Work on the strategies for capacity building
- Introduce plans for learning and relearning
- Know new online sources to get updated with contemporary programmes

PERSPECTIVE

Futurist and philosopher Alvin Toffler predicts: 'The illiterate of the 21st century will not be those who cannot read and write, but those who cannot learn, unlearn and relearn.' Actually, these words emphasise the importance of change and one's ability to adapt to change in one's life or profession. And, these words are applicable in all domains of life and practitioners of every profession. According to another popular saying, nothing stays permanent except change. It is our ability to cope with change that determines how far can we move in this world. We are living in an era where success in personal and professional life depends on how far we can adapt to new knowledge, skills, technologies and habits to make ourselves 'relevant' and 'saleable.' All of us face the constant challenge to change for growth and mobility in our career. Modern-day successful business stories feature the heroes who brilliantly mastered the art of 'change and adapt' and delivered their best to serve their organisations. You cannot be a great tennis player unless you perform with precision and show excellence on all surfaces (courts). Similarly an outstanding batsman is the one who can easily switch over from one format to another – from Test match to one-day match to T-20. The pace of change is so swift and demanding that the set of skills which were considered the most requisite ten years ago have become redundant today. And, the skills that we consider 'new' and 'updated' today may be not be desirable ten years from now. People who succeed in life are those who are constantly adapting to changes around them by unlearning old tricks and relearning new ones. Continuous learning is the new art of survival. Our willingness to learn and unlearn gives us energy to face competition successfully. Either we remain inflexible and do not let go of old skills or we learn new ones for succeeding in life and career. The choice is ours!

You don't learn to walk by following rules. You learn by doing, and by falling over.
— Richard Branson

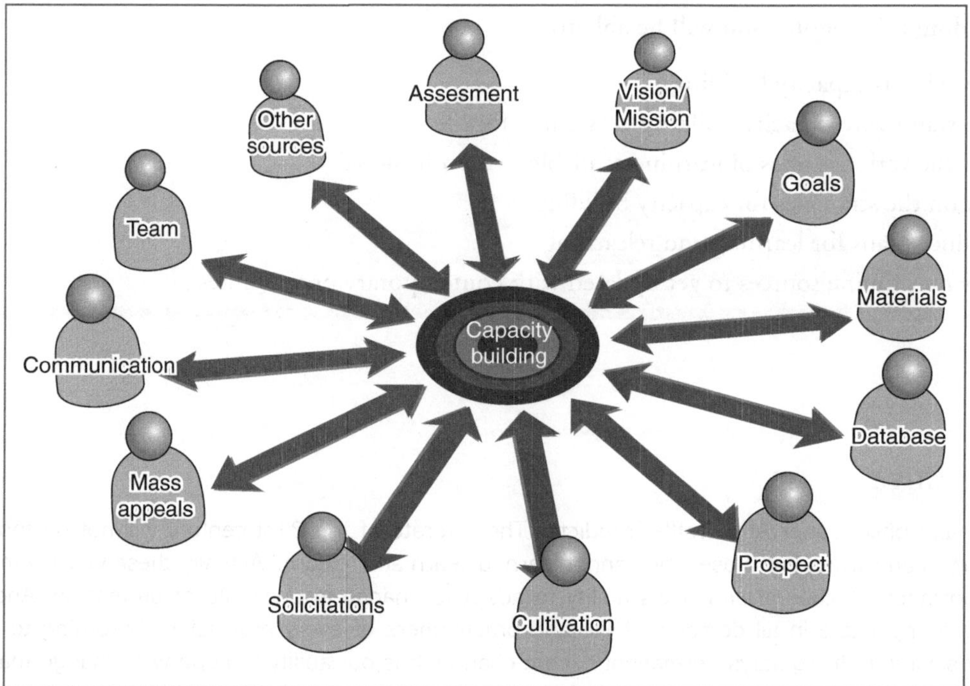

12.1 INTRODUCTION

Learning never ends. In the past, capacity building was the sole objective of university education. Learning or upgrading any skill or knowledge was just confined to the institutions of higher education. But now capacity building is mandatorily available and delivered anywhere specially at the workplace. The 21st century

We need to be creative and willing to unlearn so that we can separate our judgement from the old ways of thinking and knowledge.

workplace is volatile and demanding, be it an IT industry or a manufacturing unit or a banking organisation. The pace of change in every sphere of life and work is swift and forces people to adhere to it. To remain relevant and skilful in the workplace is a big challenge in this age of fast, continuous change and development. Therefore, to keep pace with the changes at the workplace, employees keep learning long after leaving the college. And, their quest for professional growth has shifted to a new paradigm of 'learning, unlearning and relearning' – a magical mantra that is gaining prominence at workplaces today. Continuous learning or capacity building is the real asset that professionals can bank on for facing competition successfully throughout their lives. Capacity building is the key to your survival as dramatic changes are persistently challenging the work environment. It gives you the adaptability to unlearn and relearn with the changing times and stay tuned to what's relevant in the workplace.

12.2 NEED AND IMPORTANCE OF CAPACITY BUILDING

In this era of fast and continuous development, it becomes critical for employees and organisations to move in step with the speed of the market and their competitors, otherwise they will lag behind with a severe impact on their productivity and profits. For this reason, capacity building through workplace training is vital to retain talent, keep the organisation growing and ensure development of all stakeholders. Lifelong learning for employees has become essential for increasing the productivity and efficiency of the organisation. The following are certain issues because of which capacity building has become important for employees and organisations to achieve their goals:

1. **Change is permanent:** Keeping pace with time and market is a big issue that companies and workers face every now and then. Their ability to cope with changes, particularly those brought by new technologies, HR practices, etc., makes their business or profession sustainable. Any resistance to new business learning or professional is like inviting a disaster. Learning new skills during one's job prepares one to face the dynamics of change and adapt accordingly.
2. **Technology is volatile:** Professionals cannot imagine to become resourceful, capable and productive unless they are tech-savvy. Technology empowers both employees and organisations to move forward for scaling new heights of progress.
3. **Innovation is the spice of business:** Continuous innovation by man to improve himself or being new technology is a prerequisite to survive in today's competitive market. Innovation makes things simple and people motivated. Capacity building ensures that innovative ideas are generated at the workplace to enable the organisation to handle new challenges and face competition effectively and create new growth records.

> People fear change but the pressure of change is constant to the universe. It is human and natural to be safe and static but most times, change is inevitable. It matters more how we embrace and cope with the change.

4. **It leads to greater productivity:** Capacity building improves efficiency of employees. Any training programme, aimed at capacity building, imparts new skills to employees for a better performance in workplace and in life. Such training programmes are necessary because with time, some skills of employees become useless, some do not match with new job responsibilities and some need revamping.

5. **People are our most cherished assets:** Creating an environment for every employee's growth and engaging employees creatively are the best HR practices that an organisation can follow to efficiently manage its human resource and develop it further for facing new challenges. The organisation's capacity building efforts must focus on employing its own trained and skilled human resources to nurture new talent, motivating the old guard and maximising profits.

> *I try to learn from the past, but I plan for the future by focusing exclusively on the present. That's where the fun is.*
>
> — Donald Trump

12.3 ELEMENTS OF CAPACITY BUILDING

There are three major elements of capacity building which emphasise the importance of building correct relationships and enhancing the productivity of individual and employees as well as the organisation. There are three major elements of capacity building which emphasise the importance of building correct relationships, enhancing the productivity of an individual as well as group and developing the civic bodies.

Partnership, organizational development and societal strengthening lead to capacity building.

1. **Partnership:** This element refers to the initiatives aimed at building or strengthening partnerships and enhancing resources. Good partnerships and better resources help in building capacity and promoting empowerment of each individual in the organisation, which lead to better work and maximum productivity through innovation and management.
2. **Organisational development:** Capacity building finally leads to organisational development by maximising profits and stakes. It also helps the organisation acquire a leading position in the market ahead of its competitors.
3. **Civil society strengthening:** Strengthening skills and building capacity of an organisation in the areas of strategic planning, advocacy, project development and management finally lead to the empowerment of the society and the country. These contribute to the country's progress globally recognisable progress on the economic, technological and innovation fronts.

12.4 ZONES OF LEARNING

A lucrative career is the dream of every employee. To make a dream career, learning at the workplace is essential. Workplace learning action plans are the best medium for new recruits as well as the older ones to learn and new things and unlearn obsolete ones. Successful organisations provide many opportunities for their employees to hone new skills and abilities through training. Some modes of training are described below.

12.4.1 Cross-training

Cross-training can be extremely valuable to organisations as well as employees. It is important to cross-train employees for various skill sets so that businesses do not suffer due to the absence of a key person at a critical time. Cross-training offers employees opportunity to learn jobs and assignments across a wide range of workflows. Such training makes employees flexible and multitasking to handle different workplace assignments with ease.

12.4.2 Formal Training

Formal training is a primary employee development programme for the new staff in an organisation to expose them to specific projects, technologies and procedures of the organisation. Formal training may be given in-house or through an external trainer to prepare the new staff to work in line with the organisation's objectives and future strategies.

Internal training is an in-house capacity building mechanism where senior executives train the new and junior staff about major problems, solutions, technology, resources and practices to be followed in the workplace. It takes place in a cohesive manner as trainers and trainees belong to the same organisation. In external training, experts are invited and paid a fee to train the staff in certain skills which the organisation considers necessary to face new work-related challenges.

12.4.3 Matrix Teams

The organisation forms matrix teams by taking selected people from various sections, divisions and teams to work together for resolving a common problem or for executing a project jointly. Matrix teams help utilise varied skills of different people for doing a common task.

12.4.4 Mentoring

Mentoring is the process of one person helping another to learn and grow at the workplace. Mentoring is of two types – formal and informal. In formal mentoring, the mentor and the protégé have some official agreements on roles, expectations, objectives, and meeting schedules. It is a formal commitment from both the sides in the form of an officially sponsored programme. In informal mentoring, the mentor and the protégé find some commonalities in each other in terms of skill and behaviour and agree to work together. Although, mentoring of such nature is often less structured and free to engage both of them without any fixed objectives or agreements, but the mentor offers all the requisite support, counsel and challenging situations.

12.4.5 On-the-job Training

No matter what jobs we do — professor, lawyer, doctor, software engineer, businessman, etc. — there are always new innovations, new skills, new machines. Everything changes. The best we all can do is not to stop learning to live fulfilling lives and successful careers.

In an organisation, employees are trained in their domains and departments so that they can have advantage of early learning and working on the projects or assignments that they are going to do in future. On-the-job training is quite effective as it imparts learning to employees while they work. It makes them familiar with prospective problems and solutions at the workplace. Sometimes off-the job-training is also planned with the help of consultants and experts from outside the organisation to fill the training gaps which the organisation is unable to bridge because of lack of training expertise in-house. Imparting on-the-job training is possible through various formats especially with new technologies where resource persons can directly connect to employees through Internet-enabled computers at minimal cost.

12.4.6 Job Enlargement and Job Enrichment

With diversity of workforce and global business environment, grooming and mentoring have become an integral part of any workplace leading to enhanced job satisfaction, personal excellence, and employment retention within an organisation.

To ensure that the personal growth and development objectives of employees are fulfilled, their job responsibilities are enhanced. This is done in a way so that employees could learn something of their choice while doing their regular jobs. Sometimes employees are given more tasks and assignments to expand their skills. Job enlargement also helps employees overcome boredom in the office and learn something new for their own progress.

12.4.7 Online Learning Programmes

Online courses are really the most rewarding gift for those professionals who want to update their domain knowledge and behavioural skills. Some of these programmes are absolutely free and are offered by the best universities with the support of their expert professors. These programmes truly enrich professionals with new skills and behavioural traits desired for achieving a high level of professionalism.

> *We learn by practice. Whether it means to learn to dance by practicing dancing or to learn to live by practicing living, the principles are the same. One becomes in some area an athlete of God.*
>
> — Martha Graham

12.5 IDEAS FOR LEARNING

The following ideas for learning will create more opportunities at workplace and enhance your skills, abilities and knowledge.

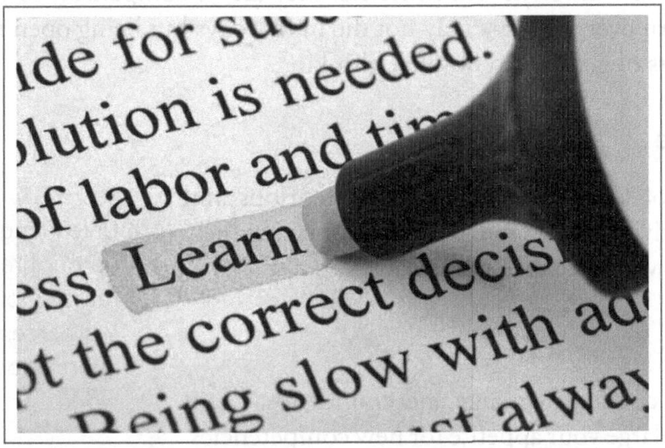

12.5.1 Just do It

One of the founding fathers of the United States, Benjamin Franklin once said, 'Tell me and I'll forget, show me and I'll remember, involve me and I learn.' This quote underlines the importance of doing something on your own in learning. In the workplace setting also, learning by doing leads to effective work management. What we see, hear, discuss and act, get imprinted in our minds. Learning becomes easy and permanent when we do it practically.

12.5.2 Welcome New Opportunities

Learning comes in different formats and installments. Many a time, our experiences teach new lessons or we discover new understanding of certain issues or tasks unexpectedly. Whether good or bad, these moments offer new learning opportunities.

12.5.3 Unlearn

Sometimes it proves good for your personal and professional progress if you get rid of some of your attitudes and thinking which are not in tune with the present times. This unlearning is essential to discover and learn new things and find out how different and beneficial they are in comparison to your earlier thinking. It is possible that what we learn over the years may not die in few days but being open to adding new knowledge will improve the prospects of getting rid obsolete thinking.

12.5.4 Be Childlike

Explore new territories of knowledge with fun. Be curious and innovative in all the activities that you perform. Learning new things becomes effortless when we take the lessons heartily.

> Unlearning is not about giving up our preserved knowledge, but rather moving beyond our existing perceptions to welcome new information and learn about the world.

12.5.5 Take Risks

Seeking new experiences demands courage and confidence. Leave your comfort zone and enlarge your appetite for new competencies.

Mr. Darwin once said, "It is not the strongest of the species that survives, nor the most intelligent. It is the one that is the most adaptable to change."

12.5.6 Learn from Mistakes

Do not get disheartened when you fail doing something. Our best lessons are only those that come after much struggle and sweat. Learning from mistakes provides a new road map for success.

12.5.7 Ask for Feedback

You can effectively manage your career graph by seeking people's feedback about your skills and behaviour. Be proactive to know what people think about your personality and the way you work with others. People's feedback gives you a clear understanding what do you have and what more you need to add to your profile.

12.5.8 Create a Continuous Learning Atmosphere

Spare some time every day to work on new expertise or skills that would empower you to handle new and sudden assignments effectively.

12.6 STRATEGIES FOR CAPACITY BUILDING

Capacity building strategies are employed on routine basis by many organisations depending upon the needs of the employees and jobs. These strategies are progressive in form allowing freedom to the professional from limitations and move them forward by offering something new and productive. The following strategies need to be focussed to build capacity and promote innovation and development in the organisations.

It is always significant to know what we are and what can we do to improve our personality.

12.6.1 Assessing the Individual

What do we know about ourselves and what can we do to improve our personality – this is an important aspect of the capacity building exercise. Our self-assessment enlightens us about our merits, demerits, abilities, attitudes, values, beliefs and overall personality. When we know ourselves better, we take right decisions while making career choices. We can enjoy no job unless we have the correct idea of what we have and what we want to do.

12.6.2 Identifying Competencies

> To help you understand yourself, self assessment is very essential. It would help you chisel your strengths, conquer your weaknesses, explore new opportunities for growth and neutralise your threats.

Our competencies, that is, our skills or personal qualities, are crucial for our progress as well as that of our organisation. Therefore, we must assess our competencies in relation to our goals and organisational objectives. The correct assessment of our competencies prepares us to deliver the best and raise the bar of professional standards.

12.6.3 Seeking the Feedback

Feedback of other people is an important indicator for validating your self-assessment – whether your perceptions about yourself match with those of others, especially your seniors, peers and subordinates. Be open to their criticisms or corrections and acknowledge that you are listening to them attentively. Being defensive about their feedback may not help you professionally but acting positively on it may take your career to new heights.

12.6.4 Assessing Organisational Needs

You should have a complete understanding of the needs of your organisation: strategic plans, management priorities, changing rules and regulations, future business trends, etc. You should be smart enough to sense the organisational setup and understand the needs of the organisation. You should channelize your capacity building exercises in tune with the organisational needs.

12.6.5 Preparing for Diverse Workforce

In today's competitive global business, it has become critical how we train ourselves to understand and adjust with a diversified multicultural workforce, a common sight in multinational organisations. Our diversity training makes us more sensitive and accommodative to the people coming from other cultures and social settings. With more and more companies getting into overseas operations, diversity training has become important for professionals to learn about cultural differences and for working efficiently in diverse groups.

12.6.6 Setting Your Goals

Set your own goals in line with the organisational vision. Goals are inspiring as they keep you learning new things in career. Our goals lead us to achieve our career objectives and guide us where we want to head in career or life. Goal setting also gives a clear idea what is most or least important for you. It does not let you get distracted from your career path. Along with goal setting, you can also have an individual development plan outlining you vision and action plan to realise it. This plan would serve as a guiding pillar to convert your goals into realities. Goal setting checks and supplements the organisational needs and individual aspirations for the future.

If you want to succeed, you need to set goals.

12.6.7 Networking with Professionals

> Networking is vital to professional growth and success. Your networking circle should include professional and personal contacts, people from alma mater, community groups, professional clubs and your colleagues.

Networking is the life-long management skill that one can develop for personal growth and building relationships. Developing a successful career or building company demands a huge amount of time and energy. So, it is critical for you to have a well-established network of friends and professionals who are willing to share their insights, learning, technical know-how and accomplishments with you. This sharing will help you overcome many a pitfall in your professional career or business. Apart from providing new opportunities and connections, networking makes you visible to people when you attend business events. You become approachable for new plans and collaborations in future.

Networking can help you establish a new business or grow an existing one.

12.6.8 Learning through Free Online Courses

On-line learning is a cool alternative to traditional education. It provides students utmost flexibility as these courses are offered asynchronously where students can enrol in any time zone, day or night.

Today, the Internet provides the learners a 'never before' and easy-to-use e-learning opportunity to enhance their domain knowledge and fulfil their professional needs and objectives. Online courses are really the most rewarding gift for those professionals who want to update their domain knowledge and behavioural skills. World's leading universities along with their scholars constitute an extraordinary online forum with an array of courses based on effective e-learning pedagogy and tools. Some of these programmes are absolutely free and offered by the best universities with the support of their expert professors. These courses help professionals learn from their homes/offices the skills and behavioural traits which are necessary to make a good career.

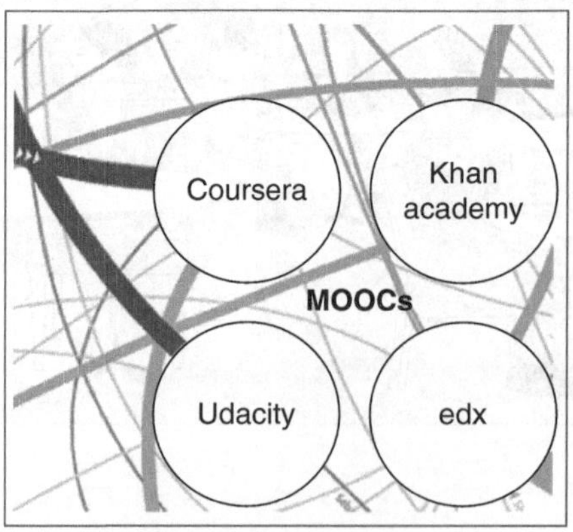

12.6.8.1 Online Learning Programmes

1. **edX:** edX offers interactive online classes and MOOCs (Massive Online Open Courses) from the world's best universities and organisations. Several global renowned educational players like MIT, Harvard, Berkeley, etc. offer their online courses through edX. These courses cater to almost everyone's aspirations and needs, ranging from economics to computer science and from food and nutrition to legal studies. The list of edX courses is quite comprehensive. These courses are taught online through newer technologies in the form of video game-like labs and 3D virtual molecule builder.
2. **OCW:** MIT OpenCourseWare (OCW) is another most valuable online learning portal that makes available almost all MIT course content. OCW is free web-based publication and delivers to the world the best learning opportunity through courses based on new and latest research inputs. It provides students cutting-edge knowledge and empowers them to contribute to solving critical problems of the world, namely, sustainable development, climate change and cancer eradication.
3. **Khan academy:** Khan Academy is a brilliant experiment in empowering people choose courses of their choice and learn them at their own pace. These courses offer unique interactive features that make learning very practical and easy with enough exercises and video content. Khan Academy is a treasure of courses right from general science to social science to fulfil expectations of varied professionals and students worldwide. It offers some exclusive programmes with specialisation in partnership with the best institutions like MIT, NASA, The Museum of Modern Art and The California Academy of Sciences.
4. **HarvardX:** Being the oldest educational institution in the United States, the Harvard University has been the global master in imparting the best practices in teaching, learning and research. It has created the global leaders in many disciplines and has more than 360,000 alumni around the world. The university has opened its classroom knowledge as 'HarvardX' to the online community worldwide and its courses can be audited free or the users can avail a verified certificate for a small fee.

Summary

We live in an era where change is the only buzzword that reverberates in every sphere of life. Today's competitive workplace demands that you continuously upgrade your skills and knowledge to remain relevant as a professional. Successful professionals keep themselves abreast with new techniques and skills in the fast-changing business world. Capacity-building is a mechanism that helps a professional in the workplace to acquire new knowledge and technical skills so that he or she can adapt to change and deliver the best. The productivity and efficiency of the organisation go down miserably if it does not care about capacity building. Capacity building strengthens the organisation to set standards of excellence and innovation, which enable it to provide unique products and services for making life better. And, in return, the organisation earns handsome profit. The capacity building exercise provides organisation an opportunity to use experienced and knowledgeable people to create more talented workforce leading to a cohesive growth environment at the workplace. Capacity building enhances the workmanship in a way that people stay longer with the companies and bring remarkable changes with their expertise and engagement. Many strategies and ways are planned by organisations for capacity building. All these efforts guide their employees towards a fruitful career.

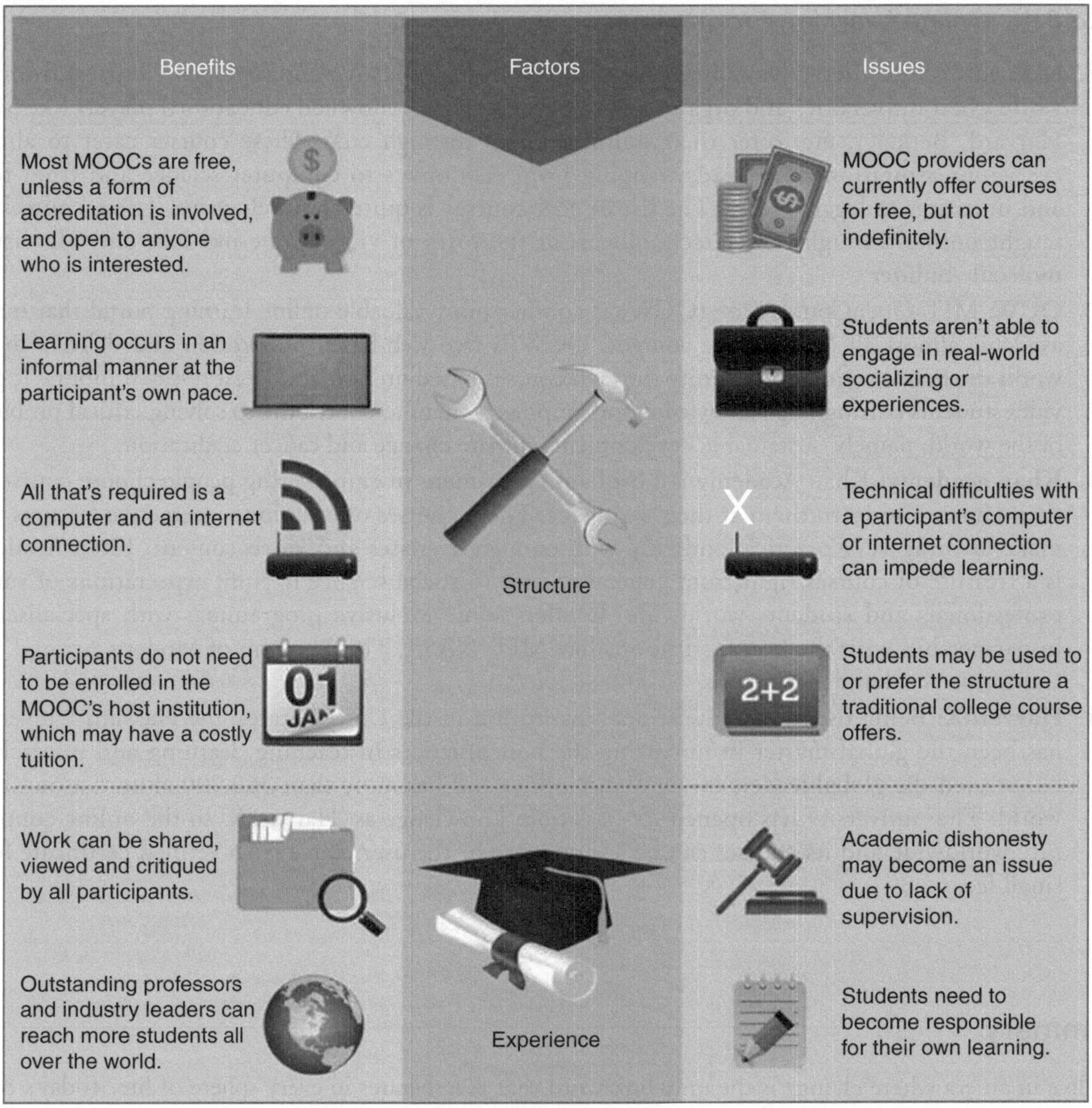

Courtesy: David Hopkins 'Technology Enhanced Learning Blog' http://www.dontwasteyourtime.co.uk/elearning/mooc-infographic/.

Chapter Review

1. Describe the issues that make capacity building important.
2. What are the elements of capacity building? Describe them.
3. What are some of the opportunities provided by organisations for their employees to hone their skills and enhance their abilities?

4. What new ideas can you explore for learning?
5. How important do you think is learning 'networking skills' for the development of an organisation?
6. How does mentoring groom a professional for professional excellence?

Direct Questions

1. What do you understand by the term 'capacity building'? Why is it important?
2. What are matrix teams?
3. What is unlearning?
4. Name and describe some online learning programmes.

Analytical Questions

1. Being the HR Manager of your organisation, which methods would you prefer to build the capacity of your employees?
2. Imagine you are a newly appointed executive. You are asked to report weekly to your mentor and get feedback from him. How would you assess the comments that you receive from your mentor and how would you apply his advice to your job?

Resources for Further Reflections

1. Azim Premji: Capacity Building Helps Ethical Behaviour. http://forbesindia.com/article/third-anniversary-special/azim-premji-capacity-building-helps-ethical-behaviour/32932/.
2. Read a book: I Have A Dream By Rashmi Bansal.
3. edX | Free online courses from the world's best universities: https://www.edx.org/.

Caselet 1

Intel India Capacity Building

Vishnu graduated from NIT Warangal in the electronics discipline. He joined Intel India as a graduate engineer trainee and was trained in the designing process of embedded systems. After training, he was posted in Bangalore, a development centre of Intel India. He was required to report to Arjun, who was his manager. When Vishnu first reported to Arjun, he found Vishnu a bright professional. Arjun placed Vishnu in a project that had to be cleared within 12 days, but most of the project work was still pending.

Vishnu saw this assignment as an opportunity and worked hard. He helped his co-employees who were quite senior to him and completed the project well before the stipulated time. Arjun felt that Vishnu had the talent to grow up the ladder quickly in the company. He thought Vishnu should be given ample opportunities to realise his potential.

One day Arjun called Vishnu to his chamber and gave him an assignment. Vishnu completed the assignment easily to Arjun's satisfaction. As a reward, Vishnu was given an advanced cross-cultural training to handle US clients. During the training, Arjun monitored Vishnu very closely and mentored him. After the training, Vishnu was sent to California for an assignment to promote their services and business. Arjun was keen to know the impact of Vishnu's plan for promoting company's services on his clients. The assignment was a success as the clients responded positively to the promotion done by Vishnu and they offered a project. This further strengthened Arjun's trust in Vishnu's talent of convincing prospective clients.

When Vishnu returned from the US, he was included in a special team which was working on an international project. It took one and half years to deliver the project to the client. Immediately after the project delivery, Vishnu was given the bigger role of a manager. He was given the authority to decide upon the organisational goals for the coming year under the guidance of Arjun. From here on, Vishnu he did not look back in his career and went to become the vice president of the engineering design division of Intel India.

Questions

1. Briefly explain how Vishnu conducts himself to build his capacity and moves up to become a business leader.
2. List the possible methods of capacity building used by the manager of Intel India?

Chapter 13

LEADERSHIP AND TEAM BUILDING

Learning Roadmap

After reading this chapter you will be able to:

- Know what make great leaders
- Learn about the traits of good leader
- Find out how leaders inculcate conducive corporate culture
- Understand different leadership styles
- Understand different stages of team building
- Know the various types of team working in the organisation

PERSPECTIVE

A leader leads by example. A leader must show the qualities that he/she expects people should have. Otherwise, he/she is not a good leader. You must have come across the term leader at a very young age. In school, you had a class leader (monitor), a band leader, a troupe leader, etc. You also have an idea of the qualities that you should display to be recognised as a leader. Some of these qualities are: command over language, friendly nature, knowing when and how to delegate work, etc. How aptly it is said by Bono, lead singer of U2, 'Real Leadership is when everyone feels in charge'. Good leaders can transform the work place into a heaven for employees where they enjoy working in collaboration with others. It is the responsibility of the leader to ensure that relations among the team members are not strained. Whenever a team shows reluctance to work, its leader plans a new strategy. If the new strategy also does not work, then the leader tries another plan. If he/she can make the team members to put in their best, then the resulting success is of the leader as well as the team members. True leaders reach new heights and also facilitate progress of their team members because they know there is no fun travelling alone. Leaders are like eagles. They do not fly with the flock; they explore new heights and challenge themselves and others to soar beyond the visible. Yet an eagle is not too obsessed with itself not to assist another eagle in distress and that is what makes an eagle a true leader. They spread their wings and soar.

13.1 INTRODUCTION

What makes a leader successful? When we remember some of the greatest statesmen of all time, we also think of the good qualities they had. What made them stand tall and different? It was indeed their power to move inspire their followers or subordinates make them partners in their mission. They were charismatic, enigmatic, and are followed as role models. They were respected not because of their position but because of their deeds. They were strategic in their moves as well as ethical in their behaviour.

Successful leaders not only nurture positive environment but also train people around them for leadership roles. Not thinking of themselves but building teams to achieve goals is the hallmark of great leaders. They are role models and source of inspiration for the members of teams they lead. They have a vision to see beyond short-term goals. They do not hesitate to use the potential of co-workers to achieve organisational goals. They also give credit to co-workers for their good work and enthusiasm. Even in times of crisis they disseminate positive energy and can-do attitude.

Among great leaders we can give the example Narayan Murthy, one of the founders of India's prestigious IT company, Infosys. It is because of Murthy's astute leadership and vision that Infosys has become globally renowned. He is a role model for many personalities not only in India but also abroad. Murthy himself is impressed by former British Prime Minister Winston Churchill, the gutsy leader who led Great Britain successfully during the turbulent times of World War II. Churchill showed immense confidence and courage to inspire his countrymen in those gloomy days. Churchill's example shows how you can inspire others to achieve goals in difficult times. A strong leader should have passion and perseverance to work tireless for his goals, whether short-term or long-term. High-level optimism and high aspirations are other qualities a leader must have.

Leaders devise innovative strategic plans to bring the changes they want. They do not get bogged down by roadblocks on the way to their goals. If a door closes for them, they do not appear crestfallen but start searching for new avenues to achieve their goals. This applies to leaders in every walk of life – politics, business, sports, science, etc. They can find opportunities even in times of crisis. Leaders are quite clear about their policies and how they want to execute them. Sometimes leaders also show flexibility in their conduct for the sake of happiness and benefit of individuals with whom they are moving toward their mission. But this does not mean that they compromise their ethical standards. Actually, the aim of their flexibility is to keep people around them inspired and full of positive energy.

The true leader moves with the team and make things happen. He leads as an example.

"Leaders don't create followers, they create more leaders."

— Tom Peters

13.2 LEADER AND LEADERSHIP

A leader is an individual and the capability to encourage the people around to work for the common goal is termed as leadership activities It is important to understand this distinction as the words 'leader' and 'manager' are used synonymously. A manager is also a leader to some extent but does not necessarily means that he/she is displaying leadership. A manager represents a formal authority in a limited sense. For business professionals, an important point to deliberate is how leadership and management are different. In the words Havard John Kotter 'Management is about coping with complexity, and leadership, in contrast, is about coping with change.' Leadership is one slice of management but management is a complete whole which includes planning, organising, staffing and controlling. Management can foresee what is coming next but leadership can also bring radical change. For the success of an organisation, it is necessary that it should have robust management as well as strong leadership.

13.3 LEADERSHIP TRAITS

There are many theories that elaborate on the qualities of a great leader. Contemporary theories stress more on action than just statements uttered by leaders. In other words, their focus is more on action than leadership qualities because if not put to good use, qualities are worthless. Whenever you think of an effective leader you associate with him/her adjectives like energetic, passionate, ambitious, intelligent, motivated, confident, dynamic, etc. These traits are essential for a leader but do not guarantee that a person having these traits will surely be an effective leader. Some people are born with these traits while others acquire them. The core characteristics of an effective leader as cited in *'Leadership: Do traits really matter?'* by SA Kirkpatrick and EA Locke are as follows:

1. Motivation
2. Drive
3. Honesty and integrity
4. Self-confidence
5. Business knowledge
6. Cognitive ability

> *I suppose leadership at one time meant muscle; but today it means getting along with people.*
> — Mahatma Gandhi

These are the traits generally required in a leader but sometimes the leader may need other qualities also depending on the environment in which he/she operates. The leader should also be able to adapt as per the requirements of time and place. But the leader's effectiveness should be assessed by his/her actions and their results rather than his/her qualities. An important role of the leader is to motivate his/her employees in the best possible way. It is not necessary that motivation comes only through monetary incentives. Motivation can also be fuelled through creative ways. A major objective of motivation is to keep employees relaxed and cope with stress in a better way. Small gestures such as keeping bean bags, providing massage chairs, etc. can be helpful in improving the work efficiency.

A leader should by his/her work and behaviour be able to motivate employees and serve as a role model for them. His role is also crucial in creating a positive, open communication environment at the workplace, which is quite instrumental in motivating employees. The leader should listen to employees patiently and facilitate frank discussion on all issues concerning employees. This way he/she can win the trust of employees. In many organisations, leaders do not have separate cabins but they sit with employees in one big hall. This arrangement is resorted to, to prevent building of any gulf between leaders and employees and to help develop a trusting relationship between them.

> Physical office environment, rejuvenating hobbies, refreshments and friendly relationship among the employees contribute to corporate culture.

Employees are motivated by giving them jobs they are interested in. The leader's task is to ensure that the employees' potential is tapped in the right way so that they could put in their best and reap the resulting rewards. The leader must develop an understanding of employees' work preferences and assign work to them accordingly. Rewards can be announced to keep the motivation of employees high.

13.4 CULTURE AND LEADERSHIP

Every organisation has a unique system of beliefs, values and ethics. This system broadly represents the corporate culture of the organisation. Corporate culture is an important element of the structure of an organisation. The corporate culture of an organisation is affected by its workplace environment, communication channels and managerial ideas and philosophies.

> The employees are contented if their potential is tapped and they do the job of their interest.

Corporate culture is an important factor contributing to the success of the organisation. Good corporate culture creates positivity and a high level of motivation and coherence among leaders and employees. If the culture is bad then it might act as a hindrance to any change in the organisation. It can act as an impediment to the good performance of the organisation. Under the influence of bad corporate culture, employees may target wrong goals and achieve dubious means to achieve them.

> *"Example is not the main thing in influencing others. It is the only thing."*
>
> — Albert Schweitzer

13.4.1 Salient Features of Corporate Culture

Some of the key features of corporate culture are as follows:

1. **Ethics:** Organisations which want to be known for good corporate culture just cannot do without ethics. In such organisations, leaders are quite clear about their duty to ensure adherence to ethics. They provide clear written information about the ethics to be followed to employees. By doing so, they facilitate enforcement of ethics among employees. They also evaluate the employees' performance by assessing their adherence to ethics.
2. **Target:** Achieving targets is essential for an organisation to progress. Leaders must have clarity about the targets of their organisation. It is their duty to explain to the employees organisational targets and make them realise the importance of their role in achieving these targets. Because it is essential for the employees to know where the organisation is heading and their role in its progress. If problems crop up in realising organisational targets, leaders can change strategies or take corrective measures to overcome the problems. For this, first, leaders themselves have to be open for change and then they should be able to convince the employees about the necessity of change.
3. **Cooperation and trust:** In an organisation the environment of openness can be created by inculcating the spirit of cooperation and trust among employees. Employees' trust in leaders is also a key measure of how effective is the leadership. For encouraging employees to work in team spirit, organisational environment will be such that leaders and employees should mutually trust each other. This helps in both leaders and employees concentrating on organisational goals which can be achieved faster.
4. **Creativity:** Creativity in the functioning of a leader implies that he/she is ready to face new challenges and think out of the box. If a problem is not solved in the usual way, creative leaders think differently. They do not hesitate in treading the path less travelled. In other words, creative leaders do not fear losing their job and challenge conventional thinking. They keep themselves in tune with the changing times.
5. **Risk:** No business or venture can be immune to risk. Therefore the ability to manage risk efficiently is an essential requirement for organisations and their leaders. They should be able to transform adverse circumstances into an opportunity to learn and grow. New strategy should be applied to draw an advantageous outcome from an adverse situation. While doing this, the reputation and good will of the organisation should also be protected.
6. **Empathy:** Employees must show empathy with those customers who are facing problems in their dealings with the organisation. They should also take the responsibility for their actions while dealing with customers. The empathetic attitude of employees helps in creating a positive environment for rendering high-quality customer service.

7. **Award:** Meeting organisational targets becomes easy if employees are rewarded based on the quality and amount of their work. While rewarding employees, ethics and fair play must be followed, leaving no room for biases. The merit-based reward system creates positive energy in the organisation and boosts work culture by fostering team spirit in employees.

Traits and qualities of a good leader.

13.5 LEADERSHIP STYLES

Although leaders or managers perform similar tasks of planning, organising, leading and controlling, they may accomplish these tasks in different ways, that is, they may have different leadership styles. Commonly followed leadership styles are: democratic, autocratic and laissez-faire. Each style has its own advantages and disadvantages. The effectiveness of each style is judged by its effect of the performance of employees.

> Just to know the well-being of your colleague can make a lot of difference.

1. **Democratic style:** Leaders or managers following this style give a lot of importance to the employees' role in decision making. For every decision, they consult the employees and take their suggestions. They give due importance to the employees' inputs while taking the decision. In the democratic style of leadership employees are made to feel important and empowered because when they are approached to give their suggestions, they get a sense of responsibility. This style enables the manager or leader to get varied perspectives on an issue or problem from employees who are closer to everyday realities. However, the leader ensures that only those employees are approached for suggestions who are experienced and matured. The uncertainty about the solution of problem is overcome with the help of knowledgeable and experienced employees.

The democratic style is also adopted to resolve the problems concerning a group or team whose leader is indecisive or cannot take a call on his/her own. However, a major drawback of this style is that it wastes a lot of time in conducting meetings. Reviewing or analysing all the suggestions of employees can also be frustrating because it requires a lot of time and effort on the part of the leader. It may also happen that every employee offers a different solution for a problem, making it difficult to come to a consensus solution. In a crisis situation or bankruptcy, when the company is on an edge, banking on employees' suggestions for a solution is risky. In such a situation, leaders or managers may have to follow other leadership styles.

2. **Autocratic style:** Leaders functioning in the autocratic style keep control over decision making, even for small tasks or issues. They do not consult employees at all. They only give directives to employees about their work and role in the organisation. The freedom of employees is curtailed and they feel unimportant because decisions are taken without their participation. The gap between employees and the leader widens because of the former's less involvement in decision making. The employees become indifferent and lose the enthusiasm and urge to show creativity at the workplace. The autocratic leadership style is losing importance as employees do not want to blindly follow the directives of their leaders or managers. The autocratic leadership style must not be adopted with the experienced employees who want to voice their opinions on important issues facing their company. However, this style can be followed when leading novice employees.

   If a big MNC follows the autocratic style of leadership, then the parent company has control over its sister concerns. In the United States of America, this leadership is popular. However, in Japan, individuals are given more importance than the leader.

3. **Laissez-fare style:** This style is based on free two-way communication between the management and employees. In the organisations following the laissez-faire style, there is no or least interference in the employees' work. Leaders give due respect to employees' freedom. Employees are not under supervision but are responsible for their decisions. They must not blame the leadership if they can take their own calls. This leadership is best when the employees are self-motivated, independent, knowledgeable and capable of decision making. This style is best for the employees who are goal-oriented, as it helps them realise their ambition. This style is not good when employees' ability is used for the advantage of the leader. Sometimes the laissez-faire style can lead to a lot of resentment and spoil the workplace environment. An employee who is recruited recently will not be able to take decisions on his/her own and that can lead to problems and the work may suffer.

   Within the same organisation different leadership styles can be followed. Often leaders have complete freedom to adopt any of style. But the happiness or sadness of employees depends on the way their leaders implement a chosen style. In addition to the above discussed styles, are two more styles called transformational leadership and transactional leadership.

4. **Transformational and transactional leadership:** These styles have robust ethical constituents and philosophical interpretations. Transformational leaders are multifaceted, talented and articulate. They have a clear vision of their goals and can put it in words appropriately. They look beyond themselves and go extra mile to make employees feel contented. They guide employees to nurture their talent and grow in the right direction. Transformational leaders are keen to get feedback or suggestions from employees. While trying to solve a problem, they do involve employees and

> Leadership styles vary according to the organisational structures and the kind of work the organisation is involved in.

encourage them to give their perspectives making them feel proud of their participation. Lots of time of transformational leaders is spent on coaching their subordinates and also in learning from them.

Transactional leaders have a centralised control over their employees. They strive for behavioural compliance by employees. They are responsible for rectifying employees' wrong moves or actions by giving them feedback, reprimand and even punishments. The employees working under transactional leaders look forward to applause and rewards for their work.

Leaders can change their style from transformational to transactional in the same situation. Actually both styles complement one another quite well. In real life, an effective leadership style could be a permutation and combination of different styles. It depends on the intelligence of the leader which particular style does he opt for in the given circumstances.

> *"Management is the art of making problems so interesting that everyone wants to get to work and deal with them."*
>
> — Paul Hawken

13.6 LEADERSHIP TRENDS

Leaders are constantly on the look-out for novel ideas and approaches to improve their understanding of the responsibilities and expectations associated with a leadership role. Described below are some current trends which are followed to build or improve leadership within organisations:

1. **Empowerment:** Today companies operate in a seamless environment where employee empowerment has become very important. Employees' participation in decision making is key to their empowerment. Through empowerment the self- esteem of employees can be bolstered, improving their satisfaction at the workplace. It helps in bringing employees together for working with enthusiasm to achieve their company's goal. It also increases the employees' pride in their work and their loyalty to the organisation.
2. **Feedback:** Constant feedback from leaders is essential for employees to improve their work and rise in their career. Leaders need to articulate their feedback positively. They must ensure that their feedback does not leave a negative impact on employees because it is meant to enable them learn from their mistakes and utilise any promotion opportunity that may come their way. Positivity is instilled by encouraging better performance and behaviour from employees, so the feedback must be given in a constructive manner. Leaders can use feedback to frankly tell employees about their mistakes, ways to rectify them and remove the misunderstandings the employees may be having about their intentions. The open environment in an organisation facilitates dissemination of proper feedback to employees and getting the desired improvement in their performance.
3. **Mentorship:** Today mentorship has become very important for organisations to face the challenges posed by their competitors. In mentorship, employees are guided to take best decisions when facing crisis or tough challenges associated with their work. The management gives employees ideas, suggestions and feedback to face challenges. Taking decisions to overcome challenges is left to employees. It must be noted that at the lower level of organisational hierarchy the mentorship has to be more rigorous because here the manager–employee interaction can be best utilised for

> Leadership styles are not compartmentalised, they change as per the need of the situation.

Friendly environment and cohesiveness in the team can do wonders in productivity.

the enhancement of employee skills. If the management is able to bolster the confidence of employees and motivate them, the latter will perform exceedingly well. The mentor should draw on the strengths of employees, channelizing them effectively for the good of both the organisation and the employee. A good mentor will also align employees' individuals goals with those of the organisation. This will facilitate personal development of employees by contributing for achievement of organisational goals. Mentors must understand that each employee is different and unique, therefore different strategies should be applied to tap the potential of an individual.

4. **Global leadership:** Today in the globalized world, organisations have to be highly competitive to grow and prosper at home as well as in international markets. To compete effectively in the international arena they must produce global leaders. Although the qualities of successful domestic and global leaders are the same, few additional qualities are required for global leaders. Global leaders need to take into consideration wider perspectives as they have to implement their strategies and ideas in foreign countries. To be successful across geographies, global leaders must understand cultures of different nations and should be sensitive to all religions, whatever may be their own religious affiliations. They must be sensitive and adaptable the lifestyle and culture of the country they are operating in. They should be flexible and also adopt the operational structure of their organisation in foreign countries, adjusting to the leadership styles prevalent there. They should be conscious not to compromise organisational ethics or values.
5. **Equal treatment:** Equal treatment of employees in an organisation infuses its workplace with positive energy. Equal treatment means treating employees according to their potential. The leader must identify the strengths and weaknesses of employees and accordingly assign them their roles. The leader should take a call whether the employee needs strict supervision or more freedom to work. A leader should know or devise the strategy to bring the best in employees and build good relations with them. This can be done by knowing each employee individually.

Good coordination and understanding make a successful team.

13.7 TEAM BUILDING

Ask yourself these questions. Can you do a big project all by yourself? Do you have enough resources to undertake the project? Do you have all the expertise to complete the project? If your answer to these questions is no, then you must form a team.

When we think of teamwork, we think of common goals of a team for which every member of the team works. Each member is equally responsible for achieving the team goals. Team building is a process where different activities are undertaken to establish positive communication among team members and encourage them to work hand-in-hand for better performance of the team. It aims to leave no room for disputes among team members and keep their morale high.

Advertising agencies use teamwork to design creative ad campaigns. An ad agency team, working on an ad campaign, includes the copywriter, one or more actors, singers, the director, the music composer, etc. Without forming a team like this, no ad agency can design an ad campaign.

In any organisation, goals are achieved only when its staff works cohesively as a well-knit team and give higher productivity. If the staff members work alone, then it will take more time for the organisation to achieve its goals. Team building is continuous process at the workplace. It enables people to work with mutual trust, support each other and also respect individual opinions of fellow team members. Team building is not an easy task. It takes lots of effort to nurture a team and keep it intact. If you have a good team, it can lead to:

1. Trust and support
2. Job satisfaction and dedication
3. Collaborative problem-solving
4. Creativity and productivity
5. Motivated employees
6. Strong policies and strategies
7. Clarity in objectives
8. Effective communication among employees

> An individual should quash self interest and work for the common goal to get satisfaction.

13.7.1 Team Development Stages

The four stages of team building are: forming, storming, norm setting and performing. It takes time to pass all these stages and build a strong team.

13.7.1.1 Forming Stage

In this stage team members are selected and team goals are defined. Those goals are set which are attainable. The selected members are delegated roles as per their individual capabilities. Normally, one dominant strength of each individual is identified, and accordingly he/she is given a role. For better team work the members should understand each other and work in an atmosphere where each member's freedom to work is respected.

While forming a team for designing an ad campaign, team goals are set for preparing and launching the ad. There will be different stages of making an ad: defining objectives, identifying targets and choosing formats, making roughs and thumbnails, proofreading and finally launching the ad in the right media. It is necessary that the schedule for reaching the team goal is set in the beginning with a proper time frame.

13.7.1.2 Storming Stage

This stage involves coordination for the activities for the work undertaken-it can be a project or a campaign. If there are problems on the way to team goals or project arrest them in the beginning. The project should start on the right track. All members of the team should work for the success of the project and shall look for any shortcomings in the project. They should continuously observe whether the project is moving in the right direction. Every member's perspective should be considered and the project should be handled creatively. Effective communication among team members is of utmost importance in this stage. For successful team work, the communication should be clear and precise. Gaps in the communication tend to create misunderstanding among members causing them stress. The communication should be task-oriented and truthful. It must be responsive, reflecting team members' willingness to collect information, taking risks and building and developing on each other's ideas.

> Success of a work depends on how smoothly the stages are completed.

13.7.1.3 Norm Setting Stage

This stage establishes tools, behaviour and rules which the team is going to follow. Rules and values are defined properly. The team reflects positive behaviour, trust, high motivation and good/open communication skills, energy and the group focus is visible. Team members recognise the potential of each other and channelize it in the right direction. There is a lot of encouragement for the team members. There is a high level of loyalty, motivation and group decision making. The energy of team is directed in one direction, that is, to work to achieve the team goals. Personal as well as team growth is encouraged throughout. Leaders also act as facilitators helping team members clarify the team objectives or goals.

13.7.1.4 Performing and Adjourning Stage

This is the final stage, where results are noticeable. This stage is marked with high productivity and a lot of support, unity and loyalty is reflected. Each member is capable of decision making by the time they come to this stage. The team work comes to an end. The work of team members is recognised and celebrated. Team member also get sentimental as they prepare for making another team. The gratitude to each other is conveyed in different forms. In new teams, individuals are put at higher level of positions and new people are also engaged. Continuity is maintained by revisiting the stages and guiding the new members.

It takes time and patience to move through various stages of team building. Every team goes through the above four stages. The timeline may vary for each stage depending on the skill and knowledge levels of team members. The leader plays a pivotal role in taking the team in the right direction.

13.8 TYPES OF TEAMS

Depending on the nature of the task to be accomplished, teams are formed. There are different types of teams. However, the most common types of teams are cross-functional and problem-solving teams.

13.8.1 Cross-functional Team

In this type of team, the level of participation of all members is same but their areas of expertise and specialisation are different. Suppose a university wants to relook into the structure of the courses in for its degree programmes, then it will form a team consisting of professors teaching all the subjects. Such a team will look into the issues related to the relevance, suitability, applicability, etc. of the existing degree programmes. Maybe towards the last stage of the team functioning experts from another university can give their inputs.

13.8.2 Problem-solving Team

Sometimes the organisation faces a particular problem to solve for which a problem-solving team is formed on temporary basis. It consists of people from all levels in the organisation, depending on the type of the problem to be solved. If the problem is related to the construction of a building, the team will include civil engineers, architects, workers, finance officers, etc. All members of the team put in concerted efforts till the problem is fully solved.

Summary

Leaders are epitome of good qualities. They are followed by the masses because of their charismatic personality and good behaviour. There is a difference between a manager and a leader but sometimes these terms are used interchangeably. For any organisation to be successful it should be working under a strong leadership. Leaders should motivate employees and inspire them to scale new heights in their careers. For this open communication is needed so that people can share their thoughts with free mind. Rewards create motivation among employees, therefore these should be given to employees from time to time. To nurture good work culture, the organisation should instil ethics, cooperation and trust, creativity, risk taking ability, empathy, etc. among its employees. There are several leadership styles and the one which suites best for the organisation should be adopted. Common leadership styles are: democratic, autocratic, laissez-faire, transformational and transactional. Each style has its advantages and disadvantages. Leaders should give equal treatment to employees. This will bring positive energy to work for achievement of organisational goals. Trust and support, job satisfaction, clarity in objectives, effective communication can be developed among team members by making them to work cohesively. The four stages of team formation are: forming, storming, norm setting and performing stages. Depending on the nature of the task to be undertaken a team can be cross-functional or problem-solving. Whatever be the type of team, there should be good understanding among its various members.

Chapter Review

1. How can you differentiate leadership from management?
2. Describe some key points of corporate culture?
3. What are the different leadership styles? Explain each of them.
4. Explain the current leadership trends.
5. What are the four stages of team building? Explain each stage briefly.
6. You have to organise the convocation in your college. What kind of teams you will form? How will you assign tasks to each team?

Direct Questions

1. How would you define a leader?
2. Which are the different traits that form the core characteristics of an effective leader?
3. What is cognitive ability?
4. What is a problem solving team?

Analytical Questions

1. Imagine you are at an interview for an important managerial post. You are asked 'What is your communication strategy as a leader? What are your communication beliefs?' Give your answer.
2. Imagine you are the person responsible for training newbies. If you could teach one thing about 'leadership that drives growth' to them, what would it be?
3. Consider yourself as an entrepreneur for a big start-up. In the initial stages, will you help people get what they want, or will you help them get what is right for them? Justify your answer.

Resources for Further Reflections

1. http://www.gallup.com/businessjournal/736/leadership-discussion-questions.aspx: Leadership Discussion Questions.
2. http://www.jqassociates.com/assessment/tools/leadership-effectiveness-analysis.asp: Leadership Effectiveness Analysis.
3. http://www.forbes.com/sites/piyankajain/2013/08/19/3-key-traits-of-head-of-analytics/: 3 Key Traits to Look For In An Analytics Leader.

Films to Watch

1. Chak de India
2. Lagaan
3. Remember the Titans
4. The imitation game

Must Read

1. Stay hungry Stay foolish by Rashmi Bansal
2. The Leader in You by Dale Carnegie
3. The seven habits of highly effective people by Stephen R. Covey
4. Team of Rivals by Doris Kearns Goodwin

Caselet 1

Maithri Industries CEO: Making of a Good Leader

Mr. Karthik was appointed the CEO of Maithri Industries in June 2012. He could not have joined the company at a more bad time — employees were resorting to frequent strikes and sit-ins to get their demands fulfilled; their productivity was very low; they lacked discipline and team spirit and had no commitment to their work. As most of the employees were illiterate, they were less competent than required to do their job efficiently.

Mr. Karthik started off with measures to solve the strike and instil discipline in the employees. He offered a new package to the employees to call off their strike. He formulated norms for completing work in time. He formed a disciplinary committee to see the work progress of the employees. Mr. Karthik did not allow the employees to directly come up to him with their problems or issues without prior permission. He asked the general manager of the company to resign when the latter was found violating the company's code of conduct. He also set targets for managers and ensured close monitoring of their work. These harsh steps compelled other managers to take their responsibility seriously.

After some time, while reviewing the outcome of his steps, Mr. Karthik found that he had succeeded in motivating the employees but due to their lack of competence they were not giving the desired productivity. To increase the employees' competence, he arranged in-house training for workers. He formed teams to make and execute plans in order to put things in order.

To win the employees' trust and confidence, Mr. Karthik visited their living quarters. To improve their living conditions, he sanctioned funds for repairing their houses, fixing new street lights and improving drinking water facilities in the workers' colony. He noticed there were grievances of workers against the authorities for not providing them with suitable houses and sent a special team to deal with the grievances. All these steps made the working environment in the company healthy and the employees became disciplined and really interested in their work. As a result, the company saw a substantial 30% increase in productivity within a year of Mr Karthik's taking charge.

In July 2013, after completing his first year in the company, Mr. Karthik reviewed his work. He noticed that the workers were more capable professionally now than before. But still there were few problems for whose solution he started devising ways. As he felt that the employees were more capable now, he made few teams with managers as their leaders for investigating problems and solving them on their own. These teams were given significant control and power to decide how the tasks given to them were to be accomplished. Mr. Karthik kept a close watch on the functioning of these teams. The leaders of these teams in turn monitored the work progress of their members. As a result, Maithri Industries reached the maximum production capacity of its plant by March 2014.

Questions

1. Explain different leadership attributes shown by Mr. Karthik in building team spirit.
2. What kind of a leader is Mr. Karthik? Justify.

Caselet 2

Coping with the HudHud Crisis: Making of a Good Leader

Mr. Nara Chandra Babu Naidu is the Chief Minister of the Andhra Pradesh State of India. He is the first Chief Minister to take office in Andhra Pradesh after the carving out of a new state, Telangana, from it. He took the chair in June 2014. However, four months later Mr Naidu's leadership qualities and managerial skills were put to test, when a severe cyclone, named HudHud, struck Andhra Pradesh.

On 7 October 2014, the Indian Meteorological Department sent out a warning to the Andhra Pradesh government about the approaching HudHud. Thereafter Chief Minister Naidu alerted the disaster management machinery and the state's police to make arrangements for protecting the lives of people living in the state's coastal areas.

Five days after the warning, on 12 October, 2014, HudHud struck Visakhapatnam, the biggest city of Andhra Pradesh, with a wind speed of 180–210 kmph. It triggered incessant rain in the districts of Visakhapatnam, Vizianagaram and Srikakulam. The road network in these three districts was paralysed because of flooding by the rain water and collapsed trees. About 70% of trees in Visakhapatnam had fallen. The airport and railway station in the city also suffered damage and were shutdown. The Rashtriya Ispat Nigam Limited, (Visakhapatnam Steel Plant) was also thrown into disarray due to heavy rains and its operations were halted. People in the city and other coastal districts lived with no electricity.

Mr. Naidu cancelled all his engagements and rushed to Visakhapatnam. But because of heavy rains and damaged road network, it took him around 18 hours to reach Visakhapatnam, which is about 600 km from the city where he was staying. On reaching Visakhapatnam, Mr. Naidu found the normal channels of communication with the local authorities were not functioning. So, it was difficult to know the extent of damage caused by the cyclone and arrange and guide rescue operations. However, he urged the officials of all departments to act fast and led them from the front for the massive rescue and restoration operation. He made restoring power supply to the city a priority of the restoration work. In just 2–3 days new electric poles were installed and power cables laid, restoring power supply in Visakhapatnam. The railway station and airport too began their operations after Mr. Naidu oversaw the making of all the necessary arrangements to make the runway and railway tracks operational.

People in Vishakhapatnam and the three coastal districts ran out of food and water. With demand of short-supply food items soaring, their prices touched the sky. To tackle food shortage, Mr. Naidu made arrangements for supplying packages of essential food items at a reasonable price to the cyclone-affected households.

The magnitude of loss caused by the cyclone was so massive that it was difficult to estimate it immediately, but the relief measures initiated by Mr. Naidu were commendable. He stayed in Visakhapatnam for almost a week, supervising the relief work closely. He kept on toes the officials in government departments making them work actively to lessen the woes of the people in the cyclone-affected districts.

Speaking about the government's relief measures, Mr. Naidu said, 'For the first time, a city was devastated by a cyclone, but the officers, who worked hard, could restore water supply in 48 hours, ease fuel supply problem, distribute six lakh food packets and carry out many other relief works. We will make people of Visakhapatnam happy with our efforts".

Questions

1. What are the qualities required in a leader to cope with a crisis?
2. Explain what is important for a leader to handle a team effectively. Give instances from this case to support your answer.

Chapter 14

DECISION MAKING AND NEGOTIATION

Learning Roadmap

After reading this chapter you will be able to:

- Learn about significance of decision making and negotiation
- Know why decision making is essential at workplace
- Understand the power of information and research data in decision making
- Know the planned steps for decision making
- Learn the techniques for effective decision making
- Understand how negotiation helps in decision making

PERSPECTIVE

Politicians, doctors, judges, corporate bosses and army officers do exhibit high-level decision making abilities even in the hour of crisis. History is replete with numerous instances where many people brought transformational changes in human civilisation with their decision making. In Hamlet, a drama by Shakespeare, 'To be or not to be' is a tough puzzle for prince Hamlet – whether to live or die. Hamlet contemplates that life has its own sufferings but opting for death is the worst thing. Just like Hamlet, we all face several decision making challenges every day. Right from choosing our toothpaste to buying a new car, we are involved in some kind of decision making – whether simple or serious. We come across several critical problems in our life but we cannot claim that we always devise right solutions for our problems. Any problem that leads us to some decision making is an opportunity for exploring new ideas. Sometimes despite having access to highly researched information on a subject, we end up taking an inappropriate decision concerning that subject. But even in the process of taking a wrong decision, we learn new things and this experience teaches us how to be better prepared for taking our next decision. In decision making the intention should be to take the most informed decision for fruitful settlement of a problem or an issue.

"Information is a source of learning. But unless it is organised, processed, and available to the right people in a format for decision making, it is a burden, not a benefit."

— William Pollard

14.1 INTRODUCTION

We take decisions every day – big or small, personal or professional. Decision making is intrinsic to our existence and growth. We all have our fair shares of decisions that we regret we should not have taken. A right decision taken at the right time leaves a significant influence on our personal and professional lives. How to take right decisions is a skill that we need to master and implement like other skills which are essential for personal and professional growth. This skill assumes importance when we take decisions for our people, organisation or nation. It is the wisdom of taking sound decisions that transforms a professional into a great leader. Often we see leaders making poor decisions because they opt for a poor choice or option. The outcome of a decision can make or mar a leader. Decision making and problem solving skills are essential for our personal and professional growth. While dealing with problems, how we balance and move forward is a strong reflection on our ability to negotiate and solve our problems. Today organisations critically assess the decision making ability of the people they recruit because decision making and negotiations play a vital role in the progress and productivity enhancement of organisations.

14.2 WHAT IS DECISION MAKING?

Whether taking up a job, selecting a college for higher education, deciding on a movie to watch, or opting for a loan, we do take decisions. Decision making is integral to our life 24 × 7. Decision making is the process of examining the available options, comparing them and choosing the most viable option in the given circumstances. An important part of any decision making process is to find a way to evaluate plenty of complex information related to the subject or issue of decision making for timely selection of the most suitable option. Great leaders are characterised by the value they add to a decision making process. They are endowed with the virtue of correctly analysing information and choosing the right course of action to settle a crisis or diffuse a dilemma. Mike Myatt endorses the need for 'hierarchy of knowledge' or the kind of information or resources available to decision making.

> Movie or magic show? Shopping or sleeping? Decision making is integral to our life. We select options and form opinions about every day issues on the basis of various reasons and emotions.

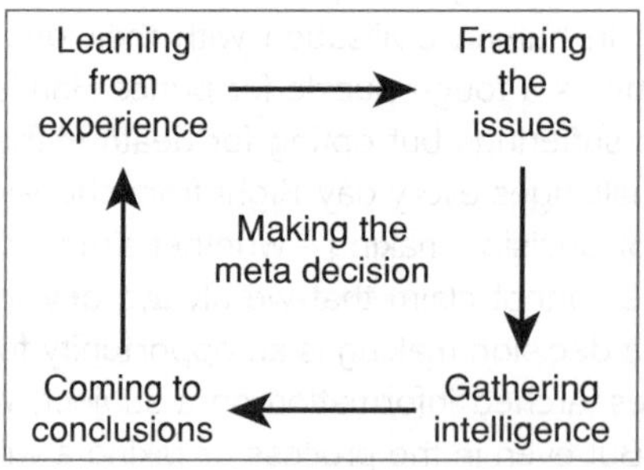

He finds that hierarchy of knowledge is instrumental in effective decision making and it could have the following attributes:

Gut feelings: Sometimes decisions taken on the basis of gut feelings turn out to be good decisions. However, it is not prudent to always take decisions purely on the basis of gut feelings or instincts. Gut feelings operate like an emotional filter in the absence of other decisive filters to support a decision. Our instincts work great when we combine them with other reliable analytics to arrive at a decision.

Data: Raw data is just a complex set of facts, statistics or inadequate resources that may not be of much value in decision making. Poor and incomplete data may lead to worst decision making.
Information: It is somewhat complete and independent data set that has been gathered after processing random facts and statistics. It is considered a more clear and valuable form of knowledge for use in decision making.
Knowledge: It is the best form of information which results from in-depth analysis and verification. It is high-quality robust knowledge based on research that leads to real performance and right decision making. It is real action oriented insight that you amass after churning up the oceans of information. It is 'doable' thing that gives authenticity and confidence of decision making to leaders as it is based on research and testing.

The hierarchy of knowledge is the most critical factor for consistent sound decision-making. The better the source of knowledge, the easier we can move from speculations to making strategic choices.

Unauthenticated and vague data would mislead the decision-making process.

However, it is mandatory to confirm the source of knowledge leading to a particular decision. Any bias in the inputs that go into decision making may lead to wrong decisions and their adverse impact. Sources of knowledge must be credible and what they offer and why they offer a particular information should be evaluated before using that information in decision making.

"The key to good decision making is evaluating the available information - the data - and combining it with your own estimates of pluses and minuses. As an economist, I do this every day."
— Emily Oster

14.3 STEPS FOR DECISION MAKING

Decision making is at the heart of everything that happens in an organisation: planning, organising, controlling, directing and staffing. Nothing moves at the modern workplace without decision making. Good decision making addresses all management and organisational issues, leading to meaningful solutions. To make right decisions, one must go through the steps described in the following sections.

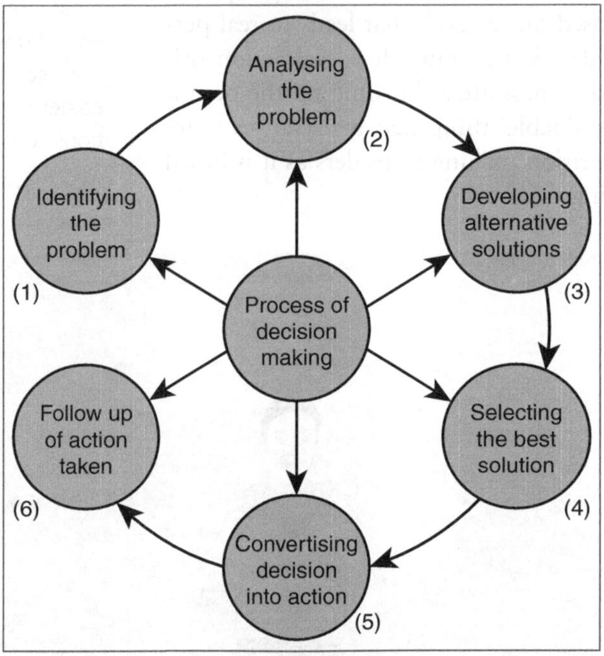

Decision-making process.

14.3.1 Know Your Problem

No decision making could be complete and meaningful unless we have a clear idea of what is to be decided. Therefore, first try to zero in on the actual problem. Smart leaders take complete stock of the situation to reach the crux of the problem.

Thinking, analysing, scrutinising and finalising involves decision making.

14.3.2 Analyse the Problem

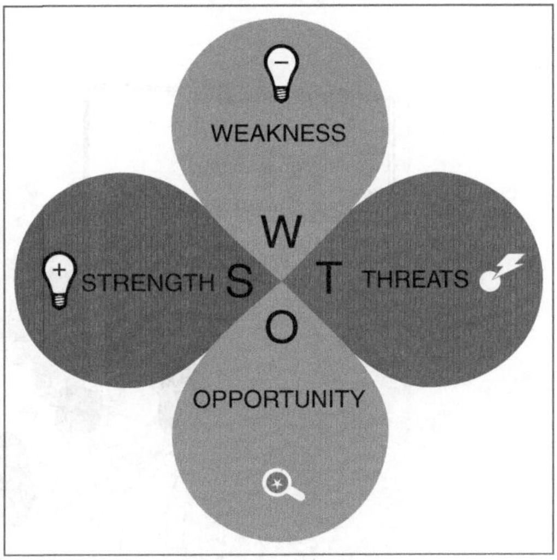

Any issue or problem that is to be settled needs thorough probing from different perspectives to avoid poor decision making about its solution. The problem must be analysed in totality. If the problem is diagnosed well, the decision regarding its solution is more likely to be positive and beneficial. You need to answer the following critical questions to investigate a problem or issue in depth:

1. How important is to make a decision?
2. What is its probable impact?
3. What would happen in case of no decision?
4. What information do you need to come to a decision?

14.3.3 Collect your Data

The kind of information or knowledge that you are going to apply to solve a specific problem matters most in effective decision making. The workplace is inundated with information easy access to which has been facilitated by communication technology. It is advantageous to have relevant and updated information that can help make decisions based on facts about reality. Use of well-researched knowledge in decision making brings clarity about possible solutions and infuses confidence in the decision makers.

14.3.4 Develop Alternatives

It is a crucial stage of the decision making process in which you think of all possible solutions that could be applied to the problem under consideration. Alternatives which are practical and cost-effective should be considered. Many factors are considered while developing alternatives. Great leaders consider time, technology, resources and budget along with other constrains while devising alternative solutions for a problem. All the people involved in finding the solution should be encouraged to expresses their ideas for the best alternatives.

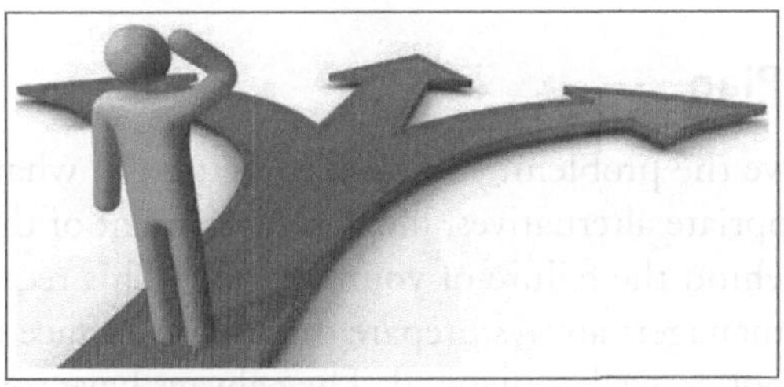

14.3.5 Choose the Best Alternative

After devising possible alternative solutions, it is the time to select the best one. The most suitable alternative usually has more merits and fewer demerits. Leaders look into each alternative in terms of its feasibility, effectiveness and consequences. Sometimes choosing the best alternative is not easy. When faced with this situation, leaders analyse probability estimates for the success of each alternative and select the one with a higher probability of acceptance or success in terms of cost, times and human resources.

14.3.6 Make the Decision

It is the moment to give your best shot. After examining thoroughly all the alternatives, you make your decision and communicate it to everyone affected by this decision. All the important stakeholders should be taken into confidence and explained how and why you have arrived at this decision. An action plan is to be put in place for implementing the solution and people should be encouraged to support the solution. A good decision creates a positive work environment by solving the problem. It gives good results and positive future directions. Further, a decision needs constant monitoring and evaluation to know how it is implemented, what are its consequences, what is people's feedback and what adjustments are needed.

14.3.7 Have a Back-up Plan

If your best decision fails to solve the problem, you need to figure out what went wrong. Improper identification of the problem, inappropriate alternatives, illogical assessment of the problem and poor implementation could be some reasons behind the failure of your decision. This requires a re-look into the problem from a new perspective. Smart managers always prepare themselves to face the adverse fallout of their decisions as they know things may not go well as planned. They always have something to fall back upon when things go wrong.

14.4 DECISION MAKING TECHNIQUES

As a leader you intend to take the best possible decision to solve a problem. However, every problem needs thorough investigation for taking the best possible decision to solve it. For this, you need to apply one or more problem-solving techniques to understand how best the problem could be resolved with available

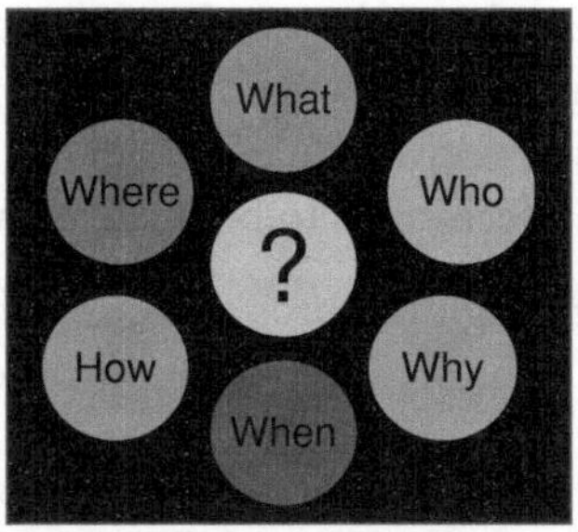

The five questions one should ask to make a decision.

alternative solutions. Described below are some of the practical and widely used techniques for finding an optimal solution of a problem:

1. **Brainstorming:** This is a clear and creative approach for developing alternatives. In brainstorming all members of a group, entrusted with solving a problem, think together about the problem and contribute their ideas to arrive the most viable solution. The basic idea behind brainstorming is to get fresh ideas from all group members. For the success of brainstorming, every idea should be welcomed and the group members should refrain from judging each other's ideas on the spot.
2. **Nominal group:** It is one step ahead of brainstorming as it includes a voting process to rank the ideas or solutions generated by group members. Every member gets equal representation in the group to contribute to decision making. First, every member states his/her solution briefly explaining the reasons why he/she opted for that solution. Then all the solutions are listed and later on ranked through voting to choose the most valued one. The idea receiving the maximum votes is accepted for implementation. In this decision making technique, it is the job of a facilitator to encourage all group members to share their choices and then invite them to rank all the choices to select the best one.
3. **Delphi technique:** This technique engages all group members to express their ideas through questionnaires about a possible solution of a specific problem. The group leader facilitates filling up questionnaires by individual members who never meet in person. This process of solution search keeps repeating as members share their responses, refines them until a consensus solution is reached.
4. **5 Whys:** No problem can have only one root cause or reason. The '5 whys' technique enables you to know the multiple causes of a problem. In this technique, a single problem is explored extensively by repeating the question 'why.' This technique is used to establish the cause and effect relationship of a given problem. The success of this technique depends on how appropriate are the questions asked to find the cause of the problem and its solution.
5. **Cost/Benefit analysis:** This technique helps in weighing the financial implication of each alternative proposed for a project or business solution. It analyses potential costs and profits associated with different alternative solutions. The best part of this analysis is that it will explain whether the cost exceeds beyond the projections or benefits fall short of expectations.
6. **Multi-voting:** Brainstorming generates many ideas to handle a problem, whereas multi-voting is effective when many people are part of decision making. Through multi-voting a large list of choices is reduced or narrowed down to a small list of top choices for further consideration or research. This technique is greatly helpful when an option or decision is favoured by most people but is not the top priority of any one of them.
7. **Decision matrix analysis:** It is a powerful technique for making a decision. It enables leaders to assess all available options and prioritise them when searching a solution for a complex problem. This technique is highly useful when you have a number of good alternatives and many other factors to look into

for taking a crucial decision. You use this technique by listing all values (options) in rows and all factors in columns in a tabular form. You can give each combination (rows and columns) a weighted ranking to ascertain which factor is crucial in decision making. All the factors under each option is added up to know the highest score about what decision is to be made or what issue is to be addressed first.

While taking any decision, leaders must weigh the pros and cons of these techniques and choose the one or may be a combination of them to serve their organisational purpose in the best possible way.

> *"During a negotiation, it would be wise not to take anything personally. If you leave personalities out of it, you will be able to see opportunities more objectively."*
>
> — Brian Koslow

14.5 NEGOTIATION FUNDAMENTALS

Negotiation is an art which you learn at every stage of life. You negotiate with people every day on various personal and professional issues. Professionally, the focus of your negotiations could be: resolving employees' issues, team work, improving business relationships, etc. Young children also negotiate with their parents to get things of their choice. They may put conditions like 'If I study, would you buy me the Firefox?' And most of the parents end up responding positively to this condition. Some people term negotiations as bargaining or haggling. However, negotiations are a means through which you can resolve your differences with people at the workplace or with your family without getting into a dispute or by resorting to heated arguments. At the workplace you negotiate because there is disagreement between you and your colleagues regarding the solution of a problem or goals of a project. If two parties conduct negotiations by keeping their ego aside, it can be beneficial to both. They also need to follow the principle of fairness to safeguard their mutual benefits and relationships. Good communication and interpersonal skills are essential to conduct effective negotiations. For successful negotiations, two parties sit across the table and discuss all possible ways to resolve some issues or finalise a business agreement. They accept the way that is most suitable to both the parties. For conducting fruitful negotiations, the following points must be taken care of.

> With all planning and preparation, a decision may go wrong but a true leader is one who emerges from such occasions and still manages the situation.

> Negotiation is a more precise and calculative work. It is highly desirable to be armed with right information supported by strong research and credible facts and figures.

'I win, you win' is the negotiation.

Preparation: Before sitting across the negotiation table, skilled negotiators do proper preparations, like determining the goal of negotiations and possible alternatives to be discussed for reaching the goal. Negotiators must look at the earlier deals where they or their colleagues had concluded agreements to reach organisational goals. Past deals can give clues about how to initiate and move forward in negotiations.

Problem analysis: Analyse the problems which are the focus of negotiations and see the benefits accruing to the negotiating parties from the resolution of the problems. All the issues – main and periphery – associated with the problems should be identified and the possible outcomes listed. A thorough preparation about all the essential elements makes you a perfect negotiator. A better agreement to a well-defined problem leads to an amicable promising solution than a great solution to an ill-conceived problem.

Emotional balance: It is very important to maintain composure during negotiations to arrive at correct decisions. Emotions have no room in negotiations they can lead to wrong decisions out of frustrations caused by emotional imbalance. If an employee has become adamant to go on leave and in the prevailing office situation, the leave cannot be allowed. But the boss because of emotional considerations allows the employee to take leave, and the office work suffers. In another example, if to keep employees in good humour, the boss takes the irrational decision of granting them pay hikes, though the company does not have enough resources to bear this hike, it will again not be a right approach to handle the situation. It is better not to negotiate and walk away from the deal with your papers than losing one' trust and temperament.

Effective listening: During negotiations it is very important that both the parties should not talk excessively. They should also be patient enough to listen to each other. They must pay full attention to non-verbal cues and interpret them properly. Non-verbal cues speak volumes about the real intention of negotiators. If you are a good listener then this will enable you to identify those points of compromise where you are not going to lose much. So do not waste your energy by indulging in unnecessary talk.

Teamwork: Negotiation is not always one-to-one. It can be many-to-many or one-to-many. If the group works according to team plan with good relations and understanding, the outcome can be favourable. Both the sides should think to work together to reach to win-win situation.

Communication with words: Articulate negotiators have an advantage over others as they can communicate with clarity and effectiveness. Good communicators leave less scope of creating misunderstandings, and therefore can come out with several permutations and combinations of the problem. You can choose passive, aggressive or assertive style while negotiating but assertive style will be the best choice to get mutually beneficial outcomes from negotiations.

> A negotiation is basically an act of giving and taking. You should know what you can give in return of what you get from other.

Interpersonal skills: Interpersonal skills are a key factor in maintaining good relationship with the people involved in negotiations. The negotiator must maintain composure and patience and should be able to persuade his/her counterpart without manipulations. This helps in maintaining a cordial relationship between negotiators.

Decision making ability: Leaders must be quick in taking right decisions during negotiations. Indecisiveness on their part can let a bargaining or beneficial opportunity slip from their hands. If decisions are not made then the deadlock will remain as it was before the start of negotiations.

Ethics: Trust between the parties involved in negotiations can be built only if both the parties conduct themselves in an ethical way. They must fulfil the promises made to each other after reaching certain decisions during negotiations. Whatever be the decisions, both the parties should respect what has been agreed upon.

> *"You can't negotiate with people who say what's mine is mine and what's yours is negotiable."*
> — John F. Kennedy

14.6 NEGOTIATION STYLES

There are three basic negotiation styles a negotiator can adopt. These styles are explained below.

14.6.1 Red Style

The Red Style negotiators' are highly competitive and therefore considered intensely competitive/ distributive bargainers. They follow the ideology that one side's gain is other side's loss (also called zero sum or value claiming). They are self-centred, hard negotiators who do not trust the other party and therefore focus on gaining the maximum share of the pie.

14.6.2 Blue Style

The Blue Style negotiators adopt a cooperative style and believe in looking for a wide range of interests to be addressed and served. They focus on building long-term relationships for mutual benefit of the parties involved in negotiations and create value for them (also called non-zero sum or value creation).

14.6.3 Purple Style

The Purple Style negotiators represent a fusion of Red and Blue Style negotiators. They believe in Give/Get principle, that is having a trading behaviour where they gain something of their choice and give something of others' choice. They are called principled negotiators as they use a strict tit-for-tat strategy. They are open, learnable, cautious and decent.

14.7 MAJOR NEGOTIATION CONCEPTS

The following concepts help both the sides make informed decisions about possible options for a deal. With these concepts, they explore what are their 'best' and 'worst' points and how are they going to negotiate them along any alternative deal.

14.7.1 BATNA (Best Alternative to a Negotiated Agreement)

While preparing for negotiations, you investigate which resources you control or influence that can serve your interests. This establishes the baseline of your walking-in BATNA. This helps you create a benchmark against which you can measure whether the negotiation process is strengthening, weakening, or changing your BATNA. The term BATNA was coined by Roger Fisher and William Ury in 1981. It means the best you can do if your counterpart refuses to negotiate on terms acceptable to you. BATNA provides you a clear picture of what is in your piggy bag if you decide to walk away from the negotiation table without an agreement. For instance, you go to buy a watch. One shopkeeper offers you a watch for Rs. 2500. You move to the next shopkeeper who offers the same watch at Rs. 2550. You start negotiating for a price reduction. You already have a BATNA of Rs. 2500 and want the shopkeeper to settle for a price below Rs. 2500.

BATNA is crucial for negotiations as no decision can be made without knowing what alternatives are available. Before starting negotiations put all the possible choices on your side. Having a good BATNA enhances your negotiating power because if you are aware of good alternatives then you need not concede much. You can also force the other side harder. You will not even care much whether you achieved the target or not. If you do not have a good BATNA, then you will give in to the other person's demand. So improve your BATNA as much as possible to be a good negotiator.

> Be clear about your negotiation style. Know and chalk out your list of goals and decide which issues you can compete, compromise, or avoid to cut a deal.

14.7.2 WATNA (Worst Alternative to a Negotiated Agreement)

The term WATNA defines the leverage the other party has over you in the negotiation process. It works positively for your counterpart in negotiations than you.

14.7.3 ZOPA (Zone of Possible Agreement)

It refers to the overlapping of the aspiration ranges of the two negotiating parties. In other words, it represents a range of prices within which the negotiating parties may reach an agreement.
Before every negotiation, one should be prepared to handle the following questions:

1. What are the negotiation objectives?
2. Are you going to address critical factors like time, prices, performances and technology?
3. What is the scope of your negotiation plan? What you may surrender or what you may not compromise with?
4. Are you planning to take a greater risk for greater margins of return?
5. Are you prepared to face the consequences if negotiation breaks down?

Summary

Decision making and problem solving abilities are the key skills for doing good in business and life. How we explore a problem and come to a solution exhibit our managerial acumen and leadership vision. Decision making is the process of weighing our choices, comparing them and taking the right call. For making a good decision, a leader must have clear thinking, strong conviction and effective implementation of decision. His/her ability to take right decisions has an important bearing on the future and growth of his/her organisation. Every organisation emphasises on right and timely decision making and effective negotiations as they are vital for its progress and productivity. Effective and successful decision making requires following a systematic process: identifying and analysing a problem, gathering all the facts, pondering over available choices, choosing the best option and taking action for implementation of the chosen. There are many techniques that leaders can use, like brainstorming, multi-voting, decision matrix and nominal group, to assess their alternatives before coming to the final choice. Negotiation is the organised process through which two parties try to settle a dispute or reach an agreement. The negotiation process demands that we listen to our counterparts in negotiations, respect them and treat every issue seriously. Negotiation ability is a skills that we use all our life time. It is not about winning every time but succeeding while collaborating with others. It is exploring a common link between two or more groups to resolve a dispute and reach an agreement.

Chapter Review

1. What is decision making and why it is essential at the workplace?
2. Discuss in detail the importance of decision making and negotiations at the workplace.
3. What is the role of knowledge in decision making?
4. Explain the major techniques commonly employed to arrive at a decision.
5. How does power and trust influence the process of negotiation?

Direct Questions

1. Discuss how the brainstorming technique is different from the nominal group technique.
2. Explain the requirements for the decision making process and negotiations.
3. How would you analyse a problem for effective decision making?
4. Why decisions taken by gut instincts are not proper?
5. What are the basic steps followed for effective decision making at the workplace?

Analytical Questions

1. As a project leader usually what leads you to choose a particular alternative over others options and how often your choice proves right?
2. How important is people's feedback in decision making and how would you obtain it?

Resources for Further Reflections

1. http://smallbusiness.chron.com/importance-business-decision-making-43457.html Importance of decision making in workplace.
2. http://theconversation.com/when-negotiating-who-should-make-the-first-offer-37643when negotiating, who should make the first offer?
3. https://www.youtube.com/watch?v=NQuhJdVqxKk video on decision making and negotiation through role playing.
4. A decision making perspective to negotiation http://www.hbs.edu/faculty/Publication%20Files/10-002.pdf.

Caselet 1

Negotiating During Interview

AT and T is a Telecom giant that was started in Texas by Delaware on 5 October, 1983. Today it has several offices around the globe. It considers young minds the best talent to bank upon. So it recruits final year graduating students every year from many reputed universities. For the academic year 2014, they came for recruitment to the campus of University of Mumbai. The recruiting team comprised of University Relations Manager, HR Manager, Technical Manager and two support staff. The University Relations Manager short listed the candidates based on their requirements and the CVs of students. The Technical Manager interviewed the candidates and finally the HR Manager started conducting interviews. Soon came the turn of Harsha Vardhan, final year Electronics Department student, to face the HR Manager. The conversation between them went like this:

HR Manager: Well! Mr. Harsha, (looking at his profile) do you think you will be selected here?

Harsha: Of course, Sir.

HR Manager: Why?

Harsha: As it is clearly mentioned in my CV that I probably possess the best skills for the advertised job and have done hands-on internship in the same field.

HR Manager: So, if I recruit you, I would be able to pay you only INR 24 lakhs per annum because our company is not performing well these days. Are you ready to work for this pay?

Harsha: Sir, as you saw my profile, you understand my consistency in scoring full marks in analytical subjects and hopefully you are having my technical interview score also with you. So INR 24 lakhs is less in terms of your expectations and my expertise but I'm sure I will work for AT & T because this is my dream company.

HR Manager: OK. Then what are you expecting us to pay?

Harsha: Sir, I'm looking at INR 36 lakhs, in which case I will work with analytics team in India and if the offer is in US, I'm looking above INR 50 lakhs.

HR Manager: All right Mr. Harsha Vardhan! Wish you all the best. We will mail you the result of the interview within two days.

Harsha: Thank you, Sir.

Questions

1. If you were the HR Manager, do you think the student is an effective negotiator? Why or why not.
2. Explain the importance of making a first offer by the HR Manager.

Caselet 2

Decision Making at Swift Technologies

Swift Technologies is an engineering company which takes electrical, civil, telecom and mechanical contracts from different vendors and serves them as per their requirement. The company's clients include South Central Railways, BSNL, Railtel Corporation of India Ltd., TV Sundaram Iyengar and Sons Ltd. and many more. Surya Hanuman Sharma is the Managing Partner of the company who looks after its operations while Surya Narayana Manoj is its Executive Engineer who takes care of its finances.

The company comes to know about an open tender for overhead electrical laying work between Kirandul and Jagadalpur stations of the Waltair Division in East Coast Railways (ECoR). The contract is of INR 43 lakhs and has to be completed in six months from the date of acceptance of the offer letter.

The required number of blue collar employees required for completion of this contract in six months is 18. Presently the company has on its rolls only 12 blue collar employees. Also the client ECoR is asking for a special supervisor who at least has bachelor's degree in electrical engineer.
Mr. Sharma is planning to quote the tender at 9% above the tender base price. Mr. Manoj presents the following facts regarding the proposed contract when Mr. Sharma asks for a financial plan for submitting the tender quote:

- Kirandul to Jagadalpur railway track route is about 150 km.
- Overhead electrical laying work costs INR 21.50 per metre.
- The wage for a blue collar employee is INR 300 per day.
- Salary for a dedicated electrical engineer is INR 30,000 per month.

Another important aspect related to the contract is that the Kirandul–Jagadalpur railway track is in the naxal zone and hence its work may be disturbed at times due to naxalite activities. Also it is a single line track with no option to divert the trains moving on it. Hence, the train traffic on the line might delay completion of the project within specified time.

The company has to pay an EMD (*earnest money deposit*) of 2% of the total value if they secure the tender before starting the project.

Questions

1. If you were Mr. Surya Hanuman Sharma, will you quote the tender? If so, will it be at 9% above the base price or more or less? Why?
2. What factors will you consider while taking the decision?

Chapter 15

STRESS AND TIME MANAGEMENT

Learning Roadmap

After reading this chapter you will be able to:

- Know the reasons of stress in an individual's life
- Learn about the signs of stress
- Know the ways to cope with stress
- Understand the importance of time management
- Learn the four Ds of management

PERSPECTIVE

Sunil Goyal is a senior joint president in Mangalam Cements which has an annual turnover of INR 7000 crores. A chartered accountant, Sunil looks after the company's finances. He is meticulous in maintaining the company's records and directly reports to the company's chairman, Manish Patni. The chairman has full faith in Sunil and does not question him on small matters. Sunil is preparing arduously for the board meeting which is very close to his trip to US. He has kept all the papers ready for presenting in the meeting. He took almost one and a half month to prepare them. Just a day before he had the file containing all the necessary papers ready and he decided to show the file to the chairman. He took a cab to reach the chairman's office. However, while getting down from the cab, he forgot to pick the file which he had kept on the cab seat beside him. He did not realise his folly till he was about to enter the chairman's office. But now it was too late to do something to recover the file as only two minutes were left for the meeting to begin.

Sunil met the chairman without the file to show which this meeting was fixed. It was embarrassing for him to inform the chairman that he had left the file in the cab. The chairman was surprised and also angry to find Sunil so careless. He started scolding Sunil who could not bear the chairman's reprimand. Somehow he suppressed his anger and left the meeting with the promise to get all the papers in an hour. After reaching his office, Sunil started his computer to get fresh prints of all the papers he had prepared for the board meeting. However, he was shocked not finding to a single computer file of these papers. His heart was pounding and sweat drops appeared on his face. He probably had deleted all the files after taking their prints to maintain secrecy. He did not know how to deal with the situation as presenting these papers at the board meeting was solely his responsibility. Now he got so stressed and simply did not know what to do next.

"Stress kills, and concentration fulfills."

— Franklin Gillette

15.1 INTRODUCTION

With modern life becoming increasingly complicated and fast moving, the stress associated with our daily routine has increased manifold. Apparently, we think we cannot do anything about stress. For, the rush hour heavy traffic will always be there, bills will have to be paid regularly, and we just cannot ignore family obligations. Sometimes we may feel that we do not have any grip over our stressful life. But ignoring stress or taking it as something beyond our control is not the right way to cope with it. Instead we must try to find out the causes of stress in the same way as we search for the reasons of our problems. We all can have control over our life, if are able to manage stress successfully. Managing stress means taking control of our thoughts, emotions, responsibilities, etc.

We must also understand that without learning to cope with stress we just cannot build a career of our dreams. For, stress is also an important common element of a modern workplace. If not managed effectively, the workplace stress adversely affects a professional's performance preventing further development of his/her skills or realisation of his/her true potential. It also leaves a harmful effect on the professional's health. Yes, we cannot have any control over the stressful workplace environment but it does not mean that we cannot have control over ourselves. Remember with a positive attitude, we can bring a lot of difference in our behaviour and our outlook towards life and profession. We need to focus on the things we want to achieve. If we have come to a situation of stalemate, we simply need to change our path instead of remaining stuck there.

15.2 STRESS IN TODAY'S TIME

Modern life because of the uncertainty associated with troubled and shaky economies is akin to a roller coaster ride. Your emotional security is always at stake as you keep hearing words like 'layoffs', 'budget deductions' and 'uncertain transfers'. When you start feeling insecure, you come in the grip of stress. Living under continuous stress affects your health adversely. However, you can cope with stress without any adverse effects by learning how to manage it. An easy way is to check those situations from developing, which give you stress, by taking pre-emptive measures. Keep a positive attitude and spread positivity around you, so that negativity remains at bay. Your positive demeanour pulls people towards you. Having positive emotions is contagious and you affect other persons by your emotions. You can take a lead to reduce overall stress at the workplace. Get into communication to improve your relations with colleagues and boss. It shows your magnanimity if you take initiative in improving the physical and mental health of employees.

In most of the occasions stress grapples the individual because of lack of time management.

"If you are feeling stressed out, stop and take 10 deep breaths... it really does help! Then focus your mind on one thing and one thing only; things are only overwhelming when you look at them all at once."
— B. Dave Walters

15.2.1 Identify the Stress Source

When you decide to manage your stress, the first step is to identify the source of your stress. It is not an easy task because life is not well defined. You may ignore or fail to identify the real source or thought that cause you stress. The most common cause of stress among students and employees is meeting deadlines. They fail to honour deadlines due to overwork or because of their dilatory approach to work. So you must identify the real cause of stress –overburden or procrastination. You can recognise true sources of stress by analysing your attitude, behaviour and habits. You may ask these questions to yourself – Is your stress ephemeral –it just comes and goes away quickly? Or has stress become an integral part of your life and you have got habituated to it? Do you feel the cause of your stress is the people surrounding you or the events? Unless you find answers to these questions, you will remain engulfed in stress.

15.2.2 Signs of Stress

Perennial stress leads to major health problems, therefore must be kept at bay.

Signs of stress in the individual can be gauged quickly as the work efficiency mitigates. The person starts showing the following signs:

1. Lack of interest in work
2. Getting irritated at small things
3. Withdrawal from working groups
4. Muscle tension
5. Upset stomach
6. Body pain
7. Getting addicted to smoke and alcohol
8. Fatigue
9. Unable to focus
10. Depression
11. Negative approach

15.3 WAYS TO COPE WITH STRESS

Do not let stress take toll on your health.

If you regularly experience some of the symptoms of stress listed above, you need to learn how to cope with them. Prepare a journal to identify the regular reasons of stress in your life. Keep analysing them. Are your ways to deal with stress healthy or unhealthy? Many people opt for wrong ways to deal with stress which aggravates their problem. People opt for negative ways to cope with stress which cause them great problem in the long run. Some of the wrong ways to fight stress are:

1. Overeating
2. Becoming introvert
3. Showing lethargy
4. Procrastinating
5. Dozing off
6. Drinking
7. Smoking
8. Sitting too long in front of television
9. Outburst of emotions

"Stop over-loading yourself with numberless tasks. Give time to yourself for rest and positive deliberations. You can't think better and plan better when you are under stress!"

— Israelmore Ayivor

Trying to ward off stress with the ways listed above could ruin one's health and the recovery might be impossible. Therefore, one should learn the positive ways to deal with stress.

15.3.1 Healthier Ways to Combat Stress

You can cure your stress if adopt healthy ways to cope with it. Among many healthy ways that are available to manage stress, you can choose the one that suits you. The first one is you can try to change your reaction or twist the situation. After choosing a way, think about the four As: accept, alter, avoid and adapt.

Remember there cannot be one solution to the stress-related problems of all people as every individual is unique. That is why you have to experiment with different methods and strategies to zero in on those solutions which can make you calm and composed.

Identify stress at the right time and deal with them in an apposite way.

The best thing in life is to avoid the stress rather than combating it. Try to quash it at the inception level.

15.3.1.1 Step 1: Avoid Stress

Although you cannot avoid encountering every cause of stress, you may adapt the following strategies to escape stress.

1. **Do not say yes when you want to say no:** Have a true measure of your capabilities and limits. This is essential for happiness in personal life and success in professional life. Never try to appear good in others' eyes by offering to take up those tasks or responsibilities which cannot handle efficiently. This will make you unnecessarily stressed.
2. **Prepare your to-do list:** If you maintain your work schedule systematically in a diary, you would know how to manage your time. Do not maintain your schedule in a way that makes it appear cluttered. Always distinguish between 'should' and 'must' tasks. Eliminate those tasks which are completely unnecessary and give priority to the ones which are most necessary.
3. **Adjust to the environment:** Avoid anything in your environment that makes you anxious. If you do not like watching news channels, do not sit in front of television and get stressed. If you think going to the crowded market will make you stressed, start buying online.
4. **Ignore people who stress you out:** If you observe that you get irritated in the company of some people, simply ignore those people. Reduce your chances of meeting them. If you cannot ignore them completely, then limit your time with them.
5. **Avoid controversial topics:** Discussion on some topics may irk you, if while discussing such topics, like religion or politics, you end up being at loggerheads with people, avoid discussing them or when such topics crop up during a conversation, just excuse yourself.

"Both positive and negative thinking are contagious."

— Stephen Richards, Overcoming Procrastination

15.3.1.2 Step 2: Change the Situation

In some situations, you just cannot avoid being stressed. Here the way out is to try to alter your behaviour or your way of talking to prevent those situations from developing. In this regard, you can use the following tips to great advantage.

1. **Be assertive:** Do not just keep taking what is thrown by others. Deal with situations in a way that is advantageous to you. If you have a guest at home and you also have an assignment deadline to meet the next day, frankly express your limitations to the guest. He/she will surely appreciate your frankness.
2. **Be open for compromise:** Sometimes you may take an extreme stand on an issue and are not willing to budge from it. In such situations it is better to compromise by taking a middle path. You soften your stand and also request the other person to climb down from his/her stand. This approach will lead to a win-win situation for both.
3. **Express your disapproval:** If you are hurt by the language or arguments used a person, then do not keep fuming inside. Simply tell the person in a polite way that you are hurt. If you do not communicate your disapproval to the other person, he/she will not realise his/her mistake and will continue behaving with you in the same way.
4. **Manage your time well:** Time management is very important in today's fast-moving world. Wasting time on unimportant tasks can cause you a lot of stress. If you are rushing to do urgent tasks at the last minute, you make yourself prone to accidents because of pressure, risking your life. If you plan ahead, you will always be relaxed.

15.3.1.3 Step 3: Adapt Yourself

If you cannot change the reasons of your stress, take a look at yourself for making yourself adaptable to changes in your personal and professional life. You must reduce your expectations from others. The following tips can help you adapt to the changes happening around you.

1. **Look at wider perspective:** If a problem is causing you stress, ask these questions to yourself: Will the problem matter to you tomorrow? Is it really worth being upset? Is it worthwhile to be obsessed with the problem? If your answer to these questions is no, then just forget the problem.
2. **Redefine your standards:** We all want to be prefect and achieve our goals fast. This ambition is a major reason of our stress. Be ready for failures and rejections too. They are part of life. Do not set too

high standards for yourself or your employee. Failure to achieve them would cause stress. It is also fine to be just good enough.

3. **Reframe the problem:** Sometimes the grave problem can be seen from different angle and worded differently. It makes huge difference in dealing with it. A difficult situation is best dealt when that you work with more vigour and energy. Do not get stuck in a suffocating situation but pause and try to come out of it. Enjoy listening to your favourite music and just have some me-time.
4. **Bank on your positives:** When you feel down or frustrated, try to think of your positive qualities and start appreciating natural surroundings. This attitude can help you see things in a proper perspective.

"The problem with procrastination is it's been around since the beginning of time it seems."
— Stephen Richards, Overcoming Procrastination

15.3.1.4 Step 4: Accept the Situation

Sometimes you have no control over a situation that is causing you stress. For example, you cannot reverse the death of close relative. Or, you may not have a say in the decisions taken by your seniors. In this case, the best way is to accept the situation and adapt to it. There is no point brooding over it. The best thing is to change the gears. The following tips can help you accept unfavourable situations.

The problems should not scare you to the limit that you find it impossible to deal with it. Start afresh.

1. **See the other side:** The Bhagwat Geeta preaches 'as we sow, so we reap'. So, if you keep patience, you will reap benefits. When you see the positive side of life make best use of it. Encash the opportunities that come your way at the earliest and keep growing. Sometimes your bad decision can put you in a stressful situation, then do not repent, learn from your mistake and move on,
2. **Share your feelings with a friend:** If you are overpowered by a lot of negative feelings towards someone, just share them with a friend. After sharing your negative feelings with your friend, you will feel relaxed mentally. Some people feel that sharing your feelings or problems is a sign of weakness, but that is not true. It actually strengthens your bonding with the people with whom you share.
3. **Do not attempt to control uncontrollable:** It is not possible for you to change basic nature of some people or their unpleasant actions in response to some adverse situations. If you lose your cool while

dealing with these people, then it reflects poorly on your personality. Remember, you cannot change the behaviour of other people but you can change your own behaviour.

4. **Forgive and forgot:** The world has many imperfect people. Do not let your resentment against such people pile up. Show your large heartedness by forgiving such people. Otherwise, the negativity caused by your continued resentment will bring down your work efficiency.

15.3.1.5 Step 5: Find time to rejuvenate

Life is so much loaded with work pressure and meeting deadlines that we forget what we are living for. It is necessary that you should find time for fun and frolic. This will keep you stress free and increase your efficiency. Me-time is a necessity. The following tips can help you rejuvenate yourself:

1. **Set aside time for relaxation:** Do not let your working hours encroach on your personal space. Keep some time out for such activities which can relax you. To recharge your energy, you must relax, else you may fall ill.
2. **Talk to people:** You cannot remain isolated, lost in your own world for a long time. Nor you will feel happy enjoying your success alone. So, it is necessary that you stay connected with people around you by talking to them. It is important to know about others, what they are doing and telling them about yourself.
3. **Indulge in what you enjoy every day:** Whatever gives you joy, get yourself involved in that activity. It can be painting, playing badminton, listening to music or driving.
4. **Let humour be part of you:** Do laugh aloud on yourself and laugh with people. The burst of laughter keeps stress at bay.

> Me time can do wonders to individuals in rejuvenating themselves.

15.3.1.6 Step 6: Go for healthy lifestyle

Your body will have better resistance if your lifestyle is healthy. The following tips can help you make your lifestyle healthy.

1. **Eat healthy food:** Balanced and well-nourished diet can keep you healthy, so be conscious that you eat right stuff. Never skip breakfast which gives you the energy to begin your day on the right note. Later meals also should be balanced. Do not depend on junk food.
2. **Exercise regularly:** Physical activity keeps your metabolism perfect. You can increase your immunity by doing 30 minutes exercise every day. Aerobic exercise helps a great deal in reducing stress.
3. **Say no to cigarettes and alcohol:** People opt for cigarette and alcohol as easy way to release stress. But this gives them a temporary relief. Gradually, smoking and drinking also become causes of their. So do not get habituated to smoking and drinking. Rather deal with stressful situations with right frame of mind.
4. **Sleep adequately:** Deep and adequate sleep reflects healthy body and mind. Proper sleep certainly reduces stress and makes you feel fresh and active.

"Don't interpret anything too much. This is time waster number 1."

— Dee Dee Artner

15.4 STEPS TO BE TAKEN IN THE ORGANISATIONS

It is the moral responsibility of the seniors in the organization to make the environment friendly so that the employees can work with enthusiasm. The stress may be initiated because of lack of time management, but if the superior observes this problem, the measures can be taken to quash it. However, lending the ears to the person under stress can be very helpful.

> A negotiation is basically an act of giving and taking. You should know what you can give in return of what you get from others.

Remember you should not let stress take a toll on you. You must take initiatives to deal with it. However the leaders have bigger role to play. It is in their interest to be ethical and objective in their approach. They have to create positive and open communication environment that the employees feel free to share their problem. The head should listen to the problem with calmness. For this they can include:

15.4.1 Open Communication

The root cause of many of the problems is lack of communication. The restrictions in the organization can suffocate the employees. Therefore, it is important to:

1. Periodically share with your employees the important decisions taken in the organisation. It will help reduce the uncertainty that the employees might have about their future.
2. Assign clearly the job responsibility to individual employees.
3. Do not make your communication to the employees sound authoritative. Be friendly while communicating with the employees so that they not feel terrorised.
4. Create amiable social climate.
5. Give ample opportunities to the employees to come out of their shell.
6. Provide no room for harassment of any kind.
7. Management policies should be open and consistent which are ethically correct.

This will certainly reduce the workplace stress levels and motivate the employees to work with their full potential and zeal.

> *"The only time that exists in life is now."*
>
> — Ken Poirot

15.4.2 Time Management

'Time is money' is an old adage but is very appropriate in today's time. If you manage your time well, stress will not grip you. It has been found that the root cause of stress is bad time management. If you miss one deadline, it causes a chain reaction making you miss subsequent deadlines, causing you more stress. If you stay ahead of your deadlines, it will make you happy and you will enjoy your work better. It has been observed that the submission deadlines of reports, documents, etc. are met till the last hour. This is not the right practice as last-minute hassles cannot be seen. You do not have control over external factors. That is why it is of utmost importance to manage time.

Managing time properly is essential in the work environment as it keeps pressure at bay and also wards off stress. Even if you have less time but better time management will enable you to have control over yourself and the work.

Good time management does not mean that you are working more but it means that you are more focused on your work and that makes all the difference in your personal life or at work.

> If you organise your life in advance, you will find time for everything.

15.4.3 Working towards Your Goals

The first initiative for time management is to pose some questions to yourself: What do you want to achieve in your life? What is more important to you – personal life or professional life? If you are clear about your objective then you can manage your time well. Also find out your long-term and short-term goals. This will help you prioritise the goals for which you have to work first. It is better to make a list of things you have to do according to your priority. A to-do list marked with priorities and deadlines helps you focus on urgent tasks and deal with non-urgent tasks later on.

15.4.4 Smart Work

Good time management mean doing high quality work, the quantity is not important. Just doing continuous work is not smart work but doing it in an effective manner with a proper break can lead to more efficiency. Sometimes you feel frustrated thinking of the time you have spent in the office working on the desk for long hours but the result is not visible. You should not lose patience but think of the positive outcomes. If you remain frustrated for a long time, it will compound your stress and make you lethargic. Sometimes you become over-ambitious and work without taking proper breaks. But remember it may not be productive .It is a general rule that by taking a break for thirty minutes in the afternoon you will be more effective because the break replenishes your energy and zeal. During the break think and talk of something other than work and that will give you a new outlook and a renewed focus.

15.4.5 Prioritise your Tasks

Categorise your tasks into four groups

1. Urgent and important
2. Not urgent but important
3. Urgent but not important
4. Neither urgent nor important

Know how to deal with the work which is urgent and important. When you are working on urgent tasks, do not get distracted by any outside noises. For example, if your telephone is ringing, ignore it. Get back to the caller after finishing your urgent and important task. Because sometimes a small two-minute talk over the phone can distract you so much that you are unable to focus on your work for the next thirty minutes.

Categorise your work equally into four types as mentioned above and deal accordingly. Do not put too many tasks in the first category because that will make you crazy.

> *"Half our life is spent trying to find something to do with the time we have rushed through life trying to save."*
>
> — Yale Richmond

15.4.6 4 Ds of Email Decision Making

We have a very bad habit of going through our inbox a number of times daily. That makes us feel exhausted and many people suffer from this email stress. It is advisable to open your email just twice a day. This will keep you away from email stress. Donaldson-Feilder suggests to practise four Ds of decision making while dealing with emails. They are as follows:

1. **Delete:** The emails which are irrelevant must be deleted immediately.
2. **Do:** The urgent mail should be replied at earliest.
3. **Delegate:** If the mail has to be handled by someone else, forward it to that person.
4. **Defer:** If the mail needs to be answered elaborately, keep it aside to be handled later on.

Summary

In this fast moving world, everyone is loaded with a lot of stress. Remember, a few things are not in your control; therefore you must learn how to deal with it. You have no control over nature, devastations and calamities that can happen anytime. Similarly in the organisation, you have no control over the behaviour of your colleagues or your boss, but you can adapt yourself according to their behaviour. While solving problems, go for alternative ways if one does not work. You can control stress with your positive attitude. If you know the reason for your stress, avoid it. Otherwise, identify the source of stress and address it. The signs of stress are getting irritated, withdrawing from people, depression, lack of focus, negative attitude etc. These symptoms adversely affect your work and you become negative in your approach. Learn a few strategies to cope with stress, like change the situation, adapt to changes happening around you, accept the situation, find time to rejuvenate and go for a healthy lifestyle. If you encourage open communication at every level in your organisation, you can create a stress-free environment at the workplace. Time management is an important part for keeping your stress at bay. Know your priorities what you want to achieve. Focus on quality work not on quantity. Set your deadlines and adhere to them. Prioritise your tasks keeping the 4Ds of e-mail management in mind. That is, delete, do, delegate and defer.

Chapter Review

1. Rajiv, senior manager at a company, has to meet four deadlines in a day. He is caught in traffic. He is getting perplexed and stressful. What should he do?
2. What are the negative ways of coping with stress? Do those ways help in the long run?
3. How can you avoid stress and how does stress reflect on your physical health?
4. How can you change the situation during stress?
5. Are ethics and stress related in some way? Explain with proper example.
6. Explain the 4Ds of email management.

Short Questions

1. What is open communication?
2. What can you infer by good time management in terms of work?
3. What is smart work? Explain.
4. What classification should you do to prioritise your tasks?
5. Do you get affected by people who indulge in backbiting?

Analytical Questions

1. Is stress good or bad? Can you describe a situation in which stress can be helpful?
2. Imagine you are attending a technical interview. What would be your choice for last minute preparations?
3. You are a hard working employee in your organisation. Your boss has always supported you. Now it is time for you to climb the professional ladder about which your boss had given you clear indications. At the last minute, you see that another person, who is close to your boss, comes to the position which you were supposed to occupy on promotion. How would you react?
4. In an interview you are asked to describe a stressful situation which you had handled in a good manner. What would be your answer?

Resources for Further Reflections

1. Conscious Calm: Keys to Freedom From Stress and Worry (ebook) by Laura Maciuika.
2. 50 Things You Can Do Today to Manage Stress by Wendy Green.
3. Stay Calm Stay Healthy: Defend Yourself Against Stress and Improve Your Health by Linda Blair, Susan Balfour, Chris Idzikowski, Susan E. Kersley, Sheena Meredit.
4. Fighting Invisible Tigers: Stress Management for Teens (Revised & Updated Third Edition) by Earl Hipp.
5. The Inner Game of Stress: Outsmart Life's Challenges and Fulfil Your Potential (Hardcover) by W. Timothy Gallwey.
6. The Positive Power of Negative Thinking (Paperback) by Julie Norem.
7. http://www.webmd.com/balance/stress-management/stress-management-frequently-asked-questions: Stress Management Health Centre.
8. http://www.stresshacker.com/2010/07/do-you-know-the-answer-to-these-10-critical-questions-about-stress/: Some FAQ's on stress.

Caselet 1

The Stressed CGM of Maruti Udyog

Vikas, Chief General Manager (CGM) of Maruthi Udyog, is 41 years old. Born and brought in Delhi, he graduated in Mechanical Engineering from Delhi University. He got married at 28. As the CGM of Maruthi Udyog, he is responsible for INR 500 crores of annual sales. He is accountable to the President of Maruthi Udyog, Indian division. When the President asks Vikas to go to London for this year's annual meeting, he agrees to go to London.

One day before his departure to London, Vikas wakes up in the morning and looks at the wall clock in his bedroom. It is 6 am. Then it occurs to him that today he has a meeting with his president in preparation to his London trip. He also has to pack his travel bag and review a few bills. "Oh God!" he exclaims angrily. "I need to fresh up fast." With pouncing heart, Vikas jumps out of the bed and starts brushing his teeth. After taking bath, he prepares coffee for himself. He knows that soon other members of the family will up and hence he must be ready to leave for the meeting before they start their day. While sipping coffee, he starts looking at his company's quarterly report, which he had received last evening. As he is short of time, he skims the report instead of reading it thoroughly and comes to know that his division has fallen short of its annual profit target by more than INR 2 crores.

When Vikas is about leave the home, his wife Priya comes running and informs him that their son Gautham has missed the school bus. Then Vikas asks angrily, "What am I supposed to do?. I have warned Gautham many times about this lazy conduct in the morning". When Priya asks him if he could drop Gautham to school on the way to his office, Vikas refuses, saying, "I have other important things to do than driving him to school. Do not waste my time now." His wife retorts, "You will never do anything for us. Come on Gautham, Mom will drop you to your school".

After arguing with Priya, Vikas leaves for the meeting, driving 40 km to reach his office. The long drive to the office has added to his stress. In the office, he is greeted by a bad news that few labours have boycotted the employee attitude survey, which was his initiative. He mutters to himself, "How dare they? I should take strong action". Then looking at his watch he realises that he was 5 minutes late for his meeting with the President. He gets furious and rushes to the meeting room where the President is waiting for him. When the meeting begins, the president asks him about his tour plan for London and his understanding of the company's quarterly preparation. Though Vikas responds to the President's queries, the latter is not satisfied by his answers. Then the President tells him frankly, "Look, Vikas! I'm sending you to London with this report because I feel you are capable to explain the audit professionals in London why we fell short our annual target by INR 2 crores. But if you get stressed like this and do not manage your time, you'll be replaced by some other person next time". And saying this, the President leaves the meeting room.

Questions

1. Vikas should have taken his son to school. Oppose or support this statement with justification.
2. How Vikas's meeting with the President would have happened had he not been so stressed before the meeting?
3. What kind of a manager Vikas is?

Caselet 2

'Idle' Operations Manager of a Steel Plant, Dinesh

Dinesh is a mechanical engineering graduate from Viseswarayya Technological University. He always topped the college and is the recipient of the State government's gold medal for academic excellence. He likes to take up challenging work. Starting his career as a Graduate Engineer Trainee at a steel plant, he rose to his current position of the operations manager at the same plant. Dinesh's current responsibilities include inspecting the daily works at the plant and writing reports about the daily operations, working of the labours and planning day to day activities of labours.

In the beginning of his career at the steel plant, Dinesh used to handle huge work but he did it with ease. And because of his success in taking the extreme workload, he got promoted as the operations manager. Now, his daily work gets completed within 3–4 hours and he sits idle the rest of the day in his cabin and feels bored. Lately, to overcome his boredom, Dinesh has he started reading some technical write-ups and textbooks to keep pace with developments in the field of technology.

But the General Manager of the steel plant on seeing Dinesh sitting idle or reading books think he is not showing interest in his work. Since Dinesh sits idle most of the time in the plant, other employees also develop the same opinion about him as the general manager. A rumour also is spread in the plant that Dinesh is planning to leave the plant very soon and that is why he is reading technology books for preparing to face job interviews.

Due to the rumour-mongering about Dinesh and the general manager's adverse opinion about him, he does not get the increment he was expecting. He feels disappointed. He starts expressing his disappointment to other employees. He starts scolding senior labours for small mistakes and assigns them heavy tasks as punishment. When he comes to know about the rumour about him, he feels more stressed. His reputation in the company is tarnished and he becomes short tempered. The quality of his work is also declined.

Questions

1. What are the behavioural changes we can observe in Dinesh?
2. Is he underutilised in the role of general manager? If yes, suggest ways to utilise his talent in the best possible way.

Bibliography

Soft Skills vs Hard Skills

1. Klaus, Peggy. *The Hard Truth About Soft Skills: Workplace Lessons Smart People Wish They'd Learned Sooner*. Harper Business, 2008.
2. Meyer, Carolyn. *Communicating for Results: A Canadian Student's Guide.* Oxford University Press: Canada, 2014.
3. Fuller, Catherine, and Phil Taylor. *A Toolkit of Motivational Skills: Encouraging and Supporting Change in Individuals.* Wiley-Blackwell, 2008.
4. Rubin, Kenneth H., Bukowski, William M., and Brett Laursen. *Handbook of Peer Interactions, Relationships, and Groups (Social, Emotional, and Personality Development in Context).* Guilford Press, 2009.

Personality Development

1. Pedler, Mike, and John Burgoyne. *Manager's Guide to Self-Development.* Delhi: McGraw Hill Education, 2011.
2. Maslow, Abraham H. *Motivation and Personality*. Pearson, 2010.
3. Morreale, Sherwyn P., Spitzberg, Brian H., and Kevin Barge. *Human Communication: Motivation, Knowledge & Skills.* Wadsworth Publishing Co. Inc, 2000.
4. Whiteley, Philip. *Motivation: People 09.07 (Express Exec).* Capstone, 2002.
5. Gulati, Sarvesh. *Corporate Grooming and Etiquette.* Rupa, 2010.
6. Calero, Henry H. *The Power of Nonverbal Communication: How you Act is more Important than what you Say.* Silver Lake, 2005.
7. Krauss, Robert M., Chen, Yihsiu, and Purnima Chawla. *Nonverbal Behavior and Nonverbal Communication: What do Conversational Hand Gestures Tell Us?* In Advances in Experimental Social Psychology by M. Zanna (Ed.). San Diego, CA: Academic Press.

Emotional Intelligence

1. Goleman, Daniel. "Emotional Intelligence. Why It Can Matter More than IQ." *Learning* 24, no. 6 (1996): 49–50.
2. Rowe, Anita, Lee Gardenswartz, and Jorge Cherbosque. *Emotional intelligence for managing results in a diverse world: The hard truth about soft skills in the workplace.* Nicholas Brealey Publishing, 2010.

3. Lathrop, Ann, and Kathleen Foss. *Guiding students from cheating and plagiarism to honesty and integrity: Strategies for change*. Libraries Unlimited, 2005.
4. Watson, Charles E. *How honesty pays: Restoring integrity to the workplace*. Penn State Press, 2005.
5. Boyatzis, Richard E., and Annie McKee. *Resonant leadership: Renewing yourself and connecting with others through mindfulness, hope, and compassion*. Harvard Business Press, 2005.
6. Lama, HH Dalai. *Open Heart: Practising Compassion in Everyday Life*. Hachette UK, 2002.
7. Kostanski, Marion. *The Power of Compassion: An Exploration of the Psychology of Compassion in the 21st Century*. Cambridge Scholars Publishing, 2008.
8. Lopez, Shane J., and Charles R. Snyder. *Oxford handbook of positive psychology*. Oxford University Press, USA, 2009.
9. Shockley-Zalabak, Pamela. *Fundamentals of organizational communication*. Pearson Education, 2011.
10. Richards, Dick. *The art of winning commitment: 10 ways leaders can engage minds, hearts, and spirits*. Public Affairs, 2004.
11. Johnson, Larry, and Bob Phillips. *Absolute honesty: building a corporate culture that values straight talk and rewards integrity*. AMACOM Div American Mgmt Assn, 2003.
12. Killinger, Barbara. *Integrity: doing the right thing for the right reason*. McGill-Queen's Press-MQUP, 2010.

Etiquette and Mannerism

1. Bowman, Judith. *Don't Take the Last Donut: New Rules of Business Etiquette: Easyread Super Large 20pt Edition*. ReadHowYouWant.com, 2008.
2. Taylor, Shirley. *Email Etiquette: A Fresh look at dealing effectively with e-mail, developing great style, and writing clear, concise messages*. Marshall Cavendish International Asia Pte Ltd, 2009.

Communication Today

1. BoveÃ, Courtland L., John V. Thill, and Barbara E. Schatzman. "Business Communication Today, 7e." (2003).
2. Greene, John O., and Brant Raney Burleson. *Handbook of communication and social interaction skills*. Psychology Press, 2003.
3. Swales, John M., and Christine B. Feak. *Academic writing for graduate students: Essential tasks and skills*. Vol. 1. Ann Arbor, MI: University of Michigan Press, 2004.

Employment Communication: Resume and Job Application

1. Belanger, Sandra E., ed. *Business and Technical Communication: An Annotated Guide to Sources, Skills, and Samples*. No. 13. Greenwood Publishing Group, 2005.
2. Roman, Kenneth, and Joel Raphaelson. *Writing that Works*. Harper & Row, Publishers, 10 East 53rd Street, New York, NY 10022, 1981.

Professional Presentations

1. Brydon, Steven Robert, and Michael D. Scott. *Between one and many: The art and science of public speaking*. McGraw-Hill, 2003.
2. Mandel, Steve. *Effective presentation skills a practical guide for better speaking*. Crisp Learning, 2000.

Job Interviews

1. Bailo, Paul J. *The Essential Digital Interview Handbook: Lights, Camera, Interview Tips for Skype, Google Hangout, GoToMeeting, and More*. Career Press, Incorporated, 2013.

Group Discussion

1. Brilhart, John K., and Gloria J. Galanes. *Effective group discussion*. McGraw-Hill Humanities, Social Sciences & World Languages, 1992.
2. Rossiter, John R., and Gary L. Lilien. "New "brainstorming" principles."*Australian Journal of Management* 19, no. 1 (1994): 61–72.

Creativity at Work Place

1. Glăveanu, Vlad Petre. *Distributed creativity: Thinking outside the box of the creative individual*. London: Springer, 2014.
2. Michalko, Michael. *Thinkertoys: A handbook of creative-thinking techniques*. Ten Speed Press, 2010.

Ethical Values

1. Cheney, George, Daniel J. Lair, Dean Ritz, and Brenden E. Kendall. *Just a job?: Communication, ethics, and professional life*. Oxford University Press, 2009.
2. Dixon, Ross, Simon Robinson, Christopher Preece, and Krisen Moodley. *Engineering, Business & Professional Ethics*. Routledge, 2007.
3. Sayer, Andrew. *Why things matter to people: Social science, values and ethical life*. Cambridge University Press, 2011.

Capacity Building: Learn Unlearn and Relearn

1. Surendra Verma. *Learn & Unlearn: The Novel Way To Rethink The Things That Matter In Your Life*. New Holland Australia, 2015.
2. Poet, Humble. *Unlearn: 101 Simple Truths for a Better Life*. CreateSpace Independent Publishing Platform, 2014.

Leadership and Team Building

1. Bojeun, Mark C. *Program Management Leadership: Creating Successful Team Dynamics*. CRC Press, 2013.
2. Dyer, William G., and Jeffrey H. Dyer. *Team building: Proven strategies for improving team performance*. John Wiley & Sons, 2013.

Decision making and Negotiation

1. Raiffa, Howard, John Richardson, and David Metcalfe. *Negotiation analysis: the science and art of collaborative decision making*. Harvard University Press, 2002.
2. Munier, Bertrand, and Melvin Shakun, eds. *Compromise, negotiation and group decision*. Vol. 1. Springer Science & Business Media, 2012.

Stress and Time Management

1. Barlow, David H. *Principles and practice of stress management*. Edited by Paul M. Lehrer, Robert L. Woolfolk, and Wesley E. Sime. Guilford Press, 2007.
2. Greenberg, Jerrold S. "Comprehensive stress management." (2002).
3. Zeigler, Kenneth. *Getting Organized at Work: 24 Lessons for Setting Goals, Establishing Priorities, and Managing Your Time*. McGraw Hill Professional, 2008.

Index

L

M

N

O

P

R